Spatial Schemas and Abstract Thought

Spatial Schemas and Abstract Thought

edited by Merideth Gattis

A Bradford Book
The MIT Press
Cambridge, Massachusetts
London, England

This book was set in Sabon by Asco Typesetters, Hong Kong, and was printed and bound in the United States of America.

First printing, 2001

Library of Congress Cataloging-in-Publication Data

Spatial schemas and abstract thought / edited by Merideth Gattis.
     p.   cm.
"A Bradford book."
Includes bibliographical references and index.
ISBN 0-262-07213-0 (alk. paper)
1. Cognitive maps (Psychology)—Congresses. 2. Human information processing—Congresses. 3. Spatial behavior—Congresses. 4. Spatial behavior in animals—Congresses. I. Gattis, Merideth.
BF314 .S63   2001
152.14′2—dc21   00-038675

Contents

Acknowledgments

This volume grew out of a symposium held at the 1997 Conference of the Cognitive Science Society at Stanford University and a workshop sponsored by the Max Planck Institute for Psychological Research in Munich, Germany in July 1998. Both symposium and workshop were organized while I was a postdoctoral researcher at the Cognitive and Behavioral Development Unit of the Max Planck Institute for Psychological Research. I thank Franz Weinert, Director of the Cognitive and Behavioural Development Unit and Vice President of the Max Planck Society, for his generous support and wise counsel. I also thank Keith Holyoak, Asher Koriat, Barbara Tversky, and Michael Waldmann for stimulating conversations and valuable advice. I thank Amy Brand and Carolyn Gray Anderson of the MIT Press for their help with this volume. The title for this volume was originally a section title in *Learnability and Cognition: The Acquisition of Argument Structure*, by Steven Pinker (1989). I thank him for his permission to use the title here.

Spatial Schemas and Abstract Thought

Chapter 1
Space as a Basis for Abstract Thought

Merideth Gattis

How has humanity come to develop fundamental abstract abilities such as those seen in science, literature, and art? One answer is familiar to evolutionary theorists: by recruiting old parts for new uses. Pinker has suggested, for instance, that sensory processors and motor programs may have become adapted to more abstract tasks that share some of the same computational structure as sensorimotor tasks (1989). One of the primary candidates for sharing computational structure with abstract cognition is spatial cognition. As a domain, space is well learned across many species (Shettleworth, 1998), and it often involves the integration of information across multiple modalities and multiple dimensions (Millar, 1994). These characteristics make it an appropriate and appealing platform for building new structures essential for higher cognitive processes.

Whether spatial structures indeed play a significant role in abstract thought is an important question for cognitive psychologists, developmental psychologists, linguists, anthropologists, and computer scientists, and has been investigated for years in each of these disciplines. The theories and evidence from these disciplines have not yet been brought together. The aim of this book is to do so. The contributors include scientists from a variety of disciplines investigating spatial cognition and whether and how humans and other animals utilize spatial structures for abstract, non-spatial tasks. The chapters in this book primarily address three questions we take as our starting point: "What do we know about spatial cognition that may be relevant to the use of space in abstract thought?" "Is there evidence that spatial structures impact performance on abstract tasks?" "How can spatial structures be adapted for non-spatial cognition?" My hope is that in addressing these questions, this book not only assembles and evaluates current evidence for the role of spatial schemas in abstract thought, but also identifies common and discrepant paradigms and findings across different disciplines, and defines directions for future investigations.

To begin, however, we must first have an idea of how space *could* be used in abstract cognition. The first part of this introduction seeks to illustrate what is meant by spatial schemas, what is meant by abstract cognition, and how the latter may benefit from the former. In the second part, the aim is to identify two important points in formulating accounts of spatial schemas. First, our account of spatial schemas explores the idea that space can be a mechanism for cognition, not merely a metaphor for cognition. Second, our account of spatial schemas aims to identify the nature of the correspondences between space and other domains, and how those correspondences, or mappings, are established. The third part of this introduction proceeds to provide an overview of the contents of the book.

1.1   Uses of Spatial Schemas

Schemas aid cognition because they are organized: they have a familiar structure, and people can rely on that structure to facilitate memory, communication, and reasoning. Spatial schemas share these qualities. What is unusual about the use of spatial schemas in abstract thought is their source. Presumably they are first acquired in a purely spatial context—we learn spatial schemas such as linear orders, directionality, and cognitive maps by observing the locations of objects, the movement of objects and people, and the configuration of our environment. To be useful for abstract cognition, however, spatial schemas must be adapted to contexts other than those in which they were acquired. Thus the use of spatial schemas in abstract thought requires transfer across widely disparate domains. Despite the far-reaching transfer required, a look at the world around us suggests that spatial schemas are adapted for three basic purposes in abstract cognition: they are used as memorial structures, as communicative structures, and as logical structures.

Spatial Schemas as Memorial Structures

Spatial schemas provide organization, and organization—particularly organization that links elements together the way spatial schemas do— improves memory (Cofer, 1973). As Neisser (1987) points out, our memory for personal history is tied to our sense of place, "that exquisite set of mechanisms that allow us to know the layout of an environment, including positions and paths, regardless of whether we are explicitly aware of it." Many people have experienced the sensitive relationship between personal history and memory for place when re-visiting a city after many years. Standing in St. Mark's Square, for instance, may trigger a memory for the location of a particularly good gelateria, and along with that location, long-forgotten faces, emotions, or conversations.

The experience of re-visiting a place demonstrates that space can sometimes be a more powerful organizer of memory than time. When I remember a week I spent in Crete, for instance, I often don't recall the order in which events occurred, but I do remember the location in which events occurred. I can use locations to guide a mental walk through the week, a week that in my memory is now ordered by the proximity of locations rather than temporal precedence. This effect is exaggerated by the availability of external representations of space, such as cartographic maps. When I survey a map of Paris from east to west, I recall shivering in the Cimetiere du Pere Lachaise, hungrily eating a crepe in front of the Bastille, and not buying a hat on the Ile St-Louis, even though that is surely not the order in which the events occurred, because that is the order of the locations. In such circumstances, maps allow space to become a post hoc organizer of memory.

Our memory for place can be adapted for other memory tasks besides personal history. For example, the most familiar use of spatial schemas in memory is an ancient memory strategy, the method of loci, wherein a person remembers an ordered sequence of elements by attaching each to a location (Anderson, 1990; Yates, 1969). At recall the person mentally walks through the space from one location to the next, noting the elements as each is passed, much like one remembers a route by walking through it, relying on landmarks and other contextual perceptual cues to keep track of direction, turns, and so on. Interestingly, although the method of loci is highly effective for remembering serial orders, it seems to require special training to master. The method of loci thus raises two important questions about spatial schemas in abstract thought: whether adaptation of a spatial schema to abstract cognition is automatic or effortful, and the related question of how often such schemas are actually used.

The question of how frequently spatial schemas are used as memorial structures and how effortful that use is appears to be related to whether the relevant spatial organization is available in the environment or must be constructed (either internally in the form of a mental array or mental model or externally in the form of a diagram or some other spatial representation), and the processing capacity of the animal or intelligent system. When ordered elements are organized into a linear array or some other useful spatial configuration, many animals can and do use spatial cues to aid memory. Studies with rats (described in Chapter 2 by Roberts) and with young children (described in Chapter 11 by McGonigle and Chalmers) indicate that when the spatial organization of items in the environment is congruent with a to-be-remembered order of elements, both humans and other animals exploit this congruence. Simulations of the process of mapping ordered elements to an internal spatial array (described by Hummel and Holyoak in Chapter 10) demonstrate however that the relational processing involved in the construction of arrays places a heavy computational load on limited-capacity processors. The processing load imposed by mapping may be one reason for spatial schemas to be more commonly used when the spatial structures are available in the environment—whether as diagrams or other explicit spatial representations, or as metaphorical structures implied by our communicative systems.

Spatial Schemas as Communicative Structures

The order and linking characteristics of spatial schemas are also apparent when spatial schemas are adapted for use as communicative structures. Other, more complex relations may also be expressed. For instance, spatial schemas are often used to represent an opposition between two entities or categories. Robert Hertz (1909/1973) argued that the right-left asymmetry of the human body, evidenced by right-handedness in a majority of people, is a universal basis for communication about social constructs. Hertz and other anthropologists (see Needham, 1973) cited numerous examples of the dual classification of social values, such as the oppositions between good and evil, superior and inferior, light and darkness, sacred and profane, all reflecting a right-left organizational scheme for social communication. In our own culture, the pervasiveness of the right-left metaphor for opposition is evidenced by the double meanings of right and left to refer to political and social orientation, and by the evaluative phrases "on the one hand ... on the other hand" and their accompanying spatial gestures. More recently, cross-cultural studies of spatial representation systems have demonstrated that which spatial metaphor a culture uses for expressing contrastive relations depends on the culture's system of spatial conception. In Chapter 5, Kita, Danziger and

Stolz report that when a culture's system of spatial conception does not include the spatial opposition of right and left, contrastive relations are communicated with an up-down or front-back spatial metaphor instead. Interestingly, though the reference frame used in spatial metaphors may vary depending upon a given culture's system of spatial conception, the use of spatial reference frames for communicating opposition appears to be common across many cultures.

In addition to conveying oppositions, spatial schemas may be used in communication to identify categories, directionality, and many other relations. When we communicate about relations using spatial schemas, the structure provided by a spatial schema facilitates understanding by establishing a metaphor for the relevant conceptual structure (Clark, 1973; Lakoff & Johnson, 1980). Such a metaphor may be communicated linguistically (such as the space → time metaphors discussed by Gentner in Chapter 8), visually (such as the diagrams and depictions described by Tversky in Chapter 4, and the diagrams and graphs described by Gattis in Chapter 9), or both (such as the configurations used by speakers gesturing, described in Chapter 5 by Kita, Danziger, and Stolz, and by signers signing, described in Chapter 6 by Emmorcy). These and other chapters in this volume document a variety of spatial schemas used in communication and raise two important questions about space in language. These two questions are: "What is the nature of the mapping between spatial structures and communicative structures?" and "Do spatial structures actually influence understanding?"

Spatial Schemas as Logical Structures

The use of spatial schemas in reasoning is closely related to their use in communication and in memory. We use spatial schemas in reasoning because the structure provided by a spatial schema, combined with partial knowledge of a set of elements and relations between them, allows us to infer the elements or relations that are unknown. Spatial schemas do so by marking three aspects of structure that play a significant role in logical reasoning: order within a dimension, directionality within a dimension, and relations between dimensions (Gattis & Dupeyrat, 1999).

Reasoning about ordered relations between elements, often called linear ordering or seriation, is one of the most common forms of reasoning. Social psychologists, anthropologists, and biologists have observed that remembering and reasoning about the hierarchy of individuals in a social group is a significant problem for many species, not only humans (De Soto,

1960; Fiske, 1992). De Soto, London, and Handel (1965) have proposed that humans reason about multiple elements and the relations between them by creating a mental spatial array. For instance, when given logical reasoning tasks about relations between several persons (e.g., Tom is taller than Sam and John is shorter than Sam), many people report creating mental arrays of items and relations given in the premises (e.g., Tom-Sam-John) to make transitive inferences about the unstated relations (e.g., Tom is taller than John) (De Soto et al., 1965). Several chapters in this volume, including those from Bryant and Squire, Gattis, Gentner, McGonigle and Chalmers, Hummel and Holyoak, and Roberts, examine the role of spatial representation in linear ordering, transitive inference, and other forms of reasoning, and the processing mechanisms which may underlie these forms of reasoning.

The question of whether reasoners spontaneously adopt spatial structures for reasoning remains open (see Chapters 10 and 11). As with spatial schemas in memory, the frequency and effortfulness of using spatial schemas in reasoning is in part determined by the environmental availability of spatial organization and the processing capacity of the reasoner. What is clear is that humans and other animals are good at exploiting congruence between spatial and logical structures, but selecting and adapting an appropriate spatial structure is a demanding task.

1.2   Accounts of Spatial Schemas

Metaphor or Mechanism?

A notable question that arose in our discussions, and in our writing of the chapters presented here is "Are spatial schemas expressive tools for understanding abstract cognition, or actual internal representations or mechanisms?" Scientific metaphors of mental processes grounded in space abound—particularly semantic spaces of language and categorization (Fauconnier, 1985; Langacker, 1986; Osgood, Suci & Tannenbaum, 1957), and state spaces such as the problem space metaphor (Duncker, 1945; Newell and Simon, 1972)—but most of these metaphors are intended to be scientific tools, a means of understanding mental processes rather than a proposal that the mental processes underlying categorization, language understanding, or problem solving are fundamentally spatial. Spatial metaphors such as these are of course not proposing that old parts of spatial cognition are recruited for new uses of representation and thought. In contrast, evolutionary theorists and proponents of embodied cognition propose that our experience in space and the cognitive structures we develop to perceive, navigate, and remember space are the indispensable foundation of more abstract cognitive tasks (Lakoff & Johnson, 1980; Pinker, 1989). Are spatial schemas a metaphor for cognitive processes, or a mechanism for cognitive processes?

A recurrent theme in all of these chapters is the importance of relational processing in abstract thought. It is this cognitive task—sometimes called relational learning, other times called relational coding, or relational reasoning—that more than any other seems to benefit from adaptation of spatial structures. This is not surprising. As Bryant and Squire note in Chapter 7, space *is* relational, and even young children demonstrate an understanding of the relational nature of space. In addition, space is a flexible base domain. As the wide-ranging content of these chapters demonstrates, spatial structures may be adapted for representing an enormous variety of abstract structures and concepts. These and other factors described throughout the book suggest that space is not simply a metaphor for abstract thought, it may actually be a basis for abstract thought. Nonetheless, as Hummel and Holyoak point out in Chapter 10, if spatial structures are to serve as the basis for abstract tasks such as reasoning about transitive relations, the mental representation involved "must make the mapping from non-spatial relations ... onto spatial predicates transparent, and the cognitive architecture must be configured to exploit this language."

Mapping Concepts to Space

A second significant question thus emerges: How is the mapping between spatial structures and non-spatial structures accomplished? Gentner (Chapter 8) suggests four possible levels of mapping from space to abstract cognition. The lowest level of interaction occurs when lexical relations for space and another domain are purely local, and no conceptual mapping exists. In this case, no causal link between space and another domain exists. Space and abstract cognition interact slightly more, though only as parallel domains, at the next level, that of structural parallelism. At this level of mapping, the similarity of structures common to both space and some other domain may be noted, but space does not structure the other domain, nor vice versa. When the structure of space has at one time been adapted for what is now an independent domain, Gentner refers to the level of mapping as cognitive archaeology, to capture the history of spatial origins and the lack of current influence of space on the abstract domain.

The strongest type of mapping between spatial structures and non-spatial structures is system mapping, in which a global spatial system is used to structure an abstract domain. These four levels of mapping provide criteria by which we can judge the extent to which space influences abstract thought, and provide hints about the origins of such mappings as well.

In my own chapter, I propose four constraints on mapping concepts to space which help to further specify how the mapping between space and abstract cognition may be accomplished. These four constraints are based on different types of similarity, ranging from perceptual similarity to abstract similarities of organizational structure. Mappings based upon similarities between linguistic and spatial representation are discussed in other chapters as well. Hummel and Holyoak's LISA model assumes that the mapping process is mediated by language, and that aspects of linguistic structure such as markedness can constrain the construction of a spatial array representing transitive relations. In fact, most of the chapters in this volume touch on the relationship between spatial structure, linguistic structure, and abstract conceptual structures, and how that relationship influences mapping, suggesting that language plays an important role in mediating the adaptation of spatial schemas to abstract thought.

1.3   Overview of the Contents of this Book

The chapters in this volume are divided into three sections, each addressing a different aspect of the question of whether spatial structures play a significant role in abstract thought. The first section examines how humans and other animals represent space, and suggests how spatial representations might influence reasoning and memory for nonspatial relations, given what we know about the representation and use of space itself. The second section documents several interesting examples of spatial representations in specific cultural contexts. Two of the chapters in this section also present evidence that spatial representations influence memory and problem solving. The third section proposes mechanisms by which spatial structures might be adapted for non-spatial purposes, and considers alternatives to spatial coding as a basis for abstract thought.

Representing and Using Space

How humans and other animals represent space is an enormous topic, one to which several excellent volumes have been dedicated (Bloom et al.,

1996; de Vega et al., 1996; Gallistel, 1990; Healy, 1998; Millar, 1994). The purpose of this section is therefore not to provide a comprehensive review of spatial representation but rather to provide a concise review with special attention to which mechanisms for navigation and spatial representation are likely or unlikely to serve the purposes of nonspatial cognition. In Chapter 2, Roberts reviews the encoding of space in animals, and discusses a wide variety of internal mechanisms available for navigating through space. In contrast to the view that animals use cognitive maps to find food and home, Roberts proposes several alternative interpretations of existing data and notes some significant methodological challenges to showing that cognitive maps actually exist. Roberts also introduces a theme repeated in several chapters throughout the book—that three very likely uses of space are encoding time, encoding number, and encoding order—and presents provocative findings suggesting that rats use a spatial array to make transitive choices in a discrimination learning task.

In Chapter 3, Liben follows on Roberts' survey of internal spatial representations with an overview of the interpretation and use of external spatial representations. Liben reviews research on children's developing understanding of maps, and proposes three principles of cartographic map understanding which determine the interpretation and use of maps (purpose, duality, and spatialization). Liben's focus on spatial representations which are external and are culturally provided relates to an important question discussed in several chapters in this volume: do people spontaneously create spatial representations in the course of reasoning, or do they only use space when it is available as a ready-made tool?

In Chapter 4, Tversky builds on this background and moves beyond maps to many other forms of spatial representation, surveying an enormous variety of graphic inventions and conventions. Tversky notes that many graphics are fundamentally spatial arrays, and that this simple spatial schema can be used to convey several different types of information (nominal, ordinal, and interval). Which of those relations people infer from an array is strongly influenced by perceptual aspects of the representation, based on Gestalt principles of perceptual organization. As Tversky demonstrates, those perceptual principles lead to some interesting and unusual inferences about conceptual relations. The inferences described by Tversky make an important point—that even when space is available as a ready-made tool for reasoning, using that tool involves going beyond the information given.

Spatial Schemas in Cultural Contexts

The question of whether the spatial schemas used in communication are culturally provided tools or are adapted on-line is relevant to Chapter 5, a study by Kita, Danziger, and Stolz of gestures produced during story-telling. People from two language groups, Yucatec and Mopan, were asked to re-tell classic myths. Their spontaneous gestures during story-telling were analyzed with respect to which spatial schemas are involved in the encoding of location, motion, flow of time, plot progression, and paradigmatic contrast. Differences in spatial conceptualization between the two languages were reflected not only in gestures referring to spatial concepts, but also those referring to nonspatial concepts. For example, one Yucatec storyteller made a sweeping gesture from right to left when talking about the passage of time from one day to the next, whereas a Mopan storyteller moved her hand forward, away from the body, when talking about the passage of time. These differences were characteristic of all Yucatec and Mopan speakers. The influence of language on spatial conceptualization and thereby on gestures suggests that culture does play an important role in providing spatial structures for thought, while the spontaneity of gesture as a medium provides possible evidence for the on-line adaptation of spatial structures for communicating about non-spatial concepts. In this light, culture and cognitive mechanism are seen as not necessarily two alternative causes, but two intertwined causes.

The mutual causality of culture and cognitive mechanism are also apparent in Chapter 6, where Emmorey describes how signers use the three-dimensional space in front of them to represent physical space as well as abstract conceptual structure. Emmorey observes that in American Sign Language, signers use physical elements—handshapes—to represent physical and conceptual elements. Signers also use movements of hand-shapes to represent motion of elements, and locations in signing space to represent both physical and conceptual locations. Similar patterns of mapping elements to elements and relations to relations are noted by Tversky and by Gattis in conventionalized and invented graphics. It makes sense then, that Emmorey argues that signing space sometimes functions much like a diagram, and offers many of the same benefits to memory and reasoning that have been noted with diagrams, both because of spatial determinacy, and because of aspects of order inherent to spatial representation. Emmorey also notes that signing space is particu-larly expedient for representing time and order (similar to the proposals of Roberts, Tversky, Kita et al., Gentner, Hummel and Holyoak, and

McGonigle and Chalmers), as well as relational aspects of conceptual structure (a point expanded upon in a later chapter by Gattis).

In Chapter 7, Bryant and Squire tackle the difficult relation between space and mathematics by examining how children's use of space can facilitate mathematical problem solving. In the face of evidence that spatial cues at times lead to misjudgments in mathematics, Bryant and Squire propose that children are poor at remembering absolute spatial values but very good at encoding spatial relations. Spatial relations plus the inferences that follow from those relations become a tool-kit for getting started in mathematics. Like Tversky, the authors make a convincing case that Gestalt principles of perceptual organization are implicated in inferencing from spatial relations, and demonstrate clearly how grouping plays a significant role in young children's solving of division problems. Bryant and Squire also note that children's ability to exploit spatial correspondence to solve problems is often matched, sometimes even exceeded, by their ability to exploit temporal correspondence to solve problems, a point returned to in the next section in a chapter by McGonigle and Chalmers.

Adapting Space for Abstract Thought

In Chapter 8, Gentner sets the stage for an examination of the relation between spatial and temporal domains by proposing four possible levels of mapping from space to abstract cognition in general (lexical relations, structural parallelism, cognitive archaeology, and system mapping, as described above in the section Mapping Concepts to Space). Gentner presents studies examining which of these mappings explains temporal reasoning with two kinds of space-time metaphors (the time-moving metaphor, and the ego-moving metaphor). From the results, Gentner concludes that spatial mappings do influence the processing of temporal metaphors, but is cautious about claiming that space structures time.

In Chapter 9, I review three constraints on mapping abstract concepts onto spatial representations (iconicity, associations, polarity), and argue that structural similarity should be considered a fourth important constraint. While the importance of structural similarity in similarity and analogy is well-established, the claim that it influences mapping between space and abstract concepts is not. To support this argument, I present recent studies with artificial sign languages and graphs. Children's and adults' interpretations of these spatial representations reflect a pattern of mapping elements to elements, relations to relations, and higher-order relations to higher-order relations.

The question of the causal precedence of spatial schemas in reasoning is addressed by McGonigle and Chalmers in Chapter 10. McGonigle and Chalmers review reasoning and seriation studies with nonhuman primates and human children, and ask whether the results of those studies indicate that spatial coding plays a role in the development and evolution of relational encoding. They point out that although some findings indicate that spatial coding does play a role in relational encoding, other findings provide evidence that temporal coding also plays an important role. They argue that spatial schemas may not be the earliest cause of the very special ability to understand order, and suggest that other mechanisms, such as rule stacks, must be considered as plausible alternatives.

Finally, in Chapter 11, Hummel and Holyoak present a process model of human transitive inference demonstrating that both structure and flexibility are important for modeling spatial schemas in abstract thought. Their LISA model, a hybrid connectionist model, creates a spatial array representation of relations between elements based on linguistic inputs such as "Bill is better than Joe. Joe is better than Sam." The spatial array representation not only allows valid inferences about relations that have not been specified, but successfully models human performance on transitive reasoning problems. Hummel and Holyoak argue that an array representation does not need to be imagistic, pointing to a crucial difference between spatial schemas in abstract thought and imagery in thought. Hummel and Holyoak also point out that they are not claiming that visuospatial processes are the only basis for reasoning, nor that they are developmentally or evolutionarily the first basis for reasoning. The success of Hummel and Holyoak's LISA model demonstrates clearly, however, that space is a possible and actual basis for reasoning.

1.4   Conclusion

The question of how spatial cognition influences abstract cognition is usually raised as a tantalizing but speculative prospect near the end of a conference or book about more well-understood research questions, rather than being given a thorough and rigorous review. This book attempts to put those tantalizing but speculative ideas to the test. Our hope is to lead you (and ourselves) to new and more vigorous questions about the role of spatial schemas in abstract thought.

Part I

Representing and Using Space

Chapter 2

Spatial Representation and the Use of Spatial Codes in Animals

William A. Roberts

A well known television program announces space as the final frontier. However, for most species of animals, space was probably a very early frontier in their evolutionary development. A characteristic of virtually all animals that move through their environment is that they show some degree of spatial competence. It is critical for an animal's survival that it know the locations of such things as its own home, water, foods of different types, and other species that might prey on it. In addition, an animal must keep track of its own travels through its environment. For example, animals that prey on nutrients found in plants rarely return to a plant previously depleted within a foraging expedition. Memory for the locations of previous visits aids in efficient foraging by preventing an animal from needlessly returning to an exhausted food site.

In his classic article, Tolman (1948) introduced the idea of cognitive maps in rats and men. Tolman advanced his theory as a cognitive alternative to the currently popular stimulus-response theories of maze learning, which suggested that each response in the maze created a stimulus for the next response. Tolman's conception was that animals had a broader appreciation of space in which goals and landmarks could be represented simultaneously. The cognitive map made it possible for animals to anticipate routes and locations to be visited and to take shortcuts through space. O'Keefe and Nadel (1978) incorporated Tolman's cognitive map into their theory of taxon and locale learning. While the taxon system was responsible for associative learning, the locale system gave rise to place learning through the formation of cognitive maps. Furthermore, it was held that the hippocampus of the mammalian brain was the organ primarily responsible for cognitive mapping ability. Although these distinctions have been criticized (Sherry & Healy, 1998; Shettleworth, 1998), the notion of a cognitive map has become very popular as a metaphor for spatial representation in animals.

In the first section of this chapter, I will argue that the term cognitive map may have outlived its usefulness. Certainly at the time it was introduced by Tolman, it served as a valuable counterweight to the dominant S-R orthodoxy of the day, and the term has clearly established the idea that animals have internal representations of space. On the other hand, it was never well defined operationally and has come to mean different things to different theorists. I will raise three implications of cognitive map theory and provide arguments and data in each case which question their validity. In the second section, I will suggest that, in place of cognitive map theory, spatial representation in animals should be thought of as a number of mechanisms and that these mechanisms operate hierarchically and interact with species and type of spatial problem encountered. In a final section, the possibility that animals might use spatial representation to deal with other cognitive problems will be discussed.

2.1 Challenges to Cognitive Map Theory

From the notion that animals form an overall representation of an experienced spatial environment, at least three implications have been drawn. One is that animals use multiple landmarks to locate important places by computing their distance and direction from these landmarks. A second implication is that animals can use the cognitive map to infer new routes or shortcuts through space that would be to their advantage. The third implication to be discussed is the suggestion that by exploring a spatial environment, an animal can form a topological map of that environment.

Relationships between Landmarks

Although some evidence suggests that animals compute positions in space by using distance and direction to several landmarks (Cheng, 1989; Suzuki, Augerinos & Black, 1980), other evidence suggests that this may not be the most common or preferred strategy. As one example, Collett, Cartwright & Smith (1986) examined gerbils' coding of the location of food buried under bedding in an open field. Two cylindrical landmarks were located in the field, and the food was hidden at equal distances between them. After gerbils had learned to search at the food location, a test was given in which the distance between the landmarks was doubled. If gerbils had coded the location of food as midway between the landmarks, they should have continued to search at the same site used in training, because this site was still an equal distance from each landmark.

Surprisingly, gerbils searched at two locations, one near the left-hand landmark and the other near the right-hand landmark. In each case, the distance between the landmark and the place searched was the same as the distance between the food location and each landmark during training. Instead, of coding the food location as being equidistant between two landmarks, the gerbils had coded it as being at fixed distances from two independent landmarks.

This coding strategy is particularly in evidence in some recent experiments carried out by Marcia Spetch and her colleagues (Spetch, Cheng & MacDonald, 1996; Spetch, Cheng, MacDonald, Linkenhoker, Kelly & Doerkson, 1997). Pigeons and humans were trained to "search" the surface of a computer monitor for a hidden goal. Four graphically created landmarks surrounded the goal. A touchscreen on the monitor recorded the location of pigeon pecks or human touches, and food reward (pigeons) or positive feedback (points for humans) was given for correct responses. Both species learned to respond in the correct area of the screen, as shown in the upper left panel of Figure 2.1. On three different types of test trials, the positions of the landmarks were expanded, either horizontally, vertically, or both horizontally and vertically (diagonal expansion). The results of these tests, shown in the remaining panels of Figure 2.1, indicate that humans continued to search in the middle of the landmark array. When asked, people indicated that the goal should continue to be in the middle of the array, equidistant from each landmark. Pigeons, on the other hand, can be seen to have searched at the same distance from landmarks as the distance used in training. Note that there were individual differences; different pigeons coded the problem by different landmarks. The difference between human and pigeon spatial coding is striking. Although humans seem to automatically compute the middle of an array, pigeons, like gerbils, compute the distances from independent landmarks. Further experiments in which pigeons and humans searched among ground arrays of landmarks confirmed these findings over a larger field in which the subjects walked to the chosen location.

In a recent series of experiments with a species of corvid, Clark's nutcracker, Kamil and Jones (1997) have reported success in finding evidence of spatial learning based on the relationship between landmarks. Nutcrackers learned to dig in bedding for a pine seed that was buried midway between a yellow cylinder on the north side of the testing room and a green cylinder on the south side. The distances between the landmarks were varied between trials, over a range of 20 to 120 cm. On test trials, the

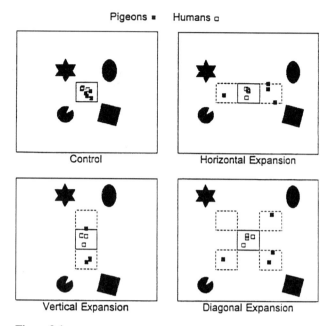

Figure 2.1
The panels show where pigeons and people searched for a goal on a touchscreen monitor after training with the four landmarks in the control configuration and after the landmarks were expanded horizontally, vertically, and diagonally.

birds were tested with five previously unused distances varying from 30 to 110 cm in 20-cm increments. It was found that nutcrackers learned to consistently search near the midpoint between landmarks on both training and test trials. The generality of this relational coding was limited. When the landmarks were rotated 90°, the nutcrackers no longer searched midway between the landmarks. Birds now searched either to the south of the yellow landmark or to the north of the green landmark. Apparently location of the hidden seed had been coded both by the relationship between landmarks and by the direction of individual landmarks. When the landmarks were rotated from their normal axis, nutcrackers resorted to a strategy based on single landmarks. These findings, combined with those of Collett and Spetch, suggest that, although animals may be able to learn locations based on relationships between landmarks, their favored strategy may be to code locations as a distance and direction from a single landmark.

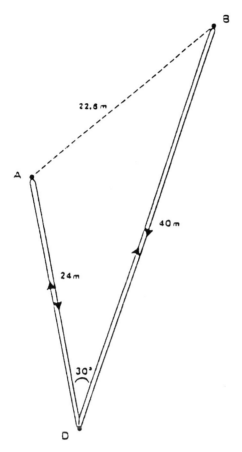

Figure 2.2
In a shortcut experiment by Chapuis and Varlet (1987), dogs were led from Point
D to a food reward at Point A and from Point D to a food reward at Point B.
Shortcut behavior was shown when a dog ran directly from A to B.

Spatial Inference

A second implication of the cognitive map is that animals should be able
to infer routes between locations, even if they have not traveled those
routes. Animals should take *shortcuts*. Figure 2.2 shows a diagram of
paths taken by Alsatian dogs over an outdoor meadow in an experiment
by Chapuis and Varlet (1987). From a starting point, Point D, a dog was
led to Point A and shown a piece of meat hidden in the grass. The dog
was returned to Point D and then led to Point B, where it was shown a
second piece of hidden meat. It was then returned to point D, where its

leash was removed, and it was free to search for the meat. Most dogs took the shorter path to the meat at Point A. The critical question was where they would go after consuming the meat at Point A. Instead of returning to Point D, all dogs took fairly direct routes to Point B. Control tests showed that the dogs were not following the odor of the hidden meat. It appears that they had inferred the shortcut between Points A and B.

Although shortcut experiments of this sort seem to imply a cognitive map, Bennett (1996) has made an important criticism of them. The problem he raises is the possibility that animals may simply be approaching landmarks encountered near rewards when visiting different locations. For example, if dogs in the Chapuis and Varlet experiment spotted certain objects, such as rocks, trees, buildings, etc., near Point B when visiting it, they may also see those objects from Point A. If those landmarks are associated with food, it is not surprising that the dog would approach the landmarks directly and thus appear to be taking a shortcut. Evidence for a cognitive map based on spatial inference in animals thus seems somewhat clouded. Resolution of this question awaits research that controls for this alternate account.

Do Animals Form Topological Maps?

If asked to, most people can draw a roughly accurate topological map of their home, workplace, or city. Such a representation is a form of cognitive map, and we can ask whether animals form such representations based on their travels through a spatial environment. An experiment performed a few years ago by Dallal and Meck (1990, Experiment 3) suggested that rats do form topological maps. Rats were trained on a 12-arm *radial maze* placed in a laboratory room. The radial maze is a popular tool used to study spatial memory in rodents. It consists of a circular central platform with a number of arms that radiate outward from it, with equal angles separating the arms. Eight randomly chosen arms always contained food on every trial. Over repeated trials, rats formed a reference memory for food locations that was shown by the fact that they preferentially visited the rewarded arms before the nonrewarded arms. The rats then were divided into two groups, one called the reversal group and the other called the nonreversal group. Both groups were taken to a new room in which a new 12-arm maze had to be learned, with eight arms rewarded. For the nonreversal group, the pattern of arm locations was exactly the same as that encountered in the first room. For the reversal group, a new random pattern of rewards was used. The interesting finding reported was that the nonreversal group learned to enter the rewarded arms far faster than the reversal group. The implication of this finding is that rats had learned the overall pattern of rewards in the first room and then transferred that pattern to the new maze in the second room. Remember that extramaze cues were of no value in transfer between mazes, because these cues were completely different in the two rooms.

In some experiments carried out recently by myself and my students (Olthof, Sutton, Slumskie, D'Addetta & Roberts, 1999), we asked if rats could transfer a learned maze pattern within the same environment. As shown in Figure 2.3, rats initially learned to find food on only six arms of a 12-arm radial maze. When they had learned to go to the baited arms preferentially, we divided the rats into two groups. One group was transferred to a 180° rotation of the rewarded arms on the same maze, and the control group was transferred to a new random selection of rewarded arms. The results of these manipulations are seen in the top two graphs of Figure 2.4. Performance was plotted as the mean number of arms visited

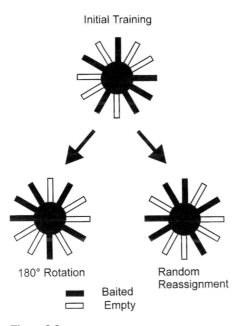

Figure 2.3
After initial training with six of the arms on a 12-arm radial maze baited in a random pattern, half the rats were tested with the pattern rotated 180°, and the other half were tested with a new random pattern.

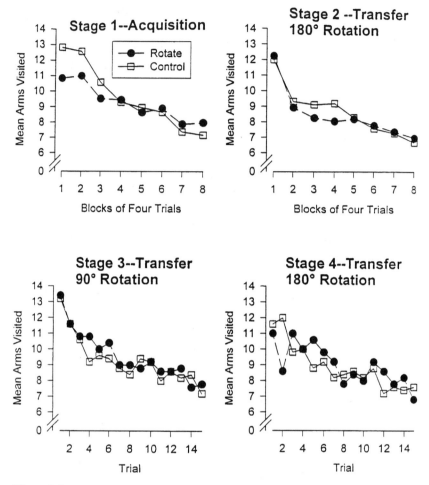

Figure 2.4
Learning curves show no differences in rates of learning between rotate and control groups throughout acquisition and three subsequent stages of pattern rotation.

in order to obtain all six rewards; perfect performance is a score of six. The left graph shows that both groups learned the task over 32 sessions of training. The right graph shows transfer performance. No evidence of positive transfer to the 180° rotation of the pattern was found. In further tests, we continued to rotate the pattern and retrain the rats. The bottom graphs show that no evidence of pattern learning appeared at subsequent 90° and 180° rotations of the pattern.

After some further failures to find evidence that rats could benefit from pattern rotation, we attempted a direct replication of the original Dallal and Meck experiment. Even when a pattern of rewarded arms was transferred to a new testing room, we found no evidence of positive transfer. Our rather extensive experiments then yielded no evidence that rats could learn a topological map of the overall locations of food on a spatial surface. On reflection, this finding makes some sense. Remember that rats, and their ancestors, essentially foraged over a two-dimensional world, with no top view of the environment. This consideration suggests it may not be surprising that they could not form a topological map. It also raises some other interesting questions. Is the human ability to form such topological representations related to the fact that the ancestors of *Homo sapiens* lived in trees? Would birds show better evidence than rats of topological maps?

Evidence has been considered regarding three different implications of cognitive map theory in animals. In none of these areas is the evidence for a cognitive map air tight. The issue of cognitive maps in animals remains controversial and in need of further well controlled research. Most importantly for this chapter, there appears to be no single well established mechanism we can point to as the essential basis of cognitive mapping.

2.2   Multiple Mechanisms

In place of the cognitive map, it will be argued that animals use a number of different mechanisms to keep track of places in space. These mechanisms can be distinguished by the type of cues used and how those cues are processed. They may be divided into two types, internal or *egocentric* mechanisms and external or *allocentric* mechanisms. Two primary egocentric mechanisms will be discussed, path integration and the use of response rules; these mechanisms are largely nonvisual and could be used by a sightless animal. Among allocentric mechanisms, the importance of the geometric frame provided by the environment will be examined, as well as the role of landmarks. Finally, the hierarchical and interactive use of these mechanisms will be emphasized through some examples.

Egocentric Mechanisms

Path integration   Ants and other insects have been observed to leave their nest and search over distant territory by taking tortuous paths. Once a morsel of food is found, however, the ant moves in a very direct line toward its nest, only stopping a few centimeters from the nest. It then appears to find the nest by a systematic search process (Gallistel, 1990). In experiments by Etienne (1992), hamsters in total darkness were observed to travel from a nest box at the periphery of an arena to a pile of hazelnuts in the center of the arena. As a hamster filled its cheek pouches with nuts, it was rotated several times. Nevertheless, the hamster then made its way directly toward the area on the periphery containing its nest. Blindfolded humans led varying distances and through several turns were asked to return to their starting point. Most were able to return to the starting point with some slight degree of error (Loomis, Klatzky, Golledge, Cicinelli, Pellegrino & Fry, 1993).

These examples indicate that widely divergent species are capable of path integration. Path integration, also called dead reckoning, is the ability to maintain an accurate heading and distance to a starting point while traveling a winding route away from the starting point. In general, the amount of error in the return heading increases with the number of turns made on the excursion away from the start. Path integration arises from the use of internal cues supplied by the semicircular canals and by motor cues from kinesthetic receptors and efference copies. The vestibular sense, in particular, may provide information about direction by sensing degree of angular rotation. Distance is sensed by proprioceptive feedback from locomotion. By updating direction and distance traveled information from these receptors, an organism can maintain a vector that will lead it directly to a location near its starting point (Etienne, Berlie, Georgakopoulos & Maurer, 1998).

Although path integration is often thought of as a simpler or more primitive spatial mechanism, some evidence suggests it may be involved in complex maze behavior in rats. In a classic experiment performed by Olton and Samuelson (1976), food was placed in a cup at the end of each of eight arms on a radial maze, and rats were allowed to explore the maze until they had entered each arm and consumed its reward. Over several trials of training, rats came to visit all eight of the arms on the maze with only a rare repeat of an entrance into an arm already visited. Various control experiments showed that rats were not accomplishing this feat by using either odor cues or response algorithms. It was concluded that they had kept track of places previously visited in a working memory for spatial locations. The Olton and Samuelson experiment and many others that replicated it were performed on open, elevated mazes placed in testing rooms with a rich supply of extramaze cues. These cues then undoubtedly provided a rich supply of information about arms visited on the maze (Suzuki et al., 1980). In other experiments, however, rats have been tested on radial mazes without visual cues. Zoladek and Roberts (1978) tested rats deprived of vision, and Brown and Moore (1997) tested rats in a radial maze that consisted of an enclosed center and arms that were made of opaque PVC tubing. In both cases, rats learned to visit all eight arms on the maze with a very low level of arm repetition. Although rats might have found some sources of intramaze cues to guide their travels, a strong possibility is that they used the same kind of internal information implicated in path integration. It may be then that even complex travels to a number of locations can be stored on the basis of internal cues. One final piece of information suggests that internal cues may be used to traverse the radial maze even when rats have normal access to visual cues. Ossenkopp and Hargreaves (1993) made vestibular lesions (labyrinthectomies) in rats and found that these rats made far more repetitive errors on an eight-arm radial maze than did control rats.

Response rules Independent of environmental cues, animals may sometime be able to solve spatial problems by learning to execute a particular response. A common example is that of an animal learning to always turn right or left in a T-maze. A somewhat more complex response rule, but one easily learned by rats, is to alternate left and right turns in a maze. In some cases, behavior that follows a complex pattern may arise from response rules. In some recent experiments by Brown and Terrinoni (1996), rats searched for food rewards placed in holes on the top of vertical poles. Rats learned to stand on their rear legs and examine the tops of poles for sucrose pellet rewards. During testing sessions, rats were allowed to explore 5×5 arrays of poles, with rewards placed only at the tops of poles in a 2×2 square pattern; the position of the 2×2 pattern within the 5×5 array of poles was changed randomly from session to session. A top view of one such testing arrangement is shown in Figure 2.5. The question

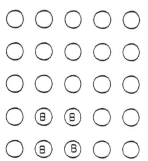

Figure 2.5
Diagram of the 5 × 5 arrangement of poles used by Brown and Terrinoni (1996) to study spatial pattern learning by rats, with four baited (B) poles forming a square pattern.

addressed was whether rats could learn to respond in a manner that suggested they had a representation of a square configuration. Although rats did not learn to execute this pattern perfectly, with sufficient training animals chose poles that possibly could complete the pattern at a higher probability than expected by chance. Thus, after discovering two rewards in a row or column, rats were more likely to choose a pole that formed the corner of square than one which extended the column or row.

Although Brown and Terrinoni (1996) suggested that these findings indicate that rats formed a geometric representation of a square, a simpler explanation is possible. Instead of forming a representation of a square, rats may have learned response rules that allowed them to choose rewarded poles more frequently than chance expectation. For example, a rat could have learned "after finding two rewards in a row or column, make a 90° turn either right or left before inspecting the next pole, and "after finding a reward following a 90° turn, make another 90° turn in the same direction and inspect the next pole." These rules require a rat to learn to respond in certain ways contingent upon its preceding response and its reward outcome, but they are reasonably simple and limited rules that could lead a rat to improve its chances of finding reward and to give the appearance of having mastered a square pattern.

Allocentric Mechanisms

Beacon homing A person I used to travel with always attempted to associate important sites with a nearby landmark, typically a tall building

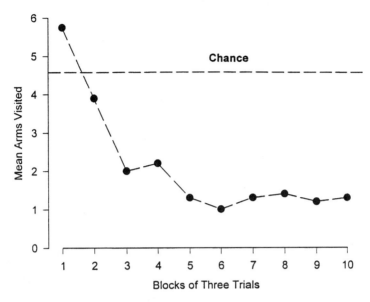

Figure 2.6
On an eight-arm radial maze containing seven black arms and one white arm, rats rapidly learned to enter the white arm first when it was the only arm containing food.

or statue. To find his way back to that site, he would search seemingly randomly until he spotted the landmark and then he would travel directly to it. This is an example of human beacon homing by following a salient cue that leads directly to the place sought. Animals make use of such beacons also, if given the opportunity to use them. In an experiment carried out in my laboratory, a black, eight-arm radial maze was used. On each trial that a rat was placed on the maze, a white metal cover was placed over one randomly chosen arm of the maze, and food reward was always placed in the goal cup at the end of that arm only. The graph presented in Figure 2.6 shows the performance of four rats trained on this task. The measure of response accuracy is the mean number of arms entered on the maze in order to obtain the reward. Each rat was tested with two trials per day for 15 days, and accuracy is plotted against blocks of three trials. The horizontal line shows the number of arm entries expected by chance alone. On the first block of trials, rats took between five and six arm entries to find the food. Over subsequent trials, mean arm entries dropped continuously to a level substantially below chance. By trial blocks 5–10, rats usually entered the white arm on the first arm entry. They had learned to the use the white arm as a beacon showing the way to food.

In the natural world, animals may sometimes be able to use beacons to navigate toward a goal. The location of food, water, or an animal's home might be at the base of a tree or near a large rock. On many other occasions, however, important sites may be located in an open, homogeneous field that offers no beacons. Nevertheless, animals are able to use cues only distantly related to the goal site to precisely track its position. The use of multiple cues to define a specific location in space is called *piloting*. We turn to some mechanisms by which animals may learn to use landmarks to pilot to a precise position.

The geometric module   Important sources of information for locating spatial position are the geometric frames within which people and animals locomote. Although you may not often be aware of them, the walls of your office or of the rooms in your home provide a background that helps to specify the location of objects in the room. Typically, we use this geometric frame in conjunction with other cues in a room, such as doors, windows, and pictures, to specify places in the room. An interesting experiment carried out by Cheng (1986) shows that, under certain conditions, a rat may be primarily dependent upon the geometric framework of its environment.

Rats were trained to dig for a piece of food buried within bedding located in a dimly illuminated rectangular box. As shown in Figure 2.7, one long wall and the two adjacent shorter walls were black, but the other long wall was white. Panels which differed in their visual appearance were placed in the corners of the box. In addition, these corner panels were further differentiated by distinctive odors placed on them. In the diagram shown in Figure 2.7, food was buried at the location of the black circle. Although rats learned to dig at that location for food, they often made errors by digging in the wrong place. When a rat made an error, it usually dug in the corner diagonally across from the one where the food was actually hidden, the location shown by the open circle in Figure 2.7. Thus, the rat dug at a location that was 180° rotated from the true location of food. Such an error should not have occurred if the rat was using the visual and/or odor cues on the panels, since both types of cues differed between these diagonal panels. Rats might have learned to dig at a certain distance from the corner in which the white wall was on the left and the

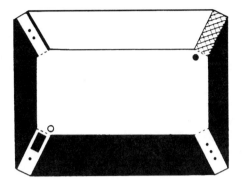

Figure 2.7
Drawing of the box used by Cheng (1986) to study the geometric module in rats. The corner panels were differentiated by visual appearance and odor. The filled circle indicates the location of reward, and the unfilled circle represents the same location rotated by 180°.

black wall was on the right. The nature of the diagonal errors suggests this was not the case, because the diagonally opposite corner had black walls on both the left and right. Cheng concluded that rats had simply coded the spatial location of food as being in the corner with a long wall on the left and a short wall on the right. Given this geometric module coding, diagonal corner errors should occur, because this corner has the same relationship to the geometric frame as the correct corner. Rats did dig more frequently in the correct corner than in the diagonal corner, suggesting that the visual and olfactory cues played some role. Nevertheless, the frequency and precision of diagonal corner errors suggested that rats represented the box primarily as an environmental frame.

It should be emphasized that the rat's dependence upon the geometric frame was caused by the use of an apparatus that allowed no orientation toward cues outside the testing arena. When rats could see room cues outside the arena, diagonal corner errors disappeared, and rats continually dug for food in the correct location (Margules & Gallistel, 1988). When the Cheng experiment was performed with humans, an interesting developmental difference appeared. Both adult students and 20-month-old children made diagonal corner errors when only cues from the geometric frame were available. If one wall was made distinguishable in color, the adults always searched in the correct corner. Children, however, continued to search as much in the diagonal corner as in the correct corner (Hermer & Spelke, 1994, 1996). It appears that dependence on the environmental frame is very strong in children and only weakens with development (Hermer-Vazquez, Spelke, & Katsnelson, 1999).

Piloting with landmarks   Although the Cheng experiment showed that animals can be almost completely dependent on the visual appearance of the geometric frame of an environment, other research indicates that animals also use isolated cues within an environment to guide their travel to particular locations. For example, rats placed within a cylindrical environment that provides no locations that are distinguished by the environmental frame still are able to locate rewarded and nonrewarded arms on a radial maze, if distinct visual cues are attached to the wall surrounding the maze (Suzuki et al., 1980).

Even more impressive is the finding that animals can find locations in areas of space that have no distinguishing characteristics. The most researched example of this capability is the study of rats' ability to find a submerged platform in a water tank (Morris, 1981). Rats were placed in a circular tank filled with an opaque mixture of milk and water. At one location in the tank, a platform was placed just beneath the surface of the water. Once the rat found this platform, it could rest on it without having to continue to swim. On initial training trials, rats swam from a fixed location on the side of the tank and took long periods of time before finding the platform. After 15 trials, however, all rats swam immediately to the platform. If they were now released from different sides of the pool, they still swam immediately to the location of the platform. In other words, the rats had learned the platform's location in space and could approach it from different directions. They were not using a response rule, and they could not have approached a beacon, because the platform was located beneath a white surface that was homogeneous with surrounding areas.

How did rats then find the platform? It appears that they must have used cues in the environment external to the water tank to *pilot* toward the location of the platform. On the two-dimensional surface of a maze or water tank, a goal location can be fixed precisely by its angular direction and distance from two external landmarks. Thus, if a rat could spot two landmarks from the goal platform, say a door and a picture on the wall, and store the angular difference between those landmarks and their distances from the platform, it could then always locate the goal by swimming to a location at which the perceived angle and distances matched its memory.

A somewhat simpler mechanism for remembering spatial location has been discovered in honeybees (Cartwright & Collett, 1983). Bees were allowed to fly into a room that was painted entirely white and to find a few drops of a sucrose solution placed in a cup. A black cylinder was placed a few centimeters from the cup. It was shown that bees used the cylinder as a landmark, because they failed to find the food readily when the cylinder was removed. Of particular interest were tests on which the size of the cylinder was varied. If it was made smaller than the training size, bees searched nearer the cylinder than the actual location of the goal, and, if it was made larger than the training size, bees searched farther away from the cylinder than the actual location of the goal. Cartwright and Collett concluded that bees were attempting to match the image of the cylinder seen to a memory of the apparent size of the cylinder or a *snapshot* taken during training. The image and memory only matched when the bee was close to a small cylinder and distant from a large cylinder.

The diagrams in Figure 2.8 show how bees make use of multiple landmarks. Bees learned to search for sucrose at fixed distances from three equally spaced landmarks, as shown in Diagram A. Variation in the size

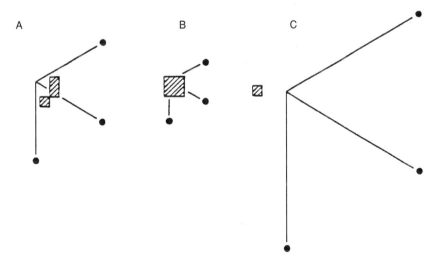

Figure 2.8
Cartwright and Collett (1983) trained bees to find food near the search area shown in Diagram A and then tested bees with the landmarks moved nearer together (Diagram B) or farther apart (Diagram C).

of the landmarks now had little effect on behavior, but the distance between landmarks had a marked effect. When the landmarks were moved
closer together (Diagram B), bees searched at a location nearer to the
landmarks than the training location. When the landmarks were moved
farther apart (Diagram C), the search location was more distant from the
landmarks than the training location. Bees searched at locations that
maintained the same compass directions between the landmarks as
those they had encountered in training. Once again, the snapshot model
accounts for these findings. The bees searched at locations where the
positions of the landmarks on its visual image matched the positions of
the landmarks on its two-dimensional snapshot taken in training.

It appears that at least some vertebrates do not use so simple a mechanism to pilot through space relative to landmarks. Collett, Cartwright and
Smith (1986) tested Mongolian gerbils in a task similar to that given bees.
Food was hidden in the bedding of an arena, and a white cylinder landmark was placed at a fixed distance from the food. Displacement tests
indicated that gerbils were using the landmark to find the food. Of particular interest, the gerbils continued to search at a fixed distance from the
landmark even when its size was changed. Unlike bees, it appears that
retinal size had little influence on gerbils' estimation of the distance of the
goal from the landmark. Similar findings have been reported in pigeon
studies (Cheng, 1988).

If rodents, birds, and presumably other vertebrates use landmark geom-
etry to pinpoint locations in space, how do they use landmarks to accomplish this feat? The Collett et al. (1986) and Spetch et al. (1996, 1997)
experiments discussed under challenges to the cognitive map indicated
that animals frequently compute the distance and direction from only a
single landmark. On some occasions, such as locating a hidden platform
in a water tank, two or more landmarks must be used. The psychologist
Ken Cheng has explored models by which birds might use multiple landmarks to find hidden food in an experimental arena. Two models have
been proposed, one called the *vector-averaging model*, and the other called
the *direction-averaging model* (Cheng, 1994). In the upper panel of Figure
2.9, a diagram of an experimental situation is shown, with differential
predictions about search behavior made for the two models. The situation
diagrammed is one in which a landmark consists of a cylinder with a
stripe painted on it. Pigeons are trained to search for food at a fixed distance from the landmark and stripe (Vector 2). It is assumed that a
pigeon will learn this position by computing distance and direction vectors

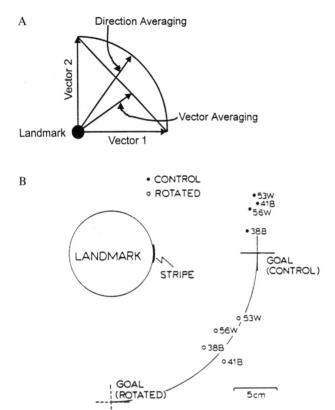

Figure 2.9
Diagram A shows predictions made by Cheng (1994) about where pigeons should search when landmark vectors indicated the location of food in two different places. Diagram B shows that pigeons in an experiment searched along the arc of the circle predicted by the direction averaging model.

from the cylinder stripe landmark and from other landmarks available in the testing environment. After control tests establish that pigeons search (dig in bedding) near the goal, the cylinder is rotated 90°, and further tests are carried out. If a pigeon were to use the goal-landmark vector indicated by the cylinder stripe alone (Vector 1), it should search at the rotated goal position. However, goal-landmark vectors based on other landmarks should tell the pigeon that the food is at the end of Vector 2. Cheng assumed that birds will average these two sources of goal information. The theoretical question that distinguishes the two models is how this averaging will take place. In the vector-averaging model, it is assumed that the pigeon will average the vectors (each based on integrated distance and direction information) that direct it to the ends of Vectors 1 and 2 and will search someplace on a the straight line between these two points. In the direction-averaging model, on the other hand, it is assumed that the pigeon computes distance and direction separately. Since the distance to the end of each vector is the same, averaging these distances leads to the prediction that the pigeon should search somewhere along the arc shown in Figure 2.9.

The lower panel in Figure 2.9 shows some actual data taken from one of Cheng's experiments in which four pigeons were tested. On control trials with the nonrotated landmark, the pigeons (indicated by their numbers) all searched a little north of the goal, but near the goal. On test trials with the goal rotated, all four pigeons searched at an intermediate direction between the location predicted by the landmark stripe and other landmarks, but they all searched near the arc predicted by the direction-averaging model. In total, Cheng carried out four experiments, and they all supported the direction-averaging model. These findings then suggest that pigeons, and perhaps other species, compute the direction and distance of landmarks from salient locations as separate pieces of information that may be independently averaged when placed in conflict.

Hierarchy and Interaction among Spatial Mechanisms

The point to be made here is that animals often have multiple cues or mechanisms available by which to encode locations in space. These mechanisms may be used redundantly, or one mechanism may replace another with experience or with the removal of a particular cue. Experiments in which the spatial environment is transformed in some way often reveal alternative spatial codes. Two examples will be discussed.

In experiments carried out by Hicks (1964) and Mackintosh (1965), rats were trained to run down a start alley and to turn right or left in a T-maze for food reward. In order to find out how rats were coding this problem, the experimenters occasionally placed the start alley on the opposite side of the maze. Thus, if rats had been trained to approach the choice point from the South, they were now tested with an approach from the North. In the early stages of learning, rats went to the same place or arm from both sides of the maze. If food was in the arm on the West side of the maze (requiring a left turn during training from the South), rats made a right turn when tested from the North and continued to go to the West. After some overtraining on this task, however, rats began to turn left on trials from both the South and North sides of the maze, thus leading them to West and East goal boxes on training and test trials, respectively. Apparently, rats initially used extramaze cues to locate the *place* where reward was located on the early trials of training but then switched to the *response rule* "always turn left" on the later trials. Perhaps a motor rule required less cognitive effort than locating extramaze cues.

Save, Poucet and Thinus-Blanc (1998) required rats to swim to a submerged platform in the corner of a rectangular tank filled with opaque water. The tank was surrounded by a curtain, and a black card placed along one wall of the tank provided the only local cue. After the rats had learned to find the platform, the card was removed. The rats' ability to find the platform initially was disrupted, showing that they were using the black card as a landmark. However, they rapidly learned to swim directly to the platform in the absence of the card landmark. Save et al. suggested that rats used some uncontrolled background cue outside the testing arena as a landmark, such as a sound or an odor. Finally, the tank was rotated 90°, and rats now swam equally often to the platform corner and to the diagonally opposite corner. When deprived of both a local cue by removing the card and of a static background cue by rotating the tank, rats now used the geometric frame of the tank as a cue to the location of the hidden platform. Thus, rats used three different spatial codes to detect a goal. When one code was no longer available, they fell back on another. Such experiments are particularly revealing of the complex multiplicity of cues animals use to code important locations.

2.3 The Possible Use of Spatial Codes in Other Cognitive Domains

Ample evidence in the literature and reviewed in this volume indicates that people use spatial representations to deal with problems in other cognitive domains. This section discusses the possibility that animals also might use spatial schemas to deal with problems in other cognitive domains. The fundamental nature of spatial representations for the survival of organisms suggests that such representations might be found in both humans and nonhumans. Two speculative examples will be discussed here.

Time, Number, and Space

Two important success stories in animal cognition are the discoveries in the last 20 years that animals are excellent timers and counters (Boysen & Capaldi, 1993; Bradshaw & Szabadi, 1997). Animals can discriminate both time durations and number of events and can accurately estimate time and number. How are time and number represented? Perhaps the best known account is the dual-mode model proposed by Meck, Church and Gibbon (1985). This model holds that time and number are represented as accumulations of pulses emitted from a pacemaker. Numbers of pulses emitted over a period of time or by a number of events are stored in a reference memory and provide criteria for timing or counting subsequent stimuli.

As an example of timing, an animal might be reinforced on a fixed-interval schedule that delivered reward for the first response made 20 seconds after a light signal was turned on. The model assumes that the light signal closes a timing switch which allows pulses to flow continuously from the pacemaker to an accumulator. If pulses are emitted from a pacemaker at the rate of 5/second, then 100 pulses would have accumulated and been sent to a working memory by 20 seconds. This total then is stored in a permanent reference memory when reward occurs. On subsequent trials, a criterion value stored in reference memory is retrieved into a comparator, where it is compared with the number of accumulating pulses in working memory. When these two values are sufficiently close to one another, a decision is made to begin responding.

The same system is used for counting by assuming that a counting switch closes for a short fixed period and then reopens each time an event to be counted occurs. Thus, if 10 light flashes were counted, each flash might cause the switch to close and allow three pulses to enter the accumulator and go to working memory. If the first response made after 10 flashes was rewarded, 30 pulses would be in working memory and would be stored in reference memory. On subsequent trials, values around 30 pulses would be retrieved from reference memory and be used as criteria for comparison with the accumulating pulses in working memory. In this case, the comparator would yield a response decision when the accumulating pulses neared 30 and the number of flashes approached 10.

An alternate way of thinking about the representation of time and number is to conceive of them as points on a spatial line. If this line extends into the distance, points equal distances apart on the line become perceptually compressed, as equal distances become compressed on the retinal image for far versus near spaces. In support of such a proposal, Staddon and Higa (1998) have suggested that subjective time may grow as the logarithm of real time. In this case, equal differences between time durations would be less discriminable for longer times than for shorter times. In the case of number, Dehaene (1997) has argued that there is a strong relationship between numbers and space, with people often reporting a number line in which numbers are ordered in quantity from left to right. This number line becomes progressively compressed at greater numbers. Dehaene further speculates that this number line may arise from a cortical spatial mapping of numbers.

One implication of the notion that time and number are represented as a progressively compressed line is that estimations of distance, time, and number all should obey Weber's law. That is, degree of error in estimating distances, lengths of time, or number of events should increase in proportion to the quantity estimated. Some evidence for this prediction from experiments with pigeons is shown in Figure 2.10. The top graph shows data from an experiment by Cheng (1990) in which pigeons had to find the location of buried food that was either 30 cm or 15 cm away from a landmark. The distributions plotted represent the time pigeons spent searching in areas near the food, with the peak of the distributions being the actual location of food. The important point to be made is that the width of the distribution for the food placed 30 cm from the landmark is about twice as great as the width of the distribution for food placed 15 cm from the landmark.

The lower left graph in Figure 2.10 shows time estimation by pigeons (Roberts, Cheng & Cohen, 1989). Pigeons were trained to peck a key that delivered food after 15 seconds when an overhead light came on or that delivered food after 30 seconds when a tone was played. These fixed interval schedules of reinforcement produce a scallop pattern in which the bird responds only at a slow rate at the beginning of an interval and then accelerates responding as the moment of reinforcement approaches. Tests eventually are given in which the light or tone signal is presented for a 90-second period, and no reinforcement is delivered. This testing procedure is called the *peak procedure*. When rate of responding in successive time bins is plotted, the curve approximates a Gaussian shape, and its peak indicates the pigeon's estimate of the length of the fixed interval. As the graph shows, the peaks of these curves are very near the reinforcement intervals of 15 and 30 seconds. Notice also, that the spread of the 30-s tone signal curve is about twice as great as that of the 15-second time signal curve. This scalar property of time estimation has been observed in many experiments with animals and people.

Finally, the curves in the lower right graph show number estimation by pigeons (Roberts & Boisvert, 1998). In this case, pigeons had to respond

A

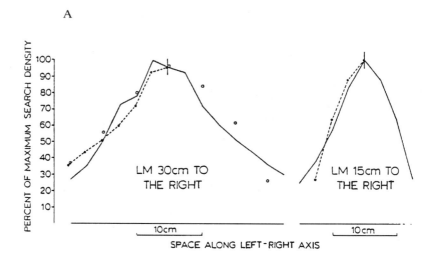

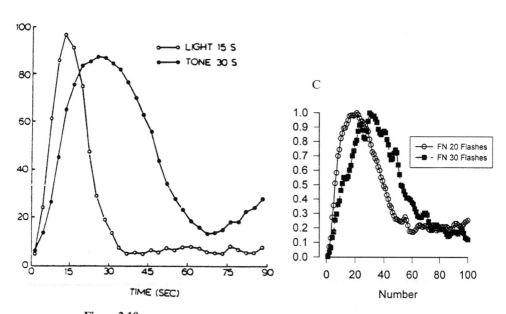

Figure 2.10
Diagram A shows the spread of spatial searching in pigeons when the goal is near
or far from a landmark. In Diagram B, the spread of time estimation in the peak
procedure is shown when pigeons have to estimate 15 seconds or 30 seconds. In
Diagram C, the spread of number estimation is shown when pigeons had to estimate 20 or 30 light flashes.

to a fixed number of red light flashes presented on a pecking key. Under one condition, reinforcement was delivered for the first response made after 20 flashes, and, under another condition, pigeons were reinforced for the first response made after 30 flashes. As was the case for time estimation, number estimation was measured by the peak procedure; test trials were introduced in which 100 flashes occurred, and no reinforcement was given. The peaks of these curves accurately reflect the criterion numbers of flashes to reinforcement in each condition. Again, the spread of the 30-flash curve is greater than that of the 20-flash curve.

These findings suggest that at least one prediction of a compressed linear representation of space, time, and number is satisfied. In all three cases, estimations of magnitude obey Weber's law by showing that error increases in proportion to the magnitude estimated.

Transitive Inference

The data in Figure 2.10 argue only indirectly for spatial representation in a different cognitive domain. Could more direct evidence of a spatial schema in animals be found by actually providing animals with a spatial code? An answer may be found in studies of transitive inference. Given a relationship between two items, such as greater than, children and adults taught that $A > B$, $B > C$, and $C > D$ are often able to reason that $A > D$, even though no relationship between A and D was ever expressed. Although transitive inference can arise from formal logical operations, several theorists have argued that humans frequently use a linear mental model to solve the problem (DeSoto, London & Handel, 1965, Huttenlocher, 1968; Sternberg, 1980; Trabasso, 1975). That is, people place stimulus items on a mental line, with the first inequality at one end and the last inequality at the other end. Relationships between any pair of items then may be easily inferred by the relative positions of the items on the line. As Hummel and Holyoak (this volume) point out, the use of such a spatial representation means that people's choice of A over D is not really an inference but simply an observation of relative position on a line. Nevertheless, the notion of a spatial code has provided considerable insight into how people actually solve transitivity problems.

How do independently presented relations between two objects become represented as a linear order? A two-stage model has been suggested in which premises are initially linguistically encoded as separate relationships or propositions; based on common terms and relationships, these initial units are placed into a linear spatial framework that not only maintains the original relationships but also shows transitive relationships (Sternberg, 1980; Kallio, 1982; Hummel & Holyoak, this volume). Given the requirement in this model of an initial stage of linguistic coding, it is quite surprising that the transitive inference phenomenon has been demonstrated in animals without language, specifically in rats, pigeons, and nonhuman primates (Davis, 1992; Fersen, Wynne, Delius & Staddon, 1991; Gillan, 1981; Roberts & Phelps, 1994). In these experiments, the relationship between two stimuli is simply instantiated by rewarding one stimulus and nonrewarding the other. A choice test is then given between two stimuli never presented together, and a preference for the transitively more valued stimulus is shown.

The details of one of these experiment will be described here. Using procedures that were developed by Davis (1992), Roberts and Phelps (1994) trained two groups of rats to make five different odor discriminations. The odors almond, cherry, vanilla, orange, and coconut were placed on the doors of tunnels. Rats were presented with two tunnels on each trial, with one tunnel containing food reward and the other tunnel empty. A correct response was made by pushing through the door of the correct tunnel. Using letters to symbolize different odor stimuli, rats learned the discriminations A+ B−, B+ C−, C+ D−, D+ E−, and E+ F−. Trials containing all of these discriminations were presented concurrently within sessions. The two groups of rats differed in the spatial positions of the stimuli used in these discriminations. As shown in Figure 2.11, the linear arrangement group always had the pairs of tunnels placed in a row, with the A+ B− problem in the first two positions, the B+ C− problem in the second and third positions, and so on to the E+ F− problem in the fifth and sixth positions. Rats in a random control group had these same problems randomly placed at different adjacent positions along this row from one trial to the next. Once these discriminations were well learned, both groups were given a choice between tunnels B and D on a Y-maze. Importantly, the Y-maze test was carried out in a different room from the original training. We reasoned that if rats in the linear arrangement group had formed a linear representation of the locations of stimuli A to F, they should be able to retrieve that representation and use it to choose the stimulus closer to the A+ end of the line (stimulus B) over the stimulus closer to the F− end of the line (stimulus D). In fact, these rats chose the stimulus B tunnel 74.3% of the time, a value that significantly exceeded the chance level of 50%. On the other hand, the random control group chose tunnel B only on 47.9% of the test trials.

LINEAR ARRANGEMENT

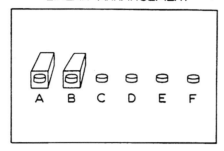

CIRCULAR ARRANGEMENT

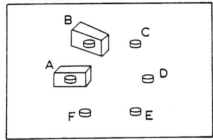

Figure 2.11
The linear and circular arrangements of tunnels used by Roberts and Phelps (1994) to study the use of a spatial code by rats given transitive inference problems.

In a second experiment, Roberts and Phelps used the circular arrangement of tunnels shown in the lower panel of Figure 2.11. In this case, stimuli A and F were placed adjacent to one another and could not serve as the endpoints of a straight line. A linear arrangement group like that run in Experiment 1 was also trained and tested. Both groups had the same pairs of odors placed at the same positions throughout training. It was predicted that the linear arrangement group, but not the circular arrangement group, would show transitive inference. When given a test between tunnels B and D in a new testing room, the linear arrangement group chose B 70% of the trials, but the circular arrangement group chose B only 52.1% of the trials. Thus, both experiments supported the contention that rats given a linear arrangement of stimuli were able to form a spatial representation that allowed them to respond correctly to stimuli never previously presented together.

What are the implications of these findings for human and animal cognition? If animals demonstrate transitive inference, this finding may imply that initial premises can be stored as nonlinguistic propositions based on the relative value of two stimuli as indicated by which is rewarded and which is nonrewarded. An animal then would somehow integrate these propositions into a linear representation. Before making this assumption, however, alternative possibilities should be considered. For example, it has been argued that "transitive inference" in pigeons may simply result from differences in associative strength conditioned to the training stimuli. Both Couvillon and Bitterman (1992) and Fersen et al. (1991) have maintained that choice of B on a B-versus-D test may arise simply because the training procedures caused more associative value to be conditioned to B than to D. This argument does not account for the Roberts and Phelps findings, however, because examination of the training data showed that stimulus D was actually rewarded on a higher proportion of trials than stimulus B. Furthermore, even when training conditions are used that prevent differences in associative strength between test stimuli, transitive inference is found in pigeons (Weaver, Steirn & Zentall, 1997).

If transitive inference in animals cannot be attributed to experimental artifact, how could an animal represent a set of stimuli as a linear array. Chalmers and McGonigle (this volume) argue that temporal order of training pairs is a primary source of linear ordering, with spatial position being a secondary factor that prevents interference in memory. As support for this position, Kallio (1982) found stronger evidence of transitive inference in children when only serial order cues were present in training than when only spatial location cues were present. On the other hand, the findings of Roberts and Phelps suggest that rats showed transitive inference when *only* spatial cues were available. The training problems were presented concurrently, so that serial order could not be used as a cue. Kallio reported that the training apparatus he used was rotated between trials and that this manipulation may have disrupted the effectiveness of spatial location cues. In addition, rotation of the training apparatus leads to an inconsistency between the training stimuli and spatial cues external to the training apparatus. Roberts and Phelps left their apparatus in a constant position and required rats to approach the stimulus boxes from opposite directions on different trials; thus, room spatial cues were always associated with proximity to the same training stimuli. When only a consistent spatial framework can be used to code the position of stimuli, rats appear to use a spatial code.

It should be noted that the control conditions of Roberts and Phelps eliminated both temporal serial order cues and spatial cues, since problems were presented concurrently and their spatial positions were either randomized (Experiment 1) or placed in a circle (Experiment 2). When both sources of ordering were removed, animals showed indifference between stimuli B and D. Could rats use just serial order as a cue? Davis (1992) trained rats with no spatial cues present but presented his training pairs in serial order. When tested, rats showed significant transitive inference. This finding, when combined with that of Roberts and Phelps, suggests that rats can use *either* spatial order or temporal order as a cue for the overall order of training stimuli. What is unknown from these observations is whether the final representations differ or are the same. That is, could a rat use temporal order to form a spatial representation of linearity or use spatial position to form a temporal representation of linearity? Such questions await further research.

2.4   Conclusions

This review of spatial representation in animals emphasizes the multiplicity of mechanisms used and the hierarchical and conditional nature of their use. Animals without vision often find their way through space by dead reckoning, and we saw evidence that even sighted animals may use this mechanism. Under dim illumination, the geometric framework within which an animal finds itself may be sufficient to guide its search for food. Although animals will readily home on beacons located near important places, they can find salient locations on an open field with no distinguishing features, such as the submerged platform in a water tank filled with opaque water. Animals undoubtedly use distant landmarks to find such locations, but the way in which they do it may vary between species and situations. Bees appear to match snapshot memories to the apparent size of landmarks, but vertebrates studied appear to compute distance and direction of landmarks. The issue of cognitive maps is controversial. None of the evidence for relational use of landmarks, shortcuts, or a topological representation of space has gone unquestioned. Although some evidence suggests that birds may be able to use the geometric relationships between landmarks to locate a goal, substantial research suggests that animals often favor locating goals relative to the distance and direction of a single landmark. Animal shortcuts may result from direct approach to cues associated with reward, and recent tests for topological representation have failed to show any transfer of learned patterns from one setting to another.

Given the unquestionable importance of spatial representation to animals, it is possible that they use such representations to deal with problems in other cognitive domains. Some evidence in support of the idea that animals might use linear spatial models to keep track of time and number and to perform transitive inference was discussed, but these possibilities remain highly speculative.

Acknowledgments

Support for preparation of this manuscript was provided by a research grant to W. A. Roberts from the Natural Sciences and Engineering Research Council of Canada.

Chapter 3

Thinking Through Maps

Lynn S. Liben

3.1 Spatial Representations and Thought

Spatial representations help us think. As illustrated by research reported throughout this volume, one important family of spatial representations for thought includes mental representations that users create in the course of reasoning. But another powerful family of spatial representations includes the ready-made, external spatial representations that are available to individuals in their educational, occupational, and everyday worlds. Given that ready-made representations are pervasive in our intellectual lives, it is important to study their contributions to cognition if we are to have a complete understanding of the ways in which spatial representations support thinking and problem solving.

But it is not only because external spatial representations are ubiquitous that they are of interest. They also provide important tools for our research. For example, by manipulating the kinds of external spatial representations that are given *to* problem solvers, we can evaluate whether novices and younger children are unable to use the kinds of representations generated by experts and older children, or if instead they simply fail to produce them on their own. By varying parameters of representations that we provide, we can investigate the effectiveness of representational techniques that would be difficult (or even impossible) to study if we had to wait for their spontaneous emergence (see Liben, 1997). Most important, external spatial representations are of interest because they may serve cognitive functions that are different from those served by spatial representations generated mentally in the course of thought.

As discussed in detail elsewhere (e.g., see Cleveland, 1985; Kosslyn, 1985, 1989; Liben, 1997, 1999; Tufte, 1983; and Tversky, this volume), there are many forms of external representations. Among them are diagrams, blueprints, graphs, computer visualizations, and—the focus of this chapter —maps. Maps are a particularly important kind of external spatial representation to study for a number of reasons. First, their referent is essential to human existence: we could not live without moving in and using the spatial environment. Second, and perhaps as a consequence of the first, maps are pervasive across time and cultures (e.g., Harley & Woodward, 1987; Stea, Blaut & Stephens, 1996). Maps are among the tools that societies use to communicate information and skills, and to socialize new generations to think about and use the large-scale environment (e.g., see Downs & Liben, 1993; Gauvain, 1993a, 1993b; Uttal, 1999).

Third, maps play an influential role in the formation of the *cognitive* map, that is, "the representation of the geographical environment as it exists within a person's mind" (Downs & Stea, 1977, 4). In other words, the way in which people come to think about the world is affected not only by their own direct physical experience in that world, but also by exposure to *representations* of that world (see Liben, 1991; Liben & Downs, 1991). The influence of representations on cognitive maps is likely to be particularly great in cases in which there is no direct experience to rely upon, either because the particular individual has not had relevant direct experience (e.g., someone who has not actually visited a particular city but has experienced it via photographs and maps), or because the human perceptual system is incapable of certain kinds of experience (e.g., our motor and visual systems do not allow us to view the entire Earth simultaneously, although we can do so via maps). Finally, and consistent with the prior assertion that external spatial representations serve functions that are different from those served by spontaneously self-generated spatial representations, maps support a wide range of thinking and problem-solving tasks.

Before launching into discussion of maps and their role in problem solving, it is useful to clarify the distinctions between the two kinds of maps just mentioned, that is, between *cognitive* maps (most commonly what is meant by the word "map" in psychological research) and *cartographic* maps (most commonly what is meant by the word "map" elsewhere, and what psychologists often refer to as "real" maps). I discuss this distinction briefly in the first section entitled "Cognitive and Cartographic Maps: Siblings, not Twins." After making the case that cognitive and cartographic maps are not identical, and that cartographic maps are an important focus of psychological study, I propose and discuss three "Principles of Cartographic Maps." These are the core principles that must be understood by the map user, irrespective of whether the user is a person on the street, a student in a classroom, or a researcher in the lab. But how do users progress in their understanding of these principles, and thus of maps? I describe this progress from the perspective of ontogenetic development in the section entitled "The Development of Map Understanding." I organize the discussion around the three core map principles, and provide illustrative empirical findings related to each. In the concluding section I return to the broader focus of this volume by discussing "Cartographic Maps as Tools for Enhancing and Studying Thought," by reviewing some of the ways that maps are (and might be) used for reasoning and problem solving.

3.2   Cognitive and Cartographic Maps: Siblings, Not Twins

As Roberts (this volume) observed in the prior chapter, the notion of the cognitive map has had a long and controversial history. Thus, my own review will necessarily be abbreviated and, no doubt, engender at least some additional controversy. (More extensive discussions may be found in Downs, 1981; and in Downs & Stea, 1977.) That disclaimer aside, I propose two fundamental, but interdependent, distinctions between cognitive and cartographic maps: (1) the medium is internal and mental in the former versus external and palpable in the latter, and (2) formats are metaphorical in the former but literal in the latter.

The first of these points implies that to examine an individual's cognitive map, it is necessary for a researcher to find some way to externalize it. Note, though, that what is externalized is a function not only of what the individual knows about the space, but also of the processes used to manipulate and communicate that knowledge. Research using a paradigm developed by Kosslyn, Pick and Fariello (1974) illustrates this point.

Preschool children and adults first learned the locations of 10 toys in a 17-ft^2 room that had been divided into quadrants by transparent and opaque barriers (low fences and hanging blankets, respectively). Of interest was whether the cognitive maps of (in fact, equal) distances between pairs of toys would differ as a function of whether direct locomotion and/or visual integration between the toys had been possible during learning. To assess cognitive maps, participants were given a referent toy, and then asked to select which of the remaining 9 toys was closest to that referent, next closest, and so on, until all toys were ranked. By repeating this procedure with different initial referent toys, and by subjecting rank orderings to multidimensional scaling (MDS), Kosslyn et al. (1974) found that children exaggerated distances of toy pairs separated by both kinds of barriers, whereas adults exaggerated across opaque barriers only. They thus concluded that direct locomotion affected preschoolers' but not adults' cognitive maps.

But do these results necessarily tell us that what children "know" about where the toys are located? Suppose, for the moment, that children have a perfectly scaled "map in the head." It still may be the case that when faced with a ranking task, children do not simply read off distances directly. They might instead, for example, take a mental walk around the map, naming toys as they encounter them, or they might be unable to convert metric distances into ordinal judgments.

To test the influence of the externalization task, we (Newcombe & Liben, 1982) asked first-graders and adults to learn the same layout, but gave half the participants the rank ordering task, and half a distance estimation task. In the latter, one toy was placed on the floor, and the second was gradually moved away by the experimenter. Participants were asked to say when the second was as far from the first as it had been in the original room. Data from the rank ordering task replicated those of Kosslyn et al. (1974). However, data from the distance estimation task showed a different pattern: only opaque barriers affected judged distance, and there was no difference in the pattern demonstrated by children and adults. One conclusion that one might take from this discrepancy is that "rank ordering is a poor tool for the study of the development of spatial representations" (Newcombe, 1997, 91), but a more general conclusion is that any behavioral measure draws upon both what information the individual has stored about the space as well as on how the individual uses or processes that knowledge (Liben, 1988).

This last point provides a good segue into the second but related distinction between cognitive and cartographic maps, namely that in the case of the cognitive map, spatial format should be taken metaphorically rather than literally. That is, any model of a cognitive space inferred by an investigator (e.g., as in the MDS solutions of Kosslyn et al., 1974) might or might not be isomorphic with the mind's eye of the participant. In contrast, any given cartographic map fixes a particular configuration of the spatial elements. For example, an individual may know isolated facts about the distance and angular relations between home and office and between home and supermarket. The individual might be able to answer a question about the relation between office and market. One might be tempted to conclude that the individual had been carrying around a mental map that integrated home, office, and market into a single map-like configuration. But this need not be the case. The individual might only have calculated the spatial relation between office and market in response to the researcher's question. In other words, information concerning the configurational relation may be *implicit* in the isolated pieces of information, without necessarily being explicitly known. To take an analogy, consider someone who knows two individual premises (e.g., A > B and B > C). That person may or may not "know" the relations implied by those premises (A > C and C < A). We would not credit the individual with knowing the inferential transitive relationship simply because it is logically implied by the (known) individual premises.

The issues discussed above are what earlier led to me to draw distinctions among three types of spatial representation (Liben, 1981). The first, *spatial storage*, was defined as information about space that is contained "in the head" in some way, but is not accessed in a conscious or reflective manner. "This information may be stored as truth propositions, pure relations, stimulus-response bonds, or in any other format, isolated or integrated" (1981, 13). For example, one might model with a cartographic map the spatial information that animals must have to enable them to behave in the various ways described by Roberts (this volume), without necessarily asserting that those animals themselves are consulting an internal map-like image. The latter would exemplify what I called *spatial thought*, that is, "thinking that concerns or makes use of space in some way. Spatial thought is knowledge that individuals have access to, can reflect upon, or can manipulate, as in spatial problem solving or spatial imagery" (Liben, 1981, 12).

Whether or not it is ever possible to distinguish empirically between spatial thought and spatial storage is questionable (because we can presumably never extract "pure" storage), but the conceptual distinction is useful. The contents of either may be called "cognitive maps," but only if that term is understood broadly to include implicit as well as explicit cognition, and only if the term is understood metaphorically such that the map-like representation may be in the mind of the investigator rather than of the subject. In any case, both may be readily distinguished from the third—*spatial products*—which are observable entities "meant to encompass any kind of external representation, regardless of medium" (Liben, 1981, 11). These include concrete, three-dimensional models, two-dimensional graphic representations, and formal language systems. A prototypical example is, of course, a cartographic map. I will return to a discussion of some of the special contributions that these external cartographic maps may offer for thinking and problem solving in the final section of this chapter. But first it is important to discuss more thoroughly cartographic maps themselves, the goal of the next section.

3.3   Principles of Cartographic Maps

Overview

The following are three essential principles of cartographic maps:

The Purpose Principle   A cartographic map has purpose: it is not only *of* something, it is *for* something.

The Duality Principle   A cartographic map has a dual existence: it *is* something and it *stands* for something.

The Spatialization Principle   A cartographic map has a spatial essence: it not only represents something, it represents something *in relation to* space.

Understanding these principles is not an all or none matter. One might, for example, understand a principle at one level of subtlety but not at another, one might understand a principle at one moment but not at another, one might understand a principle under one condition but not under another. Each principle is discussed in turn below, although they are in actuality interdependent.

The Purpose Principle

When we look at a cartographic map, we are likely to recognize immediately that it is "of" something, for example, that it is a map of the United States, or of London, or of a particular state park. Novices are less likely to appreciate as immediately that the map is also "for" something, a purpose that ideally will have affected which information about the referent space was included and which excluded, the scale of the map, its level of generalization, and so on. To the extent that one understands the Purpose Principle, one is more likely to avoid the mistaken belief that maps are simply miniaturizations (albeit flattened ones) which show some singular "reality" or "truth." Rather, there are infinite "realities" that can be expressed by maps. Furthermore, it is not only that maps communicate a particular "reality" that is already known to the cartographer. A new "reality" may emerge from the map that had been previously unrecognized even by the cartographer (e.g., see Downs, 1981; MacEachren, 1995; Monmonier, 1993).

Consider the world maps shown in Figure 3.1. For decades, maps like the first (A) have hung on classroom walls for lessons in history and politics. How do viewers understand the depicted world? Do they, for example, think that Greenland is larger than Brazil? Do they believe that Alaska is far from Russia? Many people hold mistaken beliefs like these (Nelson, 1994), apparently the consequence of repeated and perhaps even exclusive exposure to this Mercator projection of the world. The second map shown in Figure 3.1 (B) is an equal area projection. This map, too, selectively distorts spatial features of the world—as it must—because it, too, projects a three-dimensional sphere onto a two-dimensional plane. But the two maps distort *different* spatial features. The first (A) distorts area but preserves direction; the second (B) distorts direction, but preserves area. The former is thus useful for sea navigation (the purpose for which it was designed), whereas the latter would be more useful for, say, providing information about the land available for cultivation in each country. As another example, Figure 3.2 provides maps of Europe, the first (A) with north at the top as we are accustomed to seeing it, and the second (B) oriented with west at the top. The latter, modeled on one produced during World War II (Harrison, 1944), presents a "reality" about the political relations among countries that seems different from that provided by a prototypical, north-at-the-top map. It captures the vulnerability of western Europe to armies sweeping from the east. In both examples, it is not that one map is right and the other wrong. Each communicates something different about "reality." Each can lead to misunderstandings if the user takes any given map as a representation of the singular truth.

The Duality Principle

The second principle applies to any physical representation: anything that is used to stand for something else has an existence in its own right in addition to its existence in a stand-for relation to its referent. What is potentially problematic for understanding cartographic maps is distinguishing between the physical features of a map that do and do not carry representational meaning about the referent.

For example, consider an oil company road map of Pennsylvania that one might find in the glove compartment of a car. The fact that the piece of paper is flat and folds in some accordion-like manner is not meant to

(a) Mercator

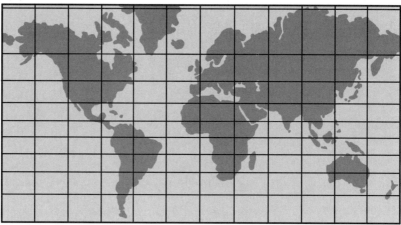

(b) Equal Area

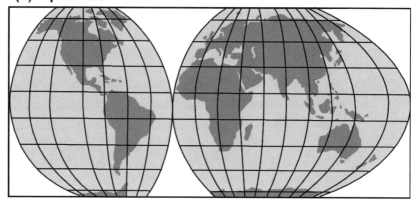

Figure 3.1
Example of two projections. Panel A shows a Mercator projection; Panel B shows an interrupted flat polar quartic equal-area projection.

(a)

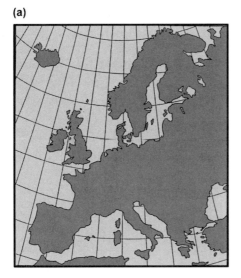

(b)

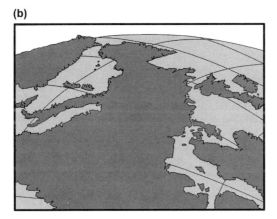

Figure 3.2
Two views of Europe. Panel A is a traditional view with north at the top; Panel B is a perspective view showing Europe as viewed from the east, based on Harrison (1944).

symbolize that Pennsylvania is a thin flat surface, amenable to accordion-like folding. These are completely *incidental* features of the representation. Other components of the map do carry representational meaning. For example, several qualities of the lines used for roads serve a representational function: the linear nature of the symbols represents the linear nature of roads, the direction and curves of the lines represent the direction and curves of the road, and different colors refer to different kinds of roads. This last representational link, unlike the first two, however, is an arbitrary one: the colors of the representations do not reflect the fact that different kinds of roads are paved in different colors. Thus, the meaning of color must be found by reference to a map key (or perhaps by surmising the meaning of red lines in general on the basis of having identified the referent of one red line in particular).

But even symbols that carry representational meaning also have features that are not referential at all. To continue with road symbols as an example, line width is typically incidental. To illustrate, if we apply the map scale to the lines used to represent interstate highways on the United States map in the *National Geographic Society Road Atlas* (1998), the roads would be calculated to be well over five miles in width! Here legibility, not representational meaning, dictates line width. As another example, consider the use of yellow squares to mark highway exits. Apart from the fact that both symbol and referent are "point" features (see Muehrcke & Muehrcke, 1998), the symbol's features are non-referential: color and shape enhance perceptual discriminability but do not carry referential meaning about exits. (Note that if, say, yellow squares were used to symbolize exits with gas stations, whereas orange squares were used to symbolize exits with both gas stations and restaurants, color would be representational rather than incidental.)

To summarize, the Duality Principle means that maps (as a whole, as well as their components) have features, some of which carry representational meaning, and some of which are only incidental. Importantly, and as demonstrated in the preceding examples, the identical feature (such as color) may be representational in one case and incidental in another. Cartographic decisions about which features serve which representational functions may be made on the basis of shared physical qualities of the referent and the representation, on the basis of psychological associations between referents and representations, or may reflect some arbitrary or aesthetic choice (e.g., see Brewer, 1997; Brewer, MacEachren, Pickle, Herrmann, 1997; MacEachren, 1995).

So far I have talked primarily about what is being represented on the map and how those referents are represented, that is, about the representational correspondences between the referent and map (see Liben & Downs, 1989). But implicit in the discussion of these symbols have been spatial qualities. For example, symbols and referents have been described as "linear" or as "point" features, they are said to be placed at various locations on a base map which itself has a particular shape and extent. It is the spatial nature of this information that leads to the third principle of map understanding.

The Spatialization Principle

The third principle concerns the centrality of space in maps, evident in the introductory description of map taken from a basic cartography text: "All maps have the same basic objective of serving as a means of communicating spatial relationships and forms" (Robinson, Sale, Morrison & Muehrcke, 1984, 4), and from a dictionary definition that begins: "a representation, usually on a flat surface, as of the features of an area of the earth or a portion of the heavens, showing them in their respective forms, sizes, and relationships according to some convention of representation" (Random House, 1997, 1173). The Spatialization Principle reminds us that—whether discussing large expanses of our universe such as Earth or small areas such as rooms—maps display spatial information. In this light, one cannot be credited with fully understanding a map on the basis of having identified only isolated referents (e.g., that its symbols show countries or pieces of furniture) unless one also appreciates spatial meaning as well. How do children come to appreciate this spatial meaning, as well as the purpose and duality of maps? It is to these developmental questions that I now turn.

3.4   The Development of Map Understanding

A General Context for Developing Map Understanding

The developing understanding of cartographic maps must be considered within a context of the developing understanding of external spatial representations, in general. Elsewhere (Liben, 1999) I proposed a six-level sequence that characterizes the individual as moving from perceptually-based identification of referents towards reflection about the purpose, form, and meaning of representations. A particularly important milestone in this progression is emergence of "representational insight" studied by

DeLoache (1987) using a paradigm in which a toy dog is hidden in either a simply-furnished room or its scale model, and the child is asked to find the analogous toy in the other space. At 3 years, children typically solve the problem without difficulty. However, at 2½ they cannot seem to understand that one space can stand in a representational relation to the other, and thus are unable to find the analogous toy. This is so even though they remember the original dog's hiding place without difficulty. Further evidence that younger children's difficulty is due to a failure to appreciate the representational function comes from what happens when the child is tricked into thinking that the original room has simply changed in size (by a shrinking or expanding machine). Under these circumstances, even younger children are able to find the hidden dog (DeLoache, Miller & Rosengren, 1997). Because the insight that one thing can stand for another is a prerequisite for understanding maps, my review of map understanding thus begins with 3-year-old children. (Readers interested in the earlier foundations for this period are referred to DeLoache, 1995; Liben, 1999; and Newcombe & Huttenlocher, in press.)

The sections below are organized using the three map principles. I have couched the discussion primarily in ontogenetic language and have emphasized illustrative empirical findings from work with children. However, I occasionally include evidence of similar phenomena in adults, and would suggest that issues that are raised with respect to children are probably also relevant for thinking about individual, group, and expertise differences in adulthood (e.g., see Downs & Liben, 1991; Eliot, 1987).

Developmental Understanding of Map Purpose

Understanding map purpose may be studied inferentially, by seeing the purposes for which maps are used, and directly, by asking individuals about the purposes of maps. In a sense, data bearing on the first of these are extensive in that any number of studies have shown that even 3-year-old children appear to understand that maps can serve location and navigational purposes. Illustrative of a location study is one by Bluestein and Acredolo (1979). Children were first familiarized with a room having uniquely marked corners and identical green boxes at the middle of each wall, and then familiarized with a room map. While the child waited outside the room, a toy elephant was placed in one of the green boxes. The child was then shown the map with an elephant sticker on one box symbol, and asked to retrieve the toy. Under simple conditions in which the map was in the room and aligned with the space, all the 4- and 5-year-olds and half the 3-year-olds succeeded.

Illustrative of a navigation study is one by Blades and Spencer (1987a). Children from 4 to 6 years were asked to navigate through a large maze drawn in chalk on their school playground. Roadblocks prevented navigation along some paths, thus requiring a map for errorless navigation. Performance was significantly better than chance in all but the youngest age group (about 4 years). The data revealed some interesting variability with respect to age and conditions, but the important point here is that children appeared to understand that the map could be used to aid navigation.

The second approach to studying individuals' understanding of map purpose is to ask direct questions about map definitions and purposes. Data from this approach also suggest that location and navigation purposes are appreciated from a young age. For example, in one study with preschoolers (Liben & Yekel, 1996), we began by saying that we would be doing some things with maps, and then asked "Do you know what a map is? What's a map?" Some preschoolers offered no or only vague answers (e.g., two children aged 4 and 5 began: "I don't know ..." and then continued, respectively, "... maybe you could do homework on it" and "... I saw one once and it looked strange"). Others, however, showed understanding of maps as archives of location information (e.g., "Where things are" and "Things with different countries") and/or as navigational aids (e.g., "Something to get around places" and "Something if you get lost, it helps you to get somewhere ... maybe home"). Responses to similar questions asked of college students (Downs & Liben, unpublished data) show that location information and wayfinding remain the most popular purposes named.

In another study relevant to young children's understanding of map purpose, we (Downs & Liben, 1987; Liben & Downs, 1991) interviewed 3- to 6-year-old preschoolers using various kinds of place representations including aerial photographs of Chicago and of the local community (State College, Pennsylvania), and a Rand McNally road map of Pennsylvania. Shown the aerial photograph of Chicago, a few children suggested that it might be used for navigation. Shown the road map of Pennsylvania, many children spontaneously labeled it as a "map," many mentioned it provided location information (e.g., "to show you where things are"), and all children talked about its wayfinding use in some way (e.g., "to show you how to go"). However, in response to the question: "Do you think you could learn anything by looking at this that would be different from what you could learn walking around the city?" only a single child offered a purpose other than wayfinding (specifically, one child answered that you can see *more* of the city from the aerial photograph of Chicago).

In summary, the developmental data available on map purpose suggest that by preschool, many children understand that maps store location information and aid navigation. Although there is no evidence that children appreciate the idea that maps may serve other purposes, it is unclear whether this reflects something about their understanding, or instead reflects the relative paucity of research addressed to this question.

Developmental Understanding of Map Duality

With respect to the Duality Principle, the first major accomplishment is coming to understand that one thing can stand for something other than itself. As discussed earlier, this idea appears to emerge quite early, as demonstrated by the 3-year-old child's ability to use a scale model (e.g., DeLoache, 1987) and maps (e.g., Bluestein & Acredolo, 1979) in a stand-for relationship. However, it takes far longer for children to differentiate consistently between referential and incidental features of particular map components.

One set of relevant data comes from the interviews of preschool children mentioned earlier. In general, preschool children had little trouble recognizing that aerial photographs, tourist maps, and road maps showed places (understanding place representations at the "holistic level," see Liben & Downs, 1989, 1991) as when an aerial photograph of Chicago was identified as showing "A city" or "Buildings and stuff." But some responses suggested a failure to understand the specificity of the link between representation and referent, as, for example, in children's suggestion that the Chicago photograph showed "The United States" or "The whole world."

In addition, all young children were able to identify the representational meaning of at least some parts of the representations (understanding at the "componential level," see Liben & Downs, 1989, 1991). There were, however, confusions in distinguishing incidental from referential features. Sometimes the assumption of fully motivated symbols facilitated correct interpretations, as when children correctly identified the Susquehanna River on the road map of Pennsylvania as a river "because it's blue" or identified roads on a black-and-white aerial photograph of Chicago because they were "grey" or "straight." But sometimes the assumption about motivated symbols worked to children's disadvantage, as when a child thought that a red line on the road map meant that the road was actually red, or as when another child denied that a field on the black-and-white photograph could be grass because "grass is green." Using a large-scale map, Blades and Spencer (1987b) reported a similar role of color: 4- to 6-year-old children were able to interpret the symbols on a simple large-scale map when color of symbol and referent matched (as when children recognized a large green area as grass), but performed poorly when they did not (e.g., school and church symbols).

Although errors that we labeled iconic overextensions (e.g., thinking a red line implies a red road or that green grass must be symbolized in green) were not common, they happened sufficiently often and with enough intensity to suggest that even after children come to understand the general notion that representations stand for referents, they continue to have trouble differentiating which aspects of a representation do and do not carry referential meaning, and whether or not the representational features are linked to the referent in a motivated or in an arbitrary fashion. It appears that children may continue to have difficulty accepting arbitrary representations even as late as the second grade: children laughed when we suggested that they might use an asterisk to represent file cabinets on their classroom maps (Liben & Downs, 1994).

But again, there are at least anecdotal reports that adults, too, may overextend qualities of symbols and referents. For example, adults often become confused when vegetation is represented by red (as it is on false color satellite images), or as when water is represented in brown (as when a New York City subway map had to be recalled because the brown used to represent rivers confused so many users). As reviewed next, confusions are not confined to interpretations of individual symbols, but are also found in the interpretation of the spatial properties of maps.

Developmental Understanding of Map Spatialization

Children's understanding of the spatial information contained in maps also undergoes gradual development. A useful way to organize discussion of developing spatial accomplishments is by reference to the three dimensions of the "cartographic eye" (Downs, 1981) or "mapmaker's vantage points" (Muehrcke & Muehrcke, 1998) relevant to any map: *viewing distance*, *viewing angle*, and *viewing azimuth*. Below I discuss age-linked data relevant to each, but end with a brief reminder that even as we attempt to generalize about development, we should remain cognizant of, and try to account for the sometimes startling variability that occurs within any single age group.

Viewing distance   Viewing distance refers to the distance from which the space is viewed, or, more accurately, the scale in which it is depicted. What is critical about scale is that for a map of any given size, (a) maps at different scales show different amounts of the referent space, and therefore (b) they present different map-to-space ratios. For example, the same 8½″ × 11″ piece of paper might show Chicago in an aerial photograph, or a line map of a room which, expressed as "map scale" (or, in cartographic terms, as a "Representative Fraction" or RF), would be representations at approximately 1:12,000 and 1:20, respectively.

When we are mapping small spaces like rooms, buildings, neighborhoods, and even towns, the ratio of map space to physical space is constant for the entire map because the curvature of the Earth is small enough over these distances that it can be disregarded (at least when one is using parallel rather than central perspective, see Muehrcke & Muehrcke, 1998). When we map larger spaces such as continents, however, the necessity of projecting the curved surface of the sphere onto the flat surface of the map yields distortions over the paper space that make the metric of the map-space relations more complex. (See, for example, the contrast in projections shown in Figure 3.1.) Here I will ignore these more complex relations, and sample research bearing on only the very basic question of whether the child understands that the representation is at a reduced scale, and is able to maintain some general understanding of proportional reduction in size across different components of the map.

There are many indications that even young children can interpret the general meaning of scaled representations. For example, we know from everyday experience that young children readily identify small models of objects (such as toy drums, tea sets, cars, and so on) and can identify objects from a distance despite changes in retinal size. But these kinds of findings do not allow us to conclude that young children understand the systematic, proportional spatial relations between a referent space and its scaled representations. On the contrary, there are data suggesting that young children have difficulty in maintaining scalar consistency when they are identifying or selecting components of representations in relation to real world referents.

In the interview study with 3- to 6-year-old children described earlier (e.g., see Liben & Downs, 1991), we found instances of scale inconsistencies in interpretations. For example, even having just identified buildings and roads on an aerial photograph of Chicago and thus demonstrating some understanding of scale reduction, some children then went on to interpret boats in Lake Michigan as "fish." And, even after showing some general understanding of an aerial photograph of his own hometown, a 4-year-old child vehemently rejected a rectangular shape as his father's office building because "His building is *huge.* . . . It's as big as this whole map!" Shown a road map, some children denied that a line could show a road, explaining, for example, "It's not fat enough for two cars to go on." Similar examples of scale inconsistencies in interpreting aerial photographs were reported by Spencer, Harrison, and Darvizeh who observed that "3 and 4 year olds do not feel constrained to maintain a size consistency within the one picture: they are quite happy to see hills as "pebbles" along side water they have identified as the sea" (1980, 61–62).

That it is challenging to maintain consistent, proportional relations has also been shown from research in which children are asked to select appropriate scaled symbols for a map. For example, Towler and Nelson (1968) showed 6- to 12-year-old children a model farm and asked them to select symbols of the appropriate size to represent the buildings. It was not until the oldest age that children were uniformly successful. However, as Spencer, Blades and Morsley (1989) note, only some, rather than all, shapes presented difficulty, suggesting that even the younger children have some understanding of scale reduction. Furthermore, anecdotal reports from geographers who teach classes on remote sensing suggest that even adults can find the maintenance of scale difficult in aerial photo interpretation.

It is possible that children's difficulties in the studies just described might reflect their lack of knowledge about the referent space itself rather than their inability to understand a representation. One way to avoid this potential problem is to teach the requisite spatial information to criterion (see Liben, 1997 for a discussion of methods more generally). Using this paradigm, Uttal (1996) first taught 4- to 6-year-old children the locations of symbols for toys on a room plan, and then asked them to place actual toys in the referent room in their correct locations. Even preschoolers were generally quite good at maintaining the configural relations among the toys' locations, showing that they could scale up from small toy symbols to real objects. They were not, however, precise in maintaining the proportional relations across components of the representation.

A second way to insure that children have access to the necessary information about the referent space is to give them mapping tasks while they are in the referent space itself. Illustrative is work in which children are asked to look around a room to find objects, and then mark the objects' locations on a map of that room (e.g., Liben & Downs, 1993; Liben & Yekel, 1996), or to go to a location marked on a map of the room in which the child is being interviewed (e.g., Bluestein & Acredolo, 1979; Presson, 1982).

Before discussing how findings from these studies illuminate children's understanding of scaled space, it is important to first differentiate between two kinds of target locations that can be used in this work: those that can be identified by topological (or landmark) cues versus those requiring metrics. To illustrate the first type of cue, consider a task in which a child is asked to place a sticker on a map to show a teddy bear's location in a room. If the bear is placed on the only piano in the room, and if that piano is symbolized on the map by a unique symbol (e.g., a rectangular shape with piano keys), the child may rely on topological reasoning (e.g., using the concept of "on" and finding the representational correspondence between piano and piano symbol). To illustrate the second, consider asking a child to show the location of the teddy bear on an open, undifferentiated area of the floor. In this situation, and assuming that placements must be reasonably precise to be scored as correct (see Liben, 1997), the child must rely upon metric reasoning (e.g., using distance along each of two intersecting walls to estimate location and scaling down).

Studies using the first kind of targets—those that provide nearby topological or landmark cues—show that even 3-year-olds seem to be able to find locations indicated on a map. For example, as discussed earlier, Bluestein and Acredolo (1979) found that half the 3-year-olds and all 4- and 5-year-olds were able to find the correct green box among four locations that could be identified by reference to nearby distinguishing landmarks (e.g., "the green box *between* the corner with the red object and the corner with the yellow object"). Presson (1982) showed that with differentiating landmarks available, kindergarten and first-grade children performed virtually perfectly in identifying the correct target location from among four identical containers as long as memory demands were removed and maps were aligned with the space.

However, studies using the second kind of target do not elicit similar levels of success. For example, when 4- to 5-year-old preschoolers were asked to place colored stickers on an aligned plan map of their familiar classroom to show the location of objects that were in view (Liben & Yekel, 1996), performance was extremely poor. This was true not only for locations in undifferentiated areas of the floor, but even for locations that were on pieces of furniture. At least part of what made even these furniture locations difficult was that the maps contained multiple instances of identical symbols (e.g., several identical circles symbolizing several round tables). Under these conditions, metric, or at least multiple topological strategies are needed to identify which of the several identical symbols is the correct one.

Older children also have difficulty when single topological cues, alone, are insufficient for solving the task. Children were asked to place stickers on a classroom map to indicate a person's location (Liben & Downs, 1993). Kindergarten children, on average, were placing stickers in the correct location less than half of the time, and first-graders about two-thirds of the time. By fifth-grade, all but a few children performed well.

In short, findings from these kinds of tasks suggest that even very young children may solve many mapping tasks by using topological concepts combined with an understanding of representational correspondences (e.g., identifying the referent of a unique piano symbol). However, the data from maps and tasks that preclude topological or landmark solutions suggest that the understanding of precise metrics of measurement and scale reduction emerge more slowly during early and middle childhood.

Viewing angle   The second spatial component showing developmental progression concerns viewing angle which refers to the direction along the vertical dimension from which the space is viewed. Viewing angles range from nadir views (also called vertical or orthogonal views) in which the space is viewed from directly overhead, through oblique views in which the space is viewed from an angle such as 45°, through to elevation views (or eye-level views) as in the way we normally view our environment while walking through it.

One approach to studying children's understanding of viewing angle has been to ask children directly about the station point of representations. For example, in our interviews with preschoolers (see Downs & Liben, 1987; Liben & Downs, 1991) we began by showing a vertical aerial photograph of Chicago, and asking children what they thought it showed. After establishing that it showed a city and that it was a photograph, we asked where they thought the camera was when the photograph was taken. Of the 30 children interviewed, only 2 mentioned that it might have been taken from far away, and only three gave responses suggesting an overhead view (e.g., "up in the sky . . . in a helicopter"). Even when children were asked directly if the photograph might have been taken from a plane, most thought not, generally explaining that they could not see the plane in the photograph.

Also suggestive that children have difficulty understanding an overhead viewing angle were some responses that would have made sense if the component of the image had been viewed in elevation (i.e., from eye-level, straight ahead). For example, trains lined up in parallel were identified as "bookshelves" and a triangular-shaped parking area was identified as a "hill." Spencer et al. (1980) also noted that although primary school children (aged 5 to 11) identified many parts of an aerial photograph correctly, there were also some angle (and scale) confusions. For example, "No children were able to see a regular pattern of lines in the corner of a park as aerially-viewed tennis courts. . . . Some children identified these lines as "doors": i.e., they found no inconsistency in seeing the lines as the panels on what would have been a pair of huge doors lying flat beside the minute blobs that they had previously identified correctly as being full sized trees" (1980, 61).

A similar kind of error was found in an investigation using maps rather than photographs: Liben and Yekel (1996) found that preschoolers had great difficulty understanding a plan map of their classroom. Consistent with the position that children may not understand the overhead viewing angle were a few cases in which children misinterpreted the plan view of the double sink as a "door," presumably because they interpreted the two rectangles representing the two halves of the sink as the upper and lower panels of a door shown in elevation (much like the tennis court example from Spencer et al., 1980).

A few empirical studies have directly contrasted children's abilities to use oblique versus vertical views. Data suggest that the former are more easily decoded, and may even support transfer to the latter. For example, Liben and Yekel (1996) found that preschool children were significantly more accurate in placing stickers on classroom maps to indicate objects' locations when the map was drawn from an oblique perspective than when drawn in plan view, and found that later performance on a plan map was significantly better when children had used the perspective map first. Some recent data collected by Blades, Hetherington, Spencer and

Sowden (1997) are also consistent with the hypothesis that a vertical or nadir view is more difficult than oblique views. Children aged 4- and 5-years, were shown 1:1,100 color aerial photographs of their school neighborhood and asked to describe what they could see and then to identify specific features. Children performed better with an oblique than with a vertical photograph, although performance was generally strong overall, perhaps due to the very large scale and familiarity of the area.

In our current work with shuttle photographs of Earth as part of our *Visualizing Earth* project (Barstow, Frost, Liben, Ride & Souviney, in progress), informal observations suggest that both children and adults find it easier to understand oblique-view images (which show the Earth's curvature) than nadir views. In short, data from maps, aerial photographs of cities, and shuttle photographs of Earth all seem to support the conclusion that children can interpret oblique angles more easily than nadir angles, and that the differential ease of interpretation continues into adulthood.

Viewing azimuth   It is the third spatial component—azimuth—that has probably attracted the greatest attention in the psychological literature. Viewing azimuth refers to the direction from which something is viewed in the horizontal plane, often referred to in everyday language as the direction or orientation from which something is viewed (e.g., facing north). Some of the earliest work relevant to children's understanding of azimuth was conducted by Piaget and Inhelder (1956) who tested children's understanding of the relation between locations in representational landscapes. Children were shown locations on one table-top model of a simple town and asked to show the analogous locations in a second, identical model, first when models were aligned, and then when the child's model was rotated 180°. Their work, as well as subsequent research using modifications of the landscape task (e.g., Laurendeau & Pinard, 1970; Liben & Downs, 1993), converge on the general conclusion that children typically fail to adjust for the 180° rotation until middle childhood.

Later investigators have examined children's ability to understand viewing azimuth in cases in which the tasks involve finding analogous locations between a real space and a representation rather than between two identical table-top representations. Illustrative are the two studies by Bluestein and Acredolo (1979) and Presson (1982) which, as discussed earlier, showed that children as young as 3 or 4 were able to find topologically-identifiable locations in a room when the map and room were aligned. In contrast, however, when the map was rotated by 180°, Bluestein and Acredolo (1979) reported success by only 8%, 25%, and 80% of the 3-, 4-, and 5-year-old children who had previously succeeded in the aligned condition (thus already a select sample), and Presson (1982) reported success by about 33% and 50% of unselected kindergarten and first-graders. In a study using a related task, Liben and Downs (1993) asked kindergarten, first-, second- and fifth/sixth-grade children to place arrow stickers on maps of their classroom to show where someone was standing and which direction he was pointing. As described earlier, by grade 2 children performed well in the aligned condition, but still had considerable difficulty when the map was rotated 180°.

Taken together, data from these and many related studies are consistent with the idea that children have trouble understanding viewing azimuth. It is, however, again important to acknowledge that adults, too, are challenged by viewing azimuths that are misaligned with the referent space. Illustrative is the research on "You Are Here" maps in which the individual's position is shown on the representation. Levine, Marchon and Hanley (1984), for example, found that when college students were asked to go to a target location indicated on a floor plan of the university library, they took significantly longer to study the map and search for the target, and were far less likely to reach the goal when maps were rotated 180° than when maps were aligned with the depicted space.

There is also growing evidence from research we are conducting as part of our *Visualizing Earth* project that reconciling viewpoints between two different representations of the same place, even apart from one's own location within that place, is difficult well into and beyond adolescence. For example, we have used a task in which a location and directional arrow is shown on one image (a plan map or oblique aerial photograph) and participants are asked to indicate the corresponding location and direction on a second image of the same region (in a different scale, azimuth, and perhaps viewing angle). Even a sample of students from a highly selective science and technology high school had great difficulty (Liben, Carlson, Szechter, Marrara, 1999). The illustrative image pair shown in Figure 3.3, for example, yielded correct directional responses (with a 45° scoring window) by about only 20% of the sample. In short, young children show skill in compensating for a changed viewing azimuth under simple conditions, but even adults can have difficulty in many circumstances.

Figure 3.3
Sample item from the Correspondences Task used by Liben et al. (1999). The top image contains an arrow pointing to a particular location in Boston, approaching Boston from a particular direction. Participants are asked to place an arrow sticker on the bottom image so that it will point to the same location and will approach the city from the same direction.

Variations on a developmental theme   In closing this section on map spatialization, it is important to reiterate that all three aspects of maps—scale, angle, and azimuth—continue to challenge even cognitively high-functioning adults. Furthermore, the age-group differences described in research reports and reviewed above often obscure striking individual differences evident at any given chronological age. For example, in our own work (e.g., Liben & Downs, 1986, 1993) we have been struck by individual first- and second-grade children who seemed to understand maps almost effortlessly, performing virtually perfectly on location and orientation tasks that most of their classmates and even many far older children found baffling. These individual differences, along with the well-established finding that (as a group) boys and men outperform girls and women on spatial tasks (e.g., see Linn & Petersen, 1985; Vasta & Liben, 1996) as well as on tests of geographic knowledge (e.g., the National Assessment of Educational Progress, see Persky et al., 1996; and the National Geography Bee, see Liben, Downs & Signorella, 1995) raise interesting questions about the factors that may help to facilitate map understanding. This understanding might have relevance not only for the ability to use maps to support navigation through the environment, but potentially for using maps to support other kinds of problem solving and reasoning. In the concluding section of this chapter, I turn to a brief discussion of these latter uses.

3.5   Concluding Comments: Cartographic Maps as Tools for Enhancing and Studying Thought

This chapter began with the straightforward assertion that "Spatial representations help us think." I argued that to understand the truth and implications of this assertion fully, we must investigate the role not only of mental or physical representations that are created by individuals in the course of reasoning and problem solving, but also the role of external representations that are provided to problem solvers. Having argued that maps are a particularly interesting subset of these external representations, I then proposed core principles of maps, and showed that understanding of these principles emerges only gradually. In closing, I return to the broader focus of this volume by asking how maps contribute to reasoning and problem solving. I begin by considering the ways in which cartographic maps are actually used, and end with a brief plea for expanding their use, both in our educational system and in our psychological research.

Real Uses of "Real" Maps

What roles do cartographic maps actually play in our everyday and scholarly worlds? Are these roles identical to those of cognitive maps? A complete answer would require, at a minimum, an introductory text on geography, but a brief overview can be provided by reproducing the succinct list entitled "Role of Maps" taken from *Map Use* (Muehrcke, 1986, 14):

1. Record and store information.
2. Serve as computational aids.
3. Serve as aids to mobility.
4. Summarize complex, voluminous data.
5. Help us to explore data (analyze, forecast, spot trends).
6. Help us to visualize what would otherwise be closed to us.
7. Serve as trigger devices to stimulate thought.

The first three roles are those that are best known outside geography. As reported earlier, definitions of maps given by both children and adults overwhelmingly focus on information storage (1) and navigation (3), which, by implication, allow computation (2), as for example, computing distances between two locations or the size of an island. These functions may, of course, also be served by cognitive maps, but cartographic maps are generally better able to provide detail and precision, and can help to correct distortions that may be introduced as a result of the user's schematic processing. To take one example, consider what typically happens when an American is asked: "What is the first foreign country you would encounter flying due south from Detroit?" The common answer is Mexico, presumably based on the "knowledge" that Mexico is the United States' closest southern neighbor. But the correct answer is Canada, an answer that becomes immediately obvious if one consults a "real" rather than a cognitive map. Or, to take an example that is perhaps better known, Stephens and Coupe (1978) found that college students were likely to judge Reno to the east of San Diego when it is, in fact, to the west. The explanation appears to lie in the "knowledge" that California is west of Nevada. The opportunity to consult a "real" map makes it immediately clear that California follows a northwest to southeast trend, and thus that a significant portion of Nevada is northwest of a significant portion of California.

Of course the availability of a "real" and cartographically correct map does not guarantee that users will draw correct inferences. Maps differ with respect to how well they display information, and users differ with respect to how well they can understand that information. To illustrate, consider a trip made by President Ford during his campaign for re-election, depicted in the top half of Figure 3.4. Ford was criticized for detouring from his tax-paid, diplomatic journey to Japan in order to make a campaign speech in Alaska. However, the appearance of a "detour" is a consequence of plotting the trip on a Mercator projection, coupled with the user's failure to understand the spatial consequences of a Mercator projection. If the trip is instead shown as a great circle route (see bottom half of Figure 3.4), it becomes clear that Ford had actually taken the shortest path and linked his speech to a standard refueling stop (Muehrcke & Muehrcke, 1998).

The remaining roles of maps (4–7) listed by Muehrcke (1986) are rarely mentioned by children and adults in answering questions about the definitions and purposes of maps, and similarly, are almost never studied in psychological research. They are, however, central to geographers. These functions may be illustrated by examining the thematic maps reproduced in Figure 3.5 (from Muehrcke & Muehrcke, 1998, 10) which show cancer rates for men and for women, by county, over a twenty-year period. Maps like these reveal patterns that would be impossible to discern if one had to rely upon mental processing of the data, and raise a host of questions. What is it about life styles, employment patterns, physical geography, water or food supplies that might co-vary with these incidence patterns? What distinguishes lives of men and women living in identical regions (e.g., in the northwest corner of Nevada) that lead one sex to show the very highest possible level of incidence and the other the very lowest?

Maps are also useful for revealing how phenomena change over time (e.g., they reveal patterns of continental drift over millennia, land use over decades, climate over the year, storms over the day), and in so doing, are likely to generate hypotheses about the causal factors that lie behind the change (e.g., hypotheses about the mechanisms responsible for dispersion of disease). Sequences of static maps can show changing distributions (as in Figure 3.6 from MacEachren, 1995, 253), although animated maps (dynamic computer displays) are even better for revealing patterns of change to the eye (e.g., see MacEachren & DiBiase, 1991;

(a) Mercator

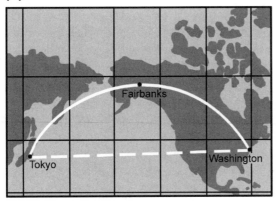

(b) Orthographic

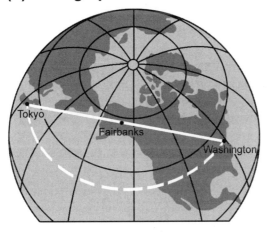

Figure 3.4
The route taken by President Gerald Ford from Washington, D.C., to Tokyo, Japan, via Fairbanks, Alaska. Panel A shows the route on a Mercator projection; Panel B shows the route as a great circle. Adapted from Muehrcke and Muehrcke (1998, 526).

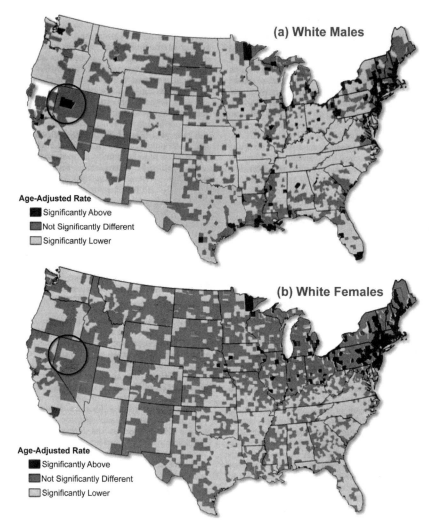

Figure 3.5
Cancer mortality for males and females in the United States, by county, 1950–
1969. Adapted from Muehrcke and Muehrcke (1998, 10).

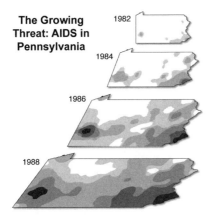

Figure 3.6
Representation of the growing dispersion of AIDS in Pennsylvania over time.
Adapted from MacEachren (1985, 253).

Harrower, Griffin & MacEachren, 1999). Again, these are patterns that would be difficult or impossible to extract without the support of external representations.

These examples illustrate the range of roles of maps listed by Muehrcke (1986). Maps allow data to be summarized in meaningful chunks; they allow patterns to emerge that would have been otherwise impossible to see, they lead us to ask questions that would never have occurred to us, and, in turn, they help us to test the resulting hypotheses. Maps help us to solve problems, be they about the spread of disease, settlement, acid rain, or the weather.

The particular illustrations of the use of maps in reasoning and problem solving cited above have all been taken from basic textbooks in geography and cartography, but similar examples could have been drawn from publications in anthropology, demography, criminal justice, epidemiology, history, astronomy, environmental science, oceanography, and political science, among others. Perhaps the best index of the wide-ranging use of maps for reasoning and problem solving comes from noting the prevalence of maps in textbooks in these and other disciplines, as well as the ever-increasing popularity of Geographic Information System (GIS) and Geographic Visualization (GVis) technology across fields (e.g., MacEachren, 1995). In short, maps not only serve to store spatial information, aid computation, and support navigation (functions that can perhaps be supported by cognitive maps, and that are perhaps shared with other animals, see Roberts, this volume), but they also support higher level reasoning and problem solving functions that are perhaps uniquely human.

Beyond "Real" Uses of "Real" Maps

The prior discussion has focused on the way that maps *are* used. In closing, I would like to extend the discussion further to propose ways that maps *could* be used, first in educational settings, and second in psychological research.

As educational tools, maps have the potential to make a number of important contributions (Liben & Downs, in press). First, and most obviously, increasing the role of maps in education could support the laudable goal of enhancing geographic knowledge about the physical and social worlds in which we live. This use of maps is thus directed to overcoming the shocking levels of geographic ignorance reported in the news, as for example, the finding that 20% of fifth graders tested in Texas misidentified Brazil as the United States on a world map, or that only about a third of the college students tested in a college in North Carolina knew that the Seine was in France (*U.S. News & World Report*, March 25, 1985).

But second, it is reasonable to suppose that placing maps more centrally in our educational curricula could promote spatial thinking and spatial skills more generally (Liben & Downs, in press; Uttal, 1999). For example, learning to understand different map projections, topographic maps, correspondences among images that depict the identical place from different viewing angles and viewing azimuths, the consequences of parallel versus central perspective, the systematic nature of proportional scale reduction and enlargement, and other map skills and concepts should contribute to the student's ability to understand and manipulate the varied diagrams and images in other disciplines such as chemistry, astronomy, and biology. Likewise, these experiences should provide a strong foundation on which to base instruction in other fields for which spatial representations are central, for example, engineering, architecture, and graphic arts.

And third, albeit speculatively, maps might also serve to enhance abstract, logical reasoning because maps give a concrete form to (or "instantiate") many basic logical relations and processes. For example, consider the act of selecting some "thing" to depict (e.g., cities) and deciding upon a means of representing that content (e.g., filled circles) on, say, a map of the United States. Inherent in this operation is classification of referents on the basis of some defining feature (e.g., some specified number of people within some specified geographic area) irrespective of numerous other differentiating features (e.g., whether they are incorporated as political units). Might experience in establishing and implementing categorical definitions or in observing the consequences of changing those definitions enhance students' ability to define and manipulate logical classes? Might the need to consider population in relation to geographic area enhance the ability to coordinate changes in two dimensions simultaneously? Or consider indicating which of the cities are state capitals by surrounding the filled circles by stars. These 50 cities are now each coded simultaneously as a "city" and as a "capital." Might working with these symbols enhance students' understanding of the logic of multiple classification? What if circles were now coded to reflect more detail about population, perhaps by using discrete categories, perhaps exploring alternative boundary definitions, or perhaps by scaling circles proportionally to population. Might experiences with systems like these facilitate understanding not only of multiple classification, but of the effects of definitional criteria, and of discrete versus continuous scales?

Or, to move to a somewhat different example, consider a map that shows a city within a county, within a state, within a region, within a country. Might experience with this map enhance students' understanding of class inclusion relations, particularly if instruction were to make explicit the embedded superordinate and subordinate class structure? Of course, maps are not the only spatial representations that can serve these roles. Tree diagrams, Venn diagrams, and many other systems may also be used to depict hierarchical relations. Maps may, however, be particularly useful because they are familiar representations used in everyday life by everyday people, and have a referential reality that may be easier to understand than more abstract systems.

Finally, and perhaps most importantly in the context of the present volume, I close with a parallel plea to expand the role of maps in psychological research. As discussed elsewhere (Liben & Downs, 1989), there is a tendency for psychologists to employ simplistic maps of impoverished, small places. Furthermore, tasks typically test only location and route understanding, and often allow solutions on the basis of understanding representational correspondences alone.

But even if the particular map, mapping task, and scoring system challenge the user's spatial understanding, if the map is of a very small space (such as a laboratory or even of a real classroom), some of the most interesting features of maps become irrelevant. First, if the space is small, the space can be experienced directly. (Contrast coming to know a classroom versus coming to know a continent.) Under these conditions, cartographic maps are not likely to be serving one of their most important roles—"to help us visualize what otherwise would be invisible" (Muehrcke & Muehrcke, 1998, 13), or "to comprehend relationships that were previously unsuspected" (Downs, 1985, 341)—and their functions may be little different from those served by cognitive maps. Furthermore, when the referent space is small, the need to represent a curved surface on a flat plane is immaterial. And yet it is the understanding of three-dimensional meaning from two-dimensional representations that is likely to be both challenging and potentially generalizable to other intellectual tasks (such as understanding the graphic representations of chemical reactions, the cross sections of organs, or the relations among celestial bodies).

In this context it is interesting to note that one of the most commonly kinds of maps used in psychological research—the room plan—is not even considered to *be* a map by the majority of people. We (Downs, Liben & Daggs, 1988) showed children and adults a collection of place images and asked "Is this a map?" with response alternatives of "Yes," "No," or "?". Whereas a world political map elicited "yes" responses from 93%, 90%, 99%, and 100% of kindergartners, first-graders, second-graders, and adults, respectively, a room plan was accepted as a map by only 12%, 17%, 30%, and 33% of these same samples. And it was not simply that respondents used the "?" response. Instead, the plan map was actively rejected (i.e., responded to with "No") by 63%, 68%, 49%, and 58% of those samples.

This should not be taken to mean that the use of room plans in research is foolish. The psychological literature is filled with valuable research in which complex processes are broken down and studied experimentally with artificial materials. We have, for example, learned a great deal about memory and language processes from research using nonsense syllables, even though people do not speak with them. Just as there is a place for using very simple prose for research and education, so too, there is a role for very simple maps in research and education. But we must be careful not to *limit* our research to these kinds of materials and tasks. To do so would be to overlook some of the most intriguing contributions of maps to human reasoning and problem solving. We need to expand our dependent measures beyond those that assess participants' success in following, reproducing, or reversing routes, or their success in reproducing locations shown on maps after delays, or in transferring those locations to a space of a different size or medium. We would be wise to look to content experts to help us select the kinds of cognitive insights that we hope will be supported by access to external spatial representations (e.g., insights about geological processes, or migration patterns, or the dispersion of disease, or the explanations of storm systems) rather than the surface-level encoding and recall of symbols on a page.

In short, just as cartographic maps have much to teach students about their geographic world, about space, about representation, and about logic, so too, they have much to teach psychologists about human cognition. It is essential to consider the richness of the kinds of reasoning and problem solving that cartographic maps (and other external spatial representations) afford. We should not become so enamored with studying the roles of our own mental representations that we overlook the roles of our equally human external representations.

I close by returning to the title of this chapter, "Thinking Through Maps." The double entendre is intentional. I urge that we *think through* maps—that is, think about maps—more thoroughly. Only then will we be able to think *through* maps—that is, think via maps—for many of the reasoning and problem-solving challenges we face in our classrooms, workplaces, psychological laboratories, and in our daily lives.

Acknowledgments

Portions of this work were supported by the National Science Foundation (#RED-9554504), although no endorsement by the NSF is implied for the opinions, findings, conclusions, or recommendations expressed here. I acknowledge with thanks the intriguing questions raised by Merideth Gattis and the reviewers of this volume; the many provocative conversations I have had with Rich Carlson as we puzzle over fascinating theoretical questions related to space and attempt to turn them into tractable empirical work; and finally, the powerful and continuing role that Roger Downs has played in helping me to think ever more like a geographer (and perhaps not *too* much less like a psychologist).

Chapter 4

Spatial Schemas in Depictions

Barbara Tversky

4.1 Overview

Depictions, such as maps, that portray visible things are ancient whereas graphics, such as charts and diagrams, that portray things that are inherently not visible, are relatively modern inventions. An analysis of historical and developmental graphic inventions suggests that they convey meaning by using elements and space naturally. Elements are based on likenesses, "figures of depiction" and analogs to physical devices. Spatial relations are used metaphorically to convey other relations, based on proximity, at nominal, ordinal, and interval levels. Graphics serve a variety of functions, among them, attracting attention, supporting memory, providing models, and facilitating inference and discovery.

4.2 Introduction: A Brief History of Graphics

We take it for granted that human beings have crafted tools to improve their physical well-being from the beginning of humanity. More recently, it has become apparent that other primates do the same (e.g., Goodall, 1986; Whiten, Goodall, Mc Grew, Nishida, Reynolds, Sugiyama, Tutin, Wrangham and Boesch, 1999). These tools augment our physical capacity, they allow us to obtain food and protection more effectively than our bodies alone could do. Less noticed is the fact that we craft tools to augment our mental capacity as well (e.g., Donald, 1991; Norman, 1993). The fabrication of cognitive tools by other primates has not been shown. One of the oldest of these tools is graphics, from maps in the sand to neon on the Ginza. The key to these is using space and elements in it to convey meaning.

Long before there was written language, there were depictions, of myriad varieties. Only a few of the multitude of cave paintings, petroglyphs, bone incisions, graffiti, clay impressions, stone carvings, and wood markings that people created and used remain from ancient cultures. Some of these depictions probably had religious significance, but many were used to communicate, to keep track of events in time, to note ownership and transactions of ownership, to map places, and to record songs and sayings (e.g., Coulmas, 1989; De Francis, 1989; Gelb, 1963; Mallery, 1893/1972; Schmandt-Besserat, 1992). As such, they served as permanent records of history, commemorations of cultural past. Because pictures represent meaning more directly than alphabetic written languages, we can guess at their meanings today. In rare cases, we have the benefit of contemporaneous translations. While collecting petroglyphs and other examples of pictographic communications from native Americans in the last century, Mallery was able to speak with many still using them (1893/1972). Several of these left by a Native American who lived near Long Lake in Maine in the mid-nineteenth century appear in Figure 4.1. They are leave-taking notices posted on bark to inform visitors where he had gone.

In many places in the world, the use of pictures to communicate developed into complete written languages. All such languages invented ways to represent concepts that are difficult to depict, such as proper names, abstract entities, causality, quantification, negations, and the like (e.g., Coulmas, 1989; DeFrancis, 1989; Gelb, 1963). As pictures evolved into written languages, two things occurred: they became schematized and they lost their transparency. Figure 4.2 shows how Sumerian characters that began as fairly transparent sketches of the concepts they conveyed became schematized in writing and lost any resemblance to those concepts. Some originally pictoric written languages transformed to use written marks to represent sound rather than meaning directly. This had two simultaneous advantages: it reduced the numbers of pictographs that had to be learned and it solved the problem of representing concepts difficult to depict. The spread of the alphabet and, much later, the invention of the printing press decreased reliance on pictures for communication. With the increasing ease of reproducing written language and increasing literacy, depictions became more decorative than communicative.

Now, pictures, depictions, and visualizations as communications are on the rise again. As with the proliferation of written language, this is partly due to technologies for creating, reproducing, and transmitting pictures.

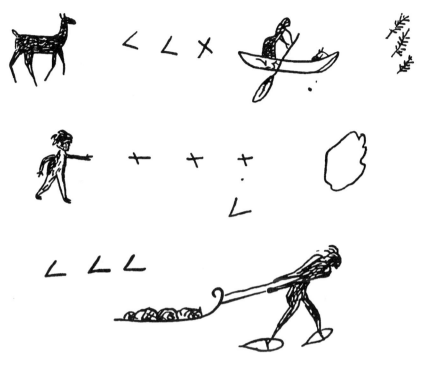

Figure 4.1
Birch bark leave notices left by a Native American living near Long Lake, Maine
in the mid-1800's. Top panel: I am going across the lake to hunt deer. Middle
panel: I am going towards the lake and will turn off at the point where there is a
pointer before reaching the lake. Lowest panel: I am going hunting and will be
gone all winter. From Mallery (1972, 331).

And as with the proliferation of written language, some of the spread
of depictions is due to intellectual insights. For this, the basic insight is
using depictions to represent abstract meaning by means of visual and
spatial metaphors and figures of depiction. Using space also capitalizes on
people's extensive experience learning about space and making spatial
inferences.

Although space in depictions has long been used to convey concrete
ideas, the use of space to convey abstract ideas is more recent. Early uses
of space in depictions for the most part portrayed things that were inherently visualizable, such as objects, buildings, or environments, in pictographs, architectural plans, or maps. Maps appear in many forms, many
taking liberty with spatial metrics, such as the T-O maps popular in

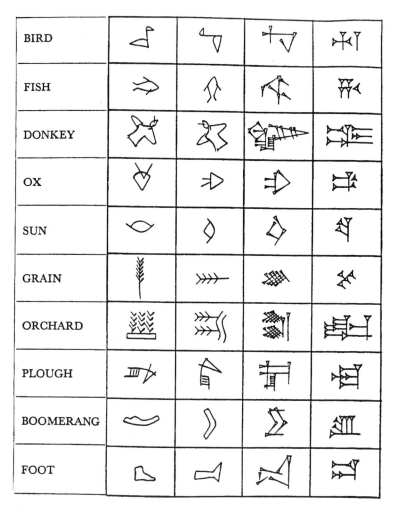

Figure 4.2
Pictorial origins of ten cuneiform signs. Note the rotation the forms underwent to accommodate production. From Gelb (1963, 70).

medieval times, so-called because they were O-shaped, with an internal T. An example appears in Figure 4.3. In these maps, East, the Orient, the rising sun, Asia, was at the top, above the crossbar of the T, which was formed by the Dan and Nile Rivers. Below the crossbar to the left was Europe and to the right, Africa, separated by the Mediterranean forming the vertical bar of T. Maps are necessarily schematic; at the least, they omit information, presumably retaining the information relevant to their expected use. Maps may even mix perspectives, as in landmark maps, appearing as early as medieval times, where countries, rivers, and roads are laid out as if from above, with landmarks portrayed frontally super-imposed. Figure 4.4 shows one of these (for more examples of maps ancient and modern, see Brown, 1979; Harley and Woodward, 1987, 1992, 1994; Southworth and Southworth, 1982). In contrast to these ancient depictions, many contemporary depictions are visualizations of things that are not inherently visualizable, such as temporal, quantitative, causal, or social relations. These depictions depend on analogy rather than schematic miniaturization or enlargement.

Graphs are perhaps the most prevalent example of depictions of abstract concepts, and were invented as recently as the late eighteenth century (e.g., Beniger and Robyn, 1978; Carswell and Wickens, 1988; Tufte, 1983), although they probably had their roots in mathematical notation, especially Cartesian coordinate systems. Two Europeans, Playfair in England and Lambert in Switzerland, are credited with being the first to promulgate their use, for the most part to portray economic and political data.

Notably, those early graphs, X-Y plots with time as one of the variables, are still the most common type of graph in scientific journals (Cleveland, 1984). This is despite the continuing clever inventions of visualizations from Florence Nightingale's polar plots of mortality across hospitals (Cohen, 1984) to box plots and stem-and-leaf diagrams (Tukey, 1977) to starfields, cone trees, and hyperbolic trees (e.g., Card, Mackinlay and Shneiderman, 1999) to the latest presentations at the InfoVis meetings or in Newsweek. Some of these visualizations have been widely adopted. Bar graphs and pie charts are common for representing quantitative data, with flow charts, trees, and networks widely used for qualitative data. Icons appear in airports, train stations, and highways all over the world, and menus of icons on information highways over the world. Many are used to portray concepts and information that are difficult to

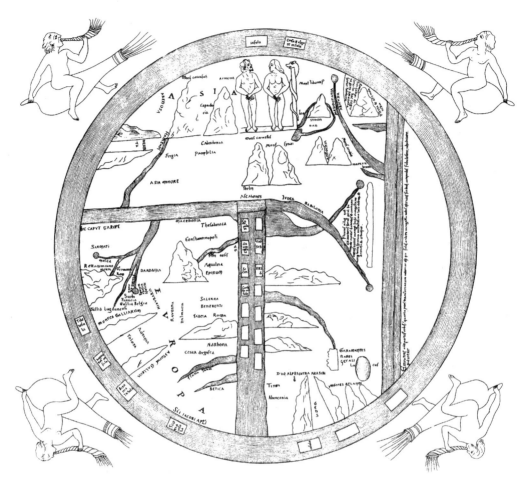

Figure 4.3
A T-O map, popular in the Middle Ages. Asia (east) is at the top, Europe (north) to the left, Africa (south) to the right. From Brown (1977, 118).

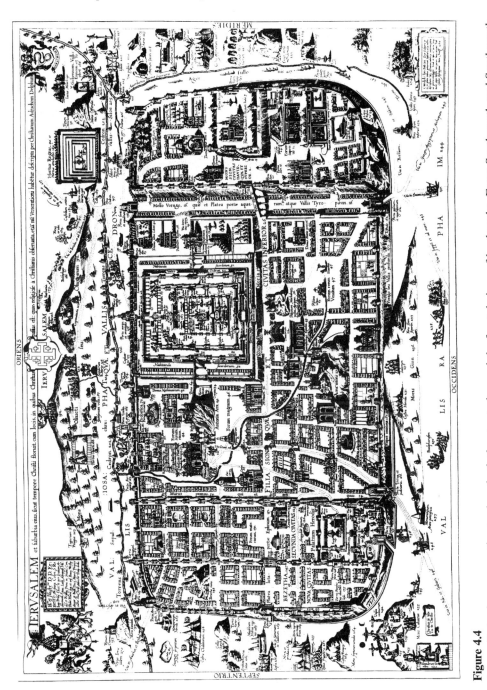

Figure 4.4
A map that mixes perspective to show both the street plan and the frontal views of landmarks. From Southworth and Southworth (1982, 74). Reprinted with permission of the Division of Rare and Manuscript Collections, Cornell University Library.

visualize, such as large data bases. Creating an effective visual webrowser continues to challenge the ingenuity of many.

4.3   How Graphics Convey Meaning

Graphics consist of elements that are systematically arranged in space. The choices of elements and spatial arrangements are usually not accidental or arbitrary. Many graphic conventions have been invented and reinvented by adults and children across cultures and time. Many have analogs in language and in gesture. Many are rooted in natural cognitive correspondences, "figures of depictions," and spatial metaphors, and have parallels in Gestalt principles of perceptual organization. In this paper, I present an analysis of graphic inventions based on how their elements and spatial arrangements are used to convey meaning. The evidence I will bring to bear is eclectic and unconventional, drawing from examinations of historical graphic inventions, children's graphic inventions, and language, as well as more conventional psychological research. Later, I examine how two contemporary graphic inventions, animation and 3-D, communicate, survey the various functions graphics serve, and draw conclusions for their design.

With some exceptions, graphic elements are generally used to represent elements in the world and graphic space is used to represent the relations between elements. One notable exception is mathematics, where elements such as + and − indicate relations. The dichotomy, into elements and relations, maps loosely onto the "what" vs. "where" distinction in vision and in spatial cognition, that is, information related to objects on the one hand and to spatial relations among objects on the other.

The fact that graphic displays are external augments many of their functions. Externalizing a representation reduces demand on memory and facilitates information processing. Spatially organized information can be accessed, integrated, and operated on quickly and easily, especially when the spatial organization reflects conceptual organization. Moreover, external representations are public. Several people can simultaneously inspect the same graphic display, and refer to it by pointing and other devices in ways apparent to all, facilitating group communication (e.g., Engle, 1998).

Elements: Figures of Depiction
Sometimes icons as elements are effective in representing meaning directly, for example, highway signs of a picnic table or a water tap on

the route to the location of actual ones. For concepts not easily depicted, icons present challenges. They can, however, represent concepts indirectly, using a number of "figures of depiction," analogous to figures of speech (Tversky, 1995). One common type of figure of depiction is metonymy, where an associated object represents the concept. In computer interfaces, a picture of a folder represents a file of words and a picture of a trash can represents a place for unwanted folders. Analogous examples in language include using "the crown" to represent the king and "the White House" to represent the president. Synecdoche, where a part is used to represent a whole, or a whole for a part, is another common figure of depiction. Returning to highway signs, an icon of a place setting near a freeway exit indicates a nearby restaurant and an icon of a gas pump a nearby gas station. Analogous examples in language include "give a hand" for help and "head count" for number of people. Figures of depiction frequent early pictographic writing (Coulmas, 1989; Gelb, 1963;). For example, early Sumerian writing used a foot to indicate "to go" and an ox's head to indicate an ox. Figure 4.5 presents early ideographs for several concepts from a number of written languages, illustrating metonymy and synecdoche. Children's spontaneous writing and depictions also illustrate these principles (e.g., Hughes, 1986; Levin and Tolchinsky-Landsman, 1989). Like the inventors of pictographic languages, children find it easier to depict objects, especially concrete ones, than operations. For abstract objects and operations, children use metonymy and synecdoche. For example, children draw hands or legs to indicate addition or subtraction. Interestingly, the latter was also used in hieroglyphics (Hughes, 1986). As seen in the examples of public icons in Figures 4.6 and 4.7, depicting objects or things is more direct than depicting relations among objects. The public symbols developed by a different local, national, and international organizations for restaurants and coffee shops are highly similar whereas those developed for purchasing tickets or for baggage claim are less so.

The meanings of these depictions are somewhat transparent. Often, they can be guessed, sometimes with help of context. Even when guessing is unsuccessful, the range of meanings possible is highly limited. Because of their transparency, these icons are easily associated to their meanings, and thus easily remembered (for similar arguments in the context of ASL and gesture, see Macken, Perry and Haas, 1993). The meanings of computer icons cannot always be conveyed by a single word. The alternatives, verbal commands, are not always transparent and frequently need to be

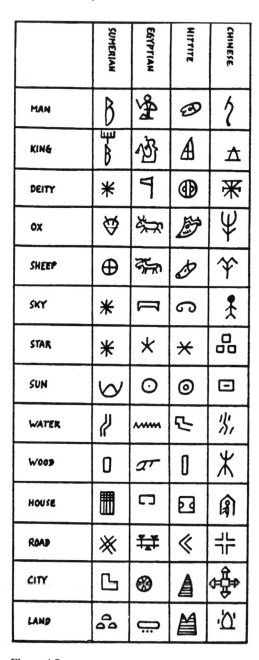

Figure 4.5
Pictorial signs in the Sumerian, Egyptian, Hittite, and Chinese languages. From Gelb (1963, 98).

learned. Does "delete" or "remove" eliminate a file? Do we "exit" or "quit" a program? Depictions have other advantages over words. Meaning is extracted from pictures faster than from words (Smith and McGee, 1980). Icons can be "read" by people who do not read the local language.

A new use of depictions has appeared in email. Seemingly inspired by smiley faces, and probably because it is inherently more casual than other written communication, computer vernacular has added signs for the emotional expression normally conveyed in face-to-face communication by intonation and gesture. These signs combine symbols found on keyboards to denote facial expressions, usually turned 90 degrees, such as :) or ;).

Spatial Arrays of Elements

Graphs, charts, and diagrams convey qualitative and quantitative information using natural correspondences and spatial metaphors, some applied to the spatial elements, and others applied to the arrays of spatial elements. For spatial arrays, the most basic metaphor is proximity: proximity in space is used to indicate proximity on some other property, such as time or value. Spatial arrays convey conceptual information metaphorically at different levels of precision, corresponding to the four traditional scale types, nominal, ordinal, interval, and ratio (Stevens, 1946). These are ordered inclusively by the degree of information preserved in the mapping. Spontaneously produced graphic displays reflect these scale types. Children, for example, represent nominal relations in graphic displays at an earlier age than ordinal relations, and ordinal relations at an earlier age than interval relations (Tversky, Kugelmass and Winter, 1991). For elements, graphic displays use a variety of visual analogs to physical devices to convey information of varying quantitative precision.

Nominal scales Nominal scales are essentially clustering by category. Here, elements are divided into classes, sharing a single property or set of properties. Graphic devices indicating nominal relations often use the simplest form of proximity, grouping. This form, like many of the uses of spatial arrangement to convey meaning, capitalizes on Gestalt principles of perceptual grouping. In perception, things that are near by in space tend to be grouped and separated from things that are distant. To use this for conveying abstract meanings simply requires placing things that are related in close proximity and placing things that are not related farther away in space. One use of this device that we take for granted are the

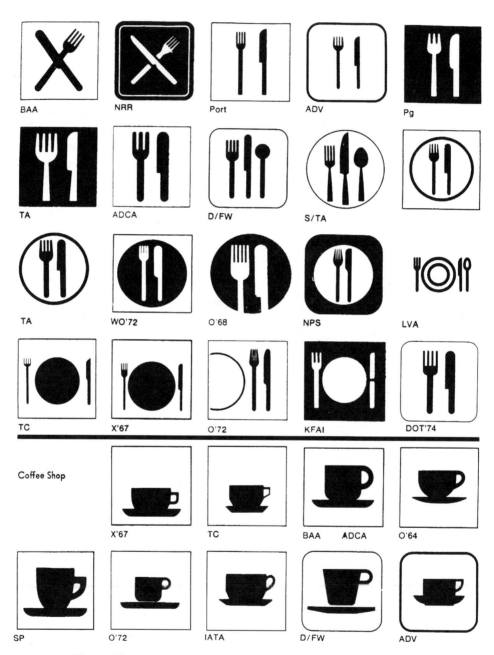

Figure 4.6
Various icons developed by civil authorities for restaurant and coffee shop. From Modley (1976, 67).

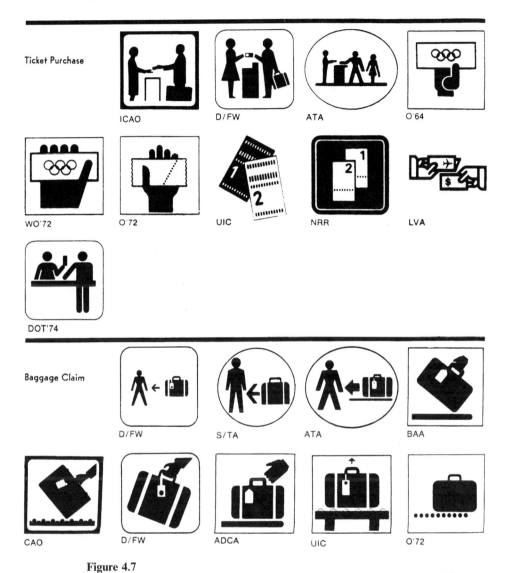

Figure 4.7
Various icons developed by civil authorities for ticket purchase and baggage claim. From Modley (1976, 70).

Table 4.1
Visual and spatial devices used to convey categorical and nominal relations

---

Categorical/Nominal Relations
spaces between words
spacing by rows and columns
( ), [ ], boxes, circles, Venn diagrams
visual devices: color, shading, cross-hatching
Ordinal
Simple subordination
  indentation
  size
  superposition
  highlighting
  punctuation
Complex subordination
  order
  trees (hierarchies)

⎯⎯

⟶

---

spaces between words in writing. Although it is easy to overlook spacing as a graphic device, early writing did not put spaces between words. The Roman alphabet for the most part maps sounds to written characters, but beyond the alphabet, many conventions of writing are based on spatial correspondences, not sound correspondences. Indentation and/or spacing before a new paragraph is another example of using separation in space to indicate separation of ideas. Some of the spatial and visual features used to convey nominal and ordinal relations appear in Table 4.1.

Another spatial device for delineating a category is a list, where all the items that need to be purchased or tasks that need to be done are written in a single column or row. Items are separated by empty space, and the items begin at the same point in each row, indicating equivalence. For lists, there is often only a single category; organization into a column indicates that the items are not randomly selected, but rather, share a property. Multiple lists are also common, for example, the list of chores of each housemate or a shopping list divided by departments or stores. A table is an elaboration of a list, using the same spatial device to organize both rows and columns (Stenning and Oberlander, 1995). A table cross-classifies items by several categories simultaneously. Items within each column and within each row are related, but on different features. In many cases, tables combine categorical and quantitative information. Examples include a list of countries with their GNP's for each of the last ten years, or a list of schools, with their average achievement scores on a variety of tests. Tables cross-classify. Items within each column and within each row are related, but on different features. Train schedules are yet another example, where the first column is typically the stations, the places where the train stops, and subsequent columns are the times for each train. For train schedules, a blank space where there would ordinarily be a time indicates a non-event, that is, this train doesn't stop at that station. Using spatially-arrayed rows and columns, tables group and juxtapose simultaneously.

Empty space is not the only spatial device used to indicate grouping. Often special signs, usually visual ones rather than strictly spatial ones, are added. These seem to fall into two classes, those based on enclosure (cf. Gestalt Principle of Grouping) and those based on similarity (cf. Gestalt Principle of Similarity). Signs used for enclosure resemble physical structures that enclose actual things, such as bowls and fences. On paper, these include parentheses, circles, boxes, and frames. Tables often add boxes to emphasize the structures of rows and columns or to enclose related items and separate different ones. Newspapers use frames to distinguish one classified ad from another. Parentheses and brackets in writing are in essence degenerate enclosures The curved or bent lines, segments of circles or rectangles, face each other to include the related words and to separate them from the rest of the sentence.

Complete circles have been useful in visualizing syllogisms and in promoting inference as in Euler or Venn diagrams or in contemporary adaptations of them (e.g., Shin, 1991; Stenning and Oberlander, 1995). Circles enclose items belonging to the same set. Circles with no physical contact indicate sets with no common items, and physically overlapping circles indicate sets with at least some common items. The classic Euler circles have been used as a reasoning heuristic as they are not sufficient for actual deduction. There are ongoing attempts to develop completely diagrammatic reasoning systems. One attempt has been to enrich Euler diagrams with spatial signs based on similarity, such as filling in similar regions with similar and dissimilar regions with different marks, color, shading, cross-hatching, and other patterns (e.g., Shin, 1991). Others have been developing heterogeneous reasoning systems based on a a combination of graphics and language, utilizing each for the contents and contexts in which inferences are easiest (Barwise and Etchemendy, 1995).

Other visual features of diagrams can be used to convey categorical relations. Maps use colors as well as lines to indicate political boundaries and geographic features. For geographic features, many of the correspondences are natural ones. For example, deserts are colored beige whereas forests are colored green, and lakes and seas are colored blue. Colors can also be used to convey quantitative information, for example, deeper (darker) blues indicating deeper water. Color categories and gradations can be used metaphorically as well. Examples include the use of colors to indicate degree of excitation in PET or fMRI images of the thinking brain. In addition to color, other visual features, such as size, shape, and font, can be used to signify groups based on similarity.

Ordinal relations   Ordinal relations can vary from a partial order, where one or more elements have precedence over others, to a complete order, where all elements are ordered with respect to some property or properties. There are two separable issues in mapping order onto space. One is the devices used to indicate order, and the other is the direction of order. The direction of indicating order will be discussed after interval relations, as the same principles apply.

Now to ways of indicating order, first using space. Many of the devices used to indicate groupings can be adapted to indicate order. Writing is ordered, so one of the simplest spatial devices to indicate rank on some property is to write items according to the order on the property, for example, writing countries in order of GNP, or people in order of age. Empty space is used to convey order, as in indentation in outlines, where successively subordinate items are successively indented relative to superordinate items.

Visual devices are also useful for indicating order. Primary among them are lines. Lines form the skeletons of trees and graphs, both of which are commonly used to display ordered concepts, to indicate asymmetry on a variety of relations, including kind of, part of, reports to, and derived from. Examples include hierarchical displays, as in linguistic trees, evolutionary trees, and organizational charts. Other visual and spatial devices used to display order rest on the metaphor of salience. More salient features have more of the relevant property. Such features include size, color, highlighting, and superposition. Some visuo/spatial devices rely on what can be called natural cognitive correspondences. For example, high temperatures or greater activity are associated with "warm" colors and low temperatures and lower activity with "cold" colors, in scientific charts. This association most likely derives from the colors of things varying in temperature, such as fire and ice.

Arrows are a special kind of line, with one end marked, inducing an asymmetry. Although they have many uses, a primary one is to indicate direction, an asymmetric relation. Like bars and lines, arrows seem to be based on physical analogs. One obvious analog is the physical object arrow, invented by many different cultures for hunting. It is not the hunting or piercing aspects of physical arrows that have been adopted in diagrams, but rather the directionality. Hunting arrows are asymmetric, as a consequence of which they fly more easily in one direction than the other. Another more abstract analog is the idea of convergence captured by the > ("V") of a diagram arrow. Like a funnel or river straits, it directs anything captured by the wide part to the point, and straight outwards from there. Arrows are frequently used to signal direction in space. In diagrams, arrows are also commonly used to indicate direction in time. Production charts and computer flow diagrams, for examples, use arrows to denote the sequence of processes. Terms for time, such as "before" and "after," and indeed thinking about time, frequently derive from terms for and thinking about space (e.g., Boroditsky, 1999; Clark, 1973; Gentner, this volume).

Interval and ratio relations   Interval and ratio relations apply more constraints of the spatial proximity metaphor than ordinal relations. In graphic displays of interval information, the distances between elements are meaningful; that is, greater space corresponds to more on the relevant dimension. This is not the case for ordinal mappings. Ratio displays of information, are even more restrictive. For them, zero and the ratios of the distances are meaningful.

The most common graphic displays of interval and ratio information are X-Y plots, where distance in the display corresponds to distance on the relevant property or properties. Musical notation is a specialized interval scale that makes use of a limited visual alphabet corresponding to modes of execution of notes as well as a spatial scale corresponding to pitch. Finally, for displaying ratio information, pie charts can be useful, where the area of the pie corresponds to the proportion on the relevant variable.

Expressing mixed cases: bars and lines   Most graphs display two variables simultaneously, average rainfall over months, school achievement scores by district, chocolate ice cream sales by stores, and so on. Bars charts are a common way to convey quantities of discrete sets. They are useful for displaying quantities for several variables at once where the height or length of the bar corresponds to the quantity on the relevant variable. Isotypes were invented by Otto and Marie Neurath in the 30's as part of a larger movement to increase communication across languages and cultures. That movement included efforts to develop picture languages and Esperanto. Isotypes combine icons and bar charts to render quantities on different variables more readily interpretable (Neurath, 1936). For example, in order to display the yearly productivity by sector for a number of countries, a unit of output for each sector is represented by an isotype, or icon that is readily interpretable, a shaft of wheat for units grain, an ingot for units of steel, an oil well for units of petroleum. The number of icons per sector is proportional to output in that sector. Because of their physical resemblance to a product of each sector, icons facilitate comparison across countries or years for the sectors.

When two variables are displayed simultaneously, one may be categorical and the other quantitative. Going from categorical grouping to conceptual ordering requires a conceptual leap. Grouping entails seeing that items in Group A share one or more properties and items in Group B share one or more different properties. Group A and Group B do not have to be related in any way; they are the proverbial "apples and oranges." Different school districts and different ice cream stores can be regarded as separate and different entities with different properties. Ordering entails seeing that Group A and Group B differ on a property (or properties) that itself differs systematically. Specifically, the systematicity underlying an order requires a property that is similar enough across groups that it can be arranged as including more or less of the property. Put differently, categorical relations depend on within group property similarity and between group property difference. Ordinal relations depend on graded property similarity between groups. Note that the division into categorical and quantitative relations depends in part on perspective. Let us return to the school district example. One way of looking at separate school districts is as separate entities. Another way of looking at them is to order them by parental income, thus turning a categorical variable into a (sensible) quantitative one.

Categorical relations separate and ordinal ones connect. Visual devices that indicate boundaries or containers are natural analogs for categories just as visual devices that indicate connections are natural analogs for orders. Visual boundaries and containers include the brackets and circles and frames discussed in the section on categorical relations. Like those, visual devices that indicate connections resemble physical structures that link things, like outstretched arms, paths, chains, and ropes. Like paths or outstretched arms, lines link one concept to another, bringing non-contiguous things into contiguity, making distal items proximal. Lines, sometimes whole and continuous (——), sometimes partial or broken (········) are used to link related items.

That categorical or discrete concepts are naturally mapped to entities that contain and ordinal concepts are naturally mapped to entities that connect seems to underlie the use and interpretation of bars and lines in graphs (Zacks and Tversky, 1999). Bars are container-like and lines connect. Zacks and Tversky (1999) distinguished two related uses. The use that is statistical lore, and sometimes explicit advice, is the bar-line data use: display discrete data with bars and continuous data with lines. But we have already seen that the same data can be viewed in different ways. The more subtle use is the bar-line message use: interpret/produce bars as discrete comparisons and lines as trends.

Evidence not only for data use but also for message use of bars and lines appeared in graphic productions and interpretations. One set of participants wrote interpretations for graphs of height of males/females, a discrete domain, or 10 year olds/12 year olds, a continuous domain. Examples appear in Figure 4.8. Discrete interpretations used terms like "higher," "less," and "fewer," whereas trend interpretations used terms like "rising" and "decreasing," and sometimes "function," "relationship," and "trend." More line graphs were interpreted as trends than bar graphs, consistent with the bar/line message use. More trend interpretations were produced for the continuous domain than for the discrete domain, consistent with the bar/line data use. Another set of participants produced graphs for discrete or trend descriptions of height in males/females or 10 year olds/12 year olds.

As for interpretations, productions showed the effects of both data and message uses of bars and lines. More line graphs were produced for trend descriptions that used terms like "increasing" than for discrete descrip-

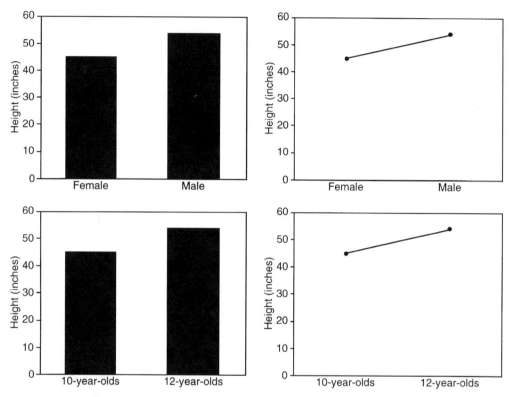

Figure 4.8
Bars and lines used by Zacks and Tversky (1999) for eliciting descriptions of
relations. Despite content, informants tended to describe relations portrayed as
bars in terms of discrete comparisons and those portrayed as lines in terms of
trends. From Zacks and Tversky (1999).

tions that used terms like "greater," supporting the bar/line message use.
More trend descriptions were produced for the continuous (age) domain
than the discrete (sex) domain, supporting the bar/line data use. Overall,
the effects of the graph form, bar or line, were stronger than the effects of
the conceptual domain, discrete or continuous.

These correspondences between choice of graphic representation and
choice of interpretation appeared despite the fact that few people in the
informant population are aware of the bar/line data use, and even fewer
of the bar/line message use. The choice of visual devices for discrete,
categorical concepts and for ordinal or continuous ones appears to be
naturally derived from physical devices that contain or connect.

Directionality   In spite of the uncountable number of possibilities for indicating order in graphic displays, the actual choices are remarkably limited. In principle, elements could be ordered in any number of orientations in a display. Nevertheless, graphic displays tend to order elements either vertically or horizontally or both. Similarly, languages are written either horizontally or vertically, in rows or in columns. There are reasons grounded in perception for the preference for vertical and horizontal orientations. The perceptual world has two dominant axes: a vertical axis defined by gravity and by all the things on earth correlated with gravity; and a horizontal axis defined by the horizon and by all the things on earth parallel to it. Vision is especially acute along the vertical and horizontal axes (Howard, 1982). Memory is poorer for the orientation of oblique lines, and slightly oblique lines are perceived and remembered as more vertical or horizontal than they were (Howard, 1982; Tversky, 1981; for exceptions that depend on graphic interpretation, see Schiano and Tversky, 1992).

Vertical asymmetry   Of all the possible orientations, then, graphic displays ordinarily only use the vertical and horizontal. What's more, they use these orientations differently. Vertical arrays take precedence over horizontal ones. Just as for the choice of dimensions, the precedence of the vertical is also rooted in perception (Clark, 1973; Cooper and Ross, 1975; Lakoff and Johnson, 1980; Franklin and Tversky, 1990). Gravity is correlated with vertical, and people are oriented vertically. The vertical axis of the world has a natural asymmetry, the ground and the sky, whereas the horizontal axis of the world does not. The dominance of the vertical over the horizontal is reflected in the dominance of columns over rows. Similarly, bar charts typically contain vertical columns (the exceptions seem to be aimed at conforming to accompanying text).

Natural correspondences with vertical   There is another plausible reason for the dominance of the vertical over the horizontal. Not only does the vertical take precedence over the horizontal, but there is a natural direction of correspondence for the vertical, though not for the horizontal. In language, concepts like more and better and stronger are associated with upward direction, and concepts like less and worse and weaker with downward direction (Clark, 1973; Cooper and Ross, 1975; Lakoff and Johnson, 1980). People and plants, indeed most life forms, grow upwards as they mature, becoming bigger, stronger, and (arguably) better. Healthy and happy people stand tall; sick or sad ones droop or lie down. More of any quantity makes a higher pile. The associations of up with quantity, mood, health, power, status, and more derive from physical correspondences in the world. It is no accident that in most bar charts and X-Y plots, increases go from down to up. The association of all good things with up is widely reflected in language as well. Inflation and unemployment are exceptions, but principled ones, as the numbers used to express inflation and unemployment go up. Language reflects these natural correspondences. We speak of someone "at the top of the heap," of doing the "highest good," of "feeling up," of being "on top of things," of having "high status" or "high ideals," of doing a "top-notch job," of reaching "peak performance," of going "above and beyond the line of duty." In gesture, we show success or approval with thumbs up, or give someone a congratulatory high five. The correspondence of pitch with the vertical seems to rest on another natural relation. We produce higher notes at higher places in the throat, and lower notes at lower places. It just so happens that higher notes correspond to higher frequency waves, but that may simply be a happy coincidence.

Horizontal neutral   In contrast, the horizontal axis is standardly used for neutral dimensions, most notably, time. Similarly, with few exceptions (curiously, economics), neutral or independent variables are plotted along the horizontal axis, and the variables of interest, the dependent variables, along the vertical axis. This arrangement of variables facilitates inferences of rates of change from line slopes (Gattis and Holyoak, 1996). Although graphic conventions stipulate that increases plotted horizontally proceed from left to right, directionality along the horizontal axis does not seem to rest in natural correspondences. The world is asymmetric along the vertical axis, but not along the horizontal axis. Right-left reflections of pictures are hardly noticed but top-bottom reflections are (e.g., Yin, 1969). Languages are just as likely to be written left to write as right to left (and in some cases, both), but they always begin at the top.

Use of space cross-culturally and developmentally   Children and adults from cultures where language is written left to right as well as from cultures where language is written right to left mapped increases on a variety of quantitative variables from down to up, but almost never mapped increases from up to down. However, people from both writing cultures mapped increases in quantity and preference from both left to right and right to left equally often. The relative frequency of using each direction to represent quantitative variables did not depend on the direction of written language (Tversky, Kugelmass and Winter, 1991). Despite the fact that most people are right-handed and that terms like dexterity derived from "right" in many languages have positive connotations and terms like sinister derived from "left" have negative connotations, the horizontal axis in graphic displays seems to be neutral. Consistent with that, we refer to one side of an issue as "on the one hand," and the other side as "on the other hand," which has prompted some politicians to ask for one-handed advisors. And in politics, both the right and the left claim the moral high ground.

Children's and adults' mappings of temporal relations showed a different pattern from their mappings of quantitative and preference relations (Tversky, Kugelmass and Winter, 1991). For time, they not only preferred to use the horizontal axis, they also used the direction of writing to determine the direction of temporal increases, so that people who wrote from left to right tended to map temporal concepts from left to right and people who wrote from right to left tended to map temporal concepts from right to left. This pattern of findings fits with the claim that neutral concepts such as time tend to be mapped onto the horizontal axis. The fact that the direction of mapping time corresponded to the direction of writing but the direction of mapping preference and quantitative variables did not may be because temporal sequences seem to be incorporated into writing more than quantitative concepts, for example, in schedules, calendars, invitations, and announcements of meetings.

Directionality in charts and diagrams   Compatible with the previous arguments and evidence, ordinal charts and networks tend to be vertically organized. A survey of the standard scientific charts in all the textbooks in biology, geology, and linguistics at the Stanford Undergraduate Library revealed vertical organization in all but two of 48 charts (Tversky, 1995). Furthermore, within each type of chart, there was agreement as to what appeared at the top. In 17 out of the 18 evolutionary charts, Homo sapiens, that is, the present age, was at the top. In 15 out of the 16 geological charts, the present era was at the top, and in 13 out of the 14 linguistic trees, the proto-language was at the top. In these charts, in contrast to X-Y graphs, time runs vertically, but time does not seem to account for the direction, partly because time is not ordered consistently across the charts. Rather, at the top of each chart is an ideal. In the case of evolution, it is humankind, regarded by some as the pinnacle of evolution, a view some biologists discourage (e.g., Gould, 1977). In the case of geology, the top is the richness and accessibility of the present era. In the case of language trees, the top is the proto-language, the most ancient theoretical case, the origin from which others diverged. In organizational charts, say of the government or large corporations, power and control are at the top. For diagramming sentences or the human body, the whole is at the top, and parts and sub-parts occupy lower levels. In charts such as these, the vertical relations are meaningful, denoting an asymmetry on the mapped relation, but the horizontal relations are often arbitrary.

4.4   Modern Graphics: 3D and Animation

Advances in computers have made more graphic devices available to professionals and amateurs alike, most notably, 3D and animation. Although both can be useful, they should come with questions: First, how well are these devices perceived and conceived? And second, what sorts of meanings do they naturally convey?

3-D

Different forms of 3-D have been used by artists all over the world. Post-Renaissance Western art has favored 1-point perspective, though modern and contemporary Western art seems to have abandoned that. Eastern art, as well as children's spontaneous art, have used other devices to convey depth, such as occlusion, size, and height in the picture plane (e.g., Braine, Schauble, Kugelmass and Winter, 1993; Willats, 1997).

For 3D, the first thought is that it is a natural for conveying information, concrete or abstract, that is inherently three-dimensional. Some encouragement for that view comes from work on drawings of objects. People naturally interpret object-like drawings, those, for example, with closed contours and hints of symmetry, as two-dimensional representations of three-dimensional objects (Hochberg, 1964; McBeath, Schiano and Tversky, 1997). Perceiving and comprehending the 3-D details, however, can be problematic from flattened images. Such perceptual difficulties abound, especially for odd views or scenes with multiple objects. The retina itself is essentially flat, and beyond small distances, perception in depth depends on a set of cues such as occlusion, foreshortening, and relative size rather than on stereoscopic vision. Those clues are only clues, however; they are fallible. Their limitations yield error in depth perception and in object recognition alike (e.g., Loomis, DaSilva, Fujita and Fukusima, 1992). 3D interfaces suffer from exactly the same limitations. Even within the bounds of stereoscopy, only one view of an object or scene is present at once. This means that mental representations of the three dimensions must be constructed from separate views. It also means that some objects may be occluded by others, as frequently happens in 3-D depth arrays of bars. Frontal views of 3-D bars often become reversible figures, hard to stabilize in order to inspect.

The difficulties of conceptualizing in three dimensions from a flat display make it no accident that maps of the three-dimensional world are schematized to two dimensions. Nor is it an accident that architects and engineers prefer to design two-dimensional planes of their projects before proceeding to three-dimensional representations (e.g., Arnheim, 1977; Suwa and Tversky, 1996). Not just production, but also interpretation of 3D graphics is difficult for novices (e.g., Cooper, Schacter, Ballesteros and Moore, 1992; Gobert, 1999). Similarly, constructing three-dimensional conceptual representations from two-dimensional graphic representations is also difficult (e.g., Shah and Carpenter, 1995). When asked to provide the information conveyed in a 2-D line graph portraying three variables, respondents described the relations between the in terms of the variables plotted on the X and Y axes rather than in terms of the indirectly represented Z axis.

Although 3D is popular, it is hard to perceive and hard to conceive, even when used for objects and scenes that are naturally three dimensional. But the proliferation of graphics software has allowed creation of 3D graphics even for things that are not naturally 3D, most notably 3-D bar graphs. This practice has been decried by many (e.g., Tufte, 1983; Wainer, 1980). The rising cost of oil, for instance, has been portrayed by proportionately larger oil barrels. Only the relative heights of the barrels are meaningful, but viewers cannot help but respond to the areas or implied volumes. Despite the difficulties of 3-D, users express preferences for 3D bars or lines in certain situations, for example, for showing data for others rather than self, or for remembering data as opposed to examining it (Levy, Zacks, Tversky and Schiano, 1996). Some of these intuitions are not off the mark. Estimates in perception from 3D bars are indeed worse than from old-fashioned 2D bars, but estimates in memory are no worse from 3D than from 2D bars (Zacks, Levy, Tversky and Schiano, 1998).

Animation

Animation, graphics that change, can be eye-catching, as web advertisers have discovered. For conveying real-time on-line processes, simple animations can be informative. Take for example, the bar that appears when accessing a website. It fills at the rate that information is downloaded, allowing the user to estimate how much time it will take to acquire the information. Because animation entails changes in graphics over time, it seems a natural for conveying actions and processes that are inherently dynamic or that take place over time. This should hold for both actions that are concrete, such as the motions of people and machines and for processes that are more abstract, such as weather systems or the temporal/causal relations of algorithms. However, as for 3D, this view does not take into account human perceptions and conceptions of dynamic events. Animations vary in complexity. One simple animation is the path of a point or object. Another is the sequential highlighting of parts of a display. Movements of two- or three-dimensional bodies, especially an irregular ones, and movements along oblique or irregular paths are more complex. Even more complex animations include the movements of parts in relation to one another, such as a system of gears or pulleys or the changes in position of the limbs during walking. Still more complex are the movements of two bodies or systems with respect to one another. For an animation to be effective, it first must be correctly perceived.

Many dynamic events, especially complex ones, take place too quickly for human observers to perceive. For example, generations of artists painted the legs of galloping horses incorrectly until Muybridge's (1957) photographs revealed the correct configuration. This is complex motion, parts moving in complex patterns relative to one another. Yet there is evidence that even the simple path of a pendulum is often misperceived. Observers who select the correct trajectory from an animation may nevertheless fail to draw the correct trajectory (Kaiser, Profitt, Whelan and Hecht, 1992). What's more paths or trajectories of moving objects are often distorted, perceived as closer to horizontal or vertical than they actually are (e.g., Pani, Jeffres, Shippey and Schwartz, 1996; Shiffrar and Shepard, 1991). Even events that are slow enough to be accurately perceived may be conceived of as discrete steps rather than as continuous movement (e.g., Zacks, Tversky and Iyer, in press). In verifying assertions about the behavior of pulley systems, people mentally animate the systems one pulley at a time in sequence rather than imagining the entire system in action (Hegarty, 1992). Put differently, people conceive of the continuous action of a pulley system as a sequence of discrete steps.

In addition to the difficulties of perceiving them accurately. animations have a substantive disadvantage relative to static diagrams. Like speech, animations are transient, ephemeral, and not readily reinspected. A series of static diagrams, freeze frames, can simultaneously portray the sequential stages of an action, like the galloping of a horse's legs or the steps in operating a coffee maker. Similarly, an annotated diagram, such as a flow chart, can show the successive steps of a complex action all at once. Compared to animations, static diagrams can more easily be inspected and reinspected, related and interrelated to insure understanding.

Misperceptions of dynamic events and conceptions of them as sequences of steps rather than continuos activity may account for many of the failures to find benefits of animation in conveying information, concrete or abstract (e.g., Kaiser, Proffitt, Whelan and Hecht 1992; Hegarty, Narayanan, Cate and Holmquist, 1999; Lowe, 1999; Pane, Corbett and John, 1996; Rieber, Boyce and Assad, 1990; Stasko and Lawrence, 1998). There are, however, some cases where animation has been more successful than static diagrams, and these cases are instructive. One notable case is in teaching speed = distance × time problems, where motion was abstracted to a moving point (Baek and Lane, 1988). Two points starting in the same place moving at different speeds and arriving at different stopping points were simple enough to perceive and interpret. In this case, the animation is not only simple, it also abstracts the information essential to solving the problems, the differences in rates of movement. Since the rates are constant and the path a straight line, the events are perceived as continuous, not likely to be conceptually segmented. Another successful application of animation also used simple animations, in this case, sequentially highlighting parts of a diagram to guide viewers' successive foci of attention. This entailed a discrete rather than continuous use of animation. Diagrams can be visually complex, but unlike for reading text, there is no established order of scanning them. Sequential highlighting can provide a sensible order of integrating parts of a diagram. It borrows a device common in language, using linear order to reveal underlying structure. For example, cities scattered spatially on a map can be organized by historical era or by size. Sequential highlighting indeed facilitated organization of a diagram by the highlighted features, determining the character of the mental representation. However, it had no benefits to memory relative to static diagrams (Betrancourt and Tversky, in press). Note that each of these animations is perceptually simple, the smooth horizontal movement of a single point or the sequential highlighting of successive parts. Note also that each animation conveys a cognitively simple idea, the relative speeds of two simultaneously moving objects or the order of spatially scattered elements.

These considerations and findings suggest that graphic animations may succeed with the right combination of information processing ease and cognitive naturalness. Animations can facilitate only when they are simple and slow enough to be perceived. Animations are natural for conveying processes or events that take place in time or for guiding focus of attention over time. Useful animations should reflect people's conceptions of the processes and events they portray; they should be continuous if conceived of as continuous, discrete if conceived of as discrete. Finally, they should abstract and portray the essence of the changes over time.

4.5   Other Approaches

The approach taken here has been to search for ways that space and the things in it have been used to represent both spatial and nonspatial elements and relations, to search for natural correspondences between space and thought. Others have analyzed graphics from different perspectives, among them, linguists, computer scientists, psychologists, statisticians, designers, and philosophers. I review these analyses briefly for the interested reader. Their insights sometimes complement and sometimes parallel the observations and findings put forth here. Some of these researchers have analyzed the graphics themselves, others have examined how people comprehend, use, or construct them, and still others have made recommendations for design. Inevitably, some have focused on more than one of these goals, as the goals interact. Analyses of actual graphics gives clues to how they are used and produced by people and how they are used gives clues to how they should be designed.

In an influential treatise, Bertin (1981) put forth a comprehensive semiotic analysis of the functions of graphics and the processes used to interpret them that established the field and defined the issues. According to Bertin, the functions of graphs are to record, communicate, and process information, and the goal of a good graphic is simplification to those ends. This work was picked up first by statisticians and designers, most notably Tufte and Wainer, and later by psychologists. Tufte (1983, 1990, 1997) has exhorted graphic designers to refrain from "chart junk," extraneous marks that convey no additional information, adopting by contrast a minimalist view that does not take into account conventions or need for redundancy. Wainer (1984, 1992) has gathered a set of useful prescriptions and insightful examples for graph construction, drawing on work in semiotics, design, and information processing.

Within psychology, the interests of researchers have varied. Ittelson (1996) has called attention to differences in information processing of "markings," deliberate, two-dimensional inscriptions on surfaces of objects and other visual stimuli that may not have communicative intent. Thus, interpreting a graphic depends on understanding that it can represent something other than itself, a concept that children gradually come to appreciate DeLoache, Miller and Rosengren (1997). After an extensive survey of graphics used primarily in education, Winn (1987) analyzed how information is conveyed in charts, diagrams, and graphs. Larkin and Simon (1987) compared sentential and diagrammatic external representations, especially in teaching, highlighting the advantages of diagrammatic ones for tasks where spatial proximity conveys useful information. Continuing this line of thinking, Stenning and Oberlander (1995) presented a formal analysis of the advantages and disadvantages of diagrammatic and sentential representations in drawing inferences. They argue that diagrams allow expression of some abstractions, much like natural language, but are not as expressive as sentential logics.

Several projects have been directly concerned with how people perceive, misperceive, interpret, remember, and produce graphics, raising implications for design. Though a statistician, Cleveland (1984; 1985) has examined the psychophysical advantages and disadvantages of using different graphic devices for conveying quantity, position, angle, length, slope, and more, for efficiency in extracting different kinds of information from displays. He and his collaborators have produced convincing cases where conventional data displays can be easily misconstrued by human users. Kosslyn (1989; 1994), using principles adopted from visual information processing and Goodman's (1978) analysis of symbol systems, has developed a set of prescriptives for graph design, based on an analysis of the syntax, semantics, and pragmatics underlying graphs. Pinker (1990) provided a framework for understanding information extraction from graphics that separates processes involved in constructing a visual description of the physical aspects of the graph from those involved in constructing a graph schema of the mapping of the physical aspects to mathematical scales. Based on Pinker's framework, Carpenter and Shah (1998) proposed a model of graph comprehension in which pattern recognition, translation of visual features to conceptual relations, and determining referents of quantified concepts, are integrated and iterated.

Carswell and Wickens (Carswell, 1992; Carswell & Wickens, 1988; 1990) have demonstrated effects of perceptual analysis of integrality on graph comprehension, and others have shown systematic biases in interpretation or memory dependent on the form of graphic displays (Gattis & Holyoak, 1996; Levy, Zacks, Tversky & Schiano, 1996; Schiano & Tversky, 1992; Shah & Carpenter, 1995; Spence & Lewandowsky, 1991; Tversky & Schiano, 1989).

A number of observers of society have discussed the role of external devices, especially visualizations, in human cognition and behavior. Donald (1991) has speculated on the effects of the creation of mental artifacts on cultural change. Norman (1993) has critiqued modern inventions that, as he says, are supposed to make us smart, but don't always succeed. Kirsh (1995) has analyzed situations, such as preparing meals, playing tetris, and counting money, in which people array artifacts spatially and manipulate those arrays to facilitate memory and inference.

Visualizations have become increasingly important in organizing large data bases and enabling efficient search through them. Navigation metaphors for these tasks abound, both in language and in graphics. Researchers in human computer interaction have also been active in the invention of graphics and visualizations, and in the development of prescriptions for design (e.g., Card, Mackinlay and Shneiderman, 1999). Their "mantra" for creating effective visualizations of large sets of data: Overview first, zoom and filter, then details-on-demand (p. 625). Though there is some support for this mantra, research in cognition on basic level concepts (e.g., Rosch, 1978) and on reasoning (e.g., Cheng and Holyoak, 1985) suggests that an effective entry into a complex system might be a thorough understanding of a concrete example. Once an exemplary example has been mastered, abstraction to generalities and inspection of details are anchored and supported.

The burgeoning interest in both descriptive and prescriptive aspects of comprehension and production of charts, graphs, and diagrams has been addressed in an increasing number of interdisciplinary conferences. Papers from the first of these, along with other seminal papers, were collected in a volume edited by Glasgow, Narayanan and Chandrasekaran (1995) that called the field diagrammatic reasoning. Comics are now regarded as serious literature. They use a variety of pictoric and spatial devices, some readily interpretable, some conventional, to convey motion, emotion, and other ideas (McCloud, 1994). A recent novel, self-described as a "Novel of Business," found it useful to include graphics as part of its' narrative (Bing, 1998).

4.6 Some Functions of Graphic Displays

Despite their variability of form and content, a number of cognitive principles underlie graphic displays. These are evident in the many functions they serve as well as in the way information is conveyed in them. Some of their many overlapping functions are reviewed below. As with functions, goals, and constraints on other aspects of human behavior, so the functions, goals, and constraints of graphic displays sometimes work at odds with each other, and sometimes work in concert.

Attract Attention and Interest

One prevalent function of graphic displays is to attract attention and interest. A related function is aesthetic; graphics may be pleasing or shocking or repulsive or calming or funny.

Record Information

An ancient function of graphics is to provide records. For example, tallies developed to keep track of property, beginning with a simple one-mark one-piece of property relation, developing into numerals as tallies became cumbersome for large sums and calculations (e.g., Schmandt-Besserat, 1992). Various native American tribes kept track of their tribal numbers with icons for members and recorded their history year by year with depictions of a major event of the year (Mallery, 1972).

Memory

A related function of graphic displays is to facilitate memory. This surely was and is one of the functions of writing, whether pictographic or alphabetic. A modern example is the use of menus, especially icon menus, in computer user interfaces. Providing a menu turns what would otherwise be a recall task into a recognition task. Instead of having to call to mind all the possible commands in a program or files on a drive, a user has only to select the command or file that is needed from a list. There is yet another way that graphs promote memory. Menus and icons are typically displayed in standard places in an array. As anyone who has returned to a previous home after a long lapse of time knows, places are excellent cues to memory. Ancient lore, the Method of Loci, and modern research support the intuition that space is not only an excellent cue but also an excellent organizer of memory (e.g., Bower, 1970; Franklin, Tversky and Coon, 1992; Small, 1997; Taylor and Tversky, 1997; Yates, 1969).

Communication

In addition to facilitating memory, graphic displays also facilitate communication. As for memory, this has also been an important function of writing, to allow communication out of earshot (or eyeshot). Graphic displays allow private, mental conceptualizations to be made public, where they can be shared, examined, and revised.

Provide Models of Actual and Theoretical Worlds

Maps, architectural drawings, molecules, circuit diagrams, organizational charts, and flow diagrams are just some of the myriad examples of diagrams serving as models of worlds and the things in them. In general, these are models, and not simply shrunken or expanded worlds. Effective diagrams omit many features of the modeled world and distort others, and even add features that are not in the modeled world. Maps, for example, are not drawn strictly to scale. Roadmaps exaggerate the sizes of highways and streets so that they can be seen and used. Maps introduce symbolic elements, for railroads, ocean depth, towns, and more, that require a key and/or convention to interpret. The essence of creating an effective external representation is to abstract those features that are essential and to eliminate those that are not, that only serve as clutter. For dynamic systems, successful diagrams must illuminate the causal chain of events over and above the parts of the systems and their interconnections (e.g., Kieras, 1992; Kieras and Bovair, 1984; Mayer and Gallini, 1990). Of course, this is not as straightforward as it sounds, partly because it is difficult to anticipate all the uses an external representation will have, partly because successful communication rests on redundancy. Well-designed diagrams facilitate learning and operation of a system but poorly-designed diagrams do not (e.g., Glenberg and Langston, 1992; Kieras and Bovair, 1984; Mayer and Gallini, 1990; Scaife and Rogers, 1996). Current trends in computer graphics go against the maxim of abstracting the essentials. The aim of at least some areas of computer graphics seems to be creating as much detail and realism as possible. At the other extreme are designers (e.g., Tufte, 1983) advocating graphic design that is so minimal that it may not give sufficient clues to interpretation.

Convey Meaning, Facilitate Discovery and Inference

Effective graphics make it easy for users to extract information and draw inferences from them. Maps, for example, facilitate determining routes and estimating distances. A map of cholera cases in London during an epidemic made it easier to find the contaminated water pump (Wainer, 1992). Plotting change rather than absolute levels of a measure can lead to very different inferences (Cleveland, 1985). Indeed, the advice in *How to Lie with Statistics* (Huff, 1954) has been used for good or bad over and over. The format of physics diagrams (Narayanan, Suwa & Motoda, 1994), architectural sketches (Suwa & Tversky, 1996), and graphs (e.g., Gattis, this volume; Gattis and Holyoak, 1996; Shah and Carpenter, 1995) bias users towards some kinds of inferences more readily than others.

4.7   Basis for Metaphors and Cognitive Correspondences

A major purpose of graphic displays is to represent visually concepts and relations that are not inherently visual. Graphic displays use representations of elements and the spatial relations among them to do so. One type of element, common in early writing systems and recent computer interfaces, is an icon, which conveys meaning naturally through resemblance to something in the world or figures of depiction. Another type of element is a schematic pictorial device, such as brackets or frames or lines, which convey meaning naturally through resemblance to physical objects that contain or link. Spatial relations convey meaning naturally by using spatial distance to represent distance on some abstract relation. Ancient graphic creations as well as recent inventions by children and professionals often spontaneously adopt these metaphoric and analogic uses of space and the things in it. People have rich experience observing and interacting with the physical world, and consequently extensive knowledge about the appearance and behavior of things in it. It is natural for this concrete experience and knowledge to serve as a basis for pictorial, verbal, and gestural expression.

This review suggests a perhaps deceptively simple maxim: use spatial elements and relations naturally. Naturalness is found in natural correspondences, "figures of depiction," physical analogs, and spatial metaphors, derived from extensive human experience with the concrete world. It is revealed in language and in gesture as well as in a long history of graphic inventions.

Acknowledgments

The author is grateful to Merideth Gattis and five anonymous reviewers for helpful comments on an earlier draft, and to Rochel Gelman, Jeff Zacks, and Julie Bauer Morrison for discussions on the general ideas. Some of the research was supported by grants from Interval Research Corporation, by NSF-IST Grant 8403273 to Stanford University, and by grants from the Human Development Institute and the Cognitive Psychology Institute of the Hebrew University. Support from ONR grant N00014-00-0649 helped in preparation of the manuscript.

Part II

Spatial Schemas in Cultural Contexts

Chapter 5

Cultural Specificity of Spatial Schemas, as Manifested in Spontaneous Gestures

Sotaro Kita, Eve Danziger, and Christel Stolz

5.1   Introduction

This paper concerns the question of how the conceptual structuring of spatial information (i.e., spatial schemas) can vary across cultures, and how this variation leads to cultural specificity in the conceptualization of abstract thought. This question is investigated by comparing individuals from two different Mayan cultures: Yucatec in Mexico and Mopan in Belize. Spatial schemas are tapped into by observing gestures that spontaneously accompany speech that expresses spatial and abstract thoughts.

Cultural Specificity of Spatial Conceptualization

In the cognitive science literature, it has been widely assumed that conceptual structuring of space varies minimally across cultures because of the common biological endowment of all humans. For example, Langacker states, "It would appear . . . promising to regard the conception of space . . . as a basic field of representation grounded in genetically determined physical properties of the human organism and constituting an intrinsic part of our inborn cognitive apparatus" (1987, 148). The conceptual use of the division of space based on the planes defined by the human body—dividing 'front' from 'back' and 'left' from 'right'—is, for example, often presumed to be a biologically determined conceptual human universal (Clark, 1973; Lyons, 1977; Miller & Lohnson-Laird 1976). Consistent with this view, some theorists maintain that metaphorical thought based on space does not vary much cross-culturally because spatial conceptualization is universal (e.g., Alverson, 1994).

This paper concerns the presumption that all cultures divide space outside of the body into two distinct regions, left and right, for conceptual purposes. The universality of this division has been questioned in recent literature (e.g., Levinson & Brown, 1994; Levinson, 1997; Pederson et al., 1998). These reports describe cultures in which the absolute frame of reference (the frame of reference based on the surrounding geography) rather than the left-right division is used in linguistic and spatial memory tasks for categorizing lateral spatial arrays in front of the body.

In this paper, we will discuss Mopan, a Mayan community in Belize, in which neither the left-right division nor the absolute frame of reference is used to categorize lateral spatial arrays in linguistic and memory tasks. As we will discuss in more detail later, we believe that Mopan Mayans in fact do not conceptually divide the lateral axis of space in front of the body. This is in sharp contrast with Yucatec, another Mayan community in Mexico. We will argue that the use and non-use of right-left contrast on the lateral axis has consequences for the spatial 'shape' of abstract thought in Mopan and Yucatec.

Conceptual Use of the Projected Lateral Axis in the Two Mayan Cultures

The two Mayan cultures that are compared in this paper share many cultural features. The two languages are genetically closely related. The main livelihood of the two groups is slash-and burn subsistence farming. They both live in small communities and have similar material cultures.

Despite these similarities, there is a crucial difference between the two groups in the conceptual structuring of space. It concerns the projected lateral axis, that is, the axis of the space in front of the torso (thus, "projected"), that is parallel to the shoulder line. For Mopan Mayans, the projected lateral axis is not contrastive in the sense that to-the-right-of and to-the-left-of relations do not play a role in the conceptual handling of space. In contrast, the projected lateral axis is contrastive for Yucatec Mayans.

This difference has been demonstrated in results from a non-linguistic pattern-matching task (Danziger & Pederson, 1998; Danziger, 1999; Danziger et al., in preparation). In this task (first used by Levinson & Brown, 1994), a simple figure and a complex figure are presented to a consultant, and the consultant is asked whether the simple figure can be found within the complex figure. In some cases, the simple figure is in fact embedded in the complex figure ("genuine part question"), and in the other cases, only the lateral mirror image of the simple figure is embedded in the complex figure ("mirror-image part question") (see Figure 5.1).

Prior to the experimental trials, training trails are administered. In the training trials, the motivation for distinguishing a genuine part from a

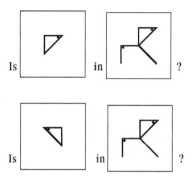

Figure 5.1
Pattern-matching task with lateral mirror-image parts. On top is a genuine part
question, and on bottom is a mirror-image part question.

mirror-image part is given by overlaying a transparent version of the
simple figure card on top of the complex figure card. All consultants are
instructed to give an affirmative answer to a genuine part question, but
not to a mirror-image part question. Only the consultants who can follow
the instruction proceed to the experimental trials.

It is found that Yucatec Mayans are likely to give an affirmative answer
to the genuine part questions, but not to the mirror-image part questions.
In other words, they consider lateral mirror image counterparts to be distinct. Thus, for Yucatec Mayans the projected lateral axis is contrastive
(i.e., when answering the questions in Figure 5.1, they use information
equivalent to saying that the slope of the longest side of the triangle runs
upward to right/left of the card). In contrast, many Mopan Mayans
give an affirmative answer to both the genuine part questions and to the
mirror-image part questions (control questions make sure that Mopan
Mayans are not giving an affirmative answer to any questions). In this
task, they do not treat lateral mirror images as distinct. This suggests that
for Mopan Mayans, different points on the projected lateral axis are not
contrastive.

Note that the difference between Mopan and Yucatec is not at the level
of visual perception, but at the level of habitual conceptualization. In the
training session, Mopan and Yucatec consultants could all "see" the difference between a genuine part and a mirror-image part, and they gave
different answers to the two types of questions. However, in the experimental trials, many Mopan consultants quickly reverted to a different way
of thinking, and started to give affirmative answers for both types of questions. In summary, there is evidence that different points on the projected

lateral axis are not contrastive in habitual Mopan conceptualization, whereas they are contrastive in habitual Yucatec conceptualization.

Cultural Specificity of Spatial Conceptualization and Metaphorical Use of Space

The cultural specificity of spatial conceptualization might have profound consequences on abstract thought by Yucatec and Mopan Mayans. This is because space is a very productive "source domain" for metaphorical projections to non-spatial "target domains." Spatial conceptualization becomes the vehicle for representing non-spatial abstract thought (Jackendoff, 1983; Johnson, 1987; Lakoff, 1987). In this view, metaphor assists abstract thought, in that the non-concrete entities of the target domain can be cognitively manipulated according to rules which apply to the more tangible components of the concrete source domain. That is, in metaphorical thought, the abstract domain is constructed to possess specific properties directly analogous to those of the source domain. If the source domain is structured differently across cultures, then it is expected that metaphorical thought in target domains would vary accordingly. This paper aims to demonstrate cultural variation of metaphorical thought due to the cultural variation in spatial conceptualization between Mopan and Yucatec already discussed.

Spatial Conceptualization as Revealed in Spontaneous Gestures

One of the ways in which we can observe how space is conceptualized is to analyze the expression of ideas in gestures that spontaneously accompany speech. Here, we are referring to spontaneous co-speech gestures with "iconic" and "deictic" (McNeill, 1992) components, whose form is determined in coordination with the speech content. Unlike "emblems" (e.g., the OK sign with a ring created by the thumb and the index finger) and sign language (cf. Emmorey, this volume), the form-function relationship of spontaneous co-speech gesture is not fully determined by convention, and thus some degree of semiotic freedom is left for idiosyncratic expression. Consequently, spontaneous co-speech gestures (henceforth simply "gesture") can reveal important aspects of the speaker's spatial thinking at the moment of speaking (McNeill, 1985, 1992; Church & Goldin-Meadow, 1986; Kita 2000).

What is revealed by gesture is not merely the speaker's strategic thinking about how to visually convey information to conversational partner via gesture. Gesture reflects a mental representation that serves not only communicative but also speaker-internal purposes (Rimé et al., 1984;

Krauss et al., 1996; de Ruiter,1998; Kita, 2000). The support for this view comes from, for example, experimental studies that indicate that people gesture without visual contact with the interlocutor (e.g., Rimé, 1983).

Speakers use the space around the body gesturally for both iconic and metaphoric signification (McNeill, 1992). They can depict spatial concepts. For example, sweeping a hand from left to right can represent a moving object. Like sign language (Emmorey, this volume), gestures can also depict the spatialization of abstract concepts. For example, sweeping a hand from left to right can represent flow of time (Calbris, 1990). Thus, using gestures as a window into the speaker's mind allows observation of both concrete and abstract use of space.

Goals of This Paper

The question arises as to whether the difference in the habitual conceptual structuring of space between Yucatec and Mopan leads to different spatialization of abstract concepts. This question is investigated through the observation of gestures.

The goal of this paper is two-fold. First, we demonstrate that the difference between Yucatec Mayans and Mopan Mayans, which is revealed by the aforementioned pattern-matching task, is replicated in gestural representation. Namely, to-the-right-of and to-the-left-of relations are relevant in the gestural representation of spatial concepts in Yucatec, but not in Mopan. Second, we show that this difference extends to the spatialization of abstract concepts, as manifested in gestures. The abstract concepts to be discussed are time flow, plot development of the story, and opposition between two similar non-spatial entities. We will conclude that a culture-specific spatial schema leads to culture-specific conceptualization of abstract thought in terms of space.

5.2   Gestures in Mopan and Yucatec Traditional Mythical Stories

In order to elicit gestures, three Yucatec Mayans and three Mopan Mayans were asked to tell a traditional mythical story of their choice (different stories were told by each speaker). All consultants are a member of a small-scale Yucatec and Mopan farming community. The stories are mythical in that they do not involve known real world locations and entities (the stories are, however, believed by the tellers to have actually occurred in some location). The consultants told their stories while seated in a familiar environment such as in their own house, with one of the investigators as well as other people in the community as audience. The story telling was video-taped with a Hi-8 camcorder. A segment from each story, roughly 10 minutes long, was selected for narrative coherence and for topical match between Yucatec and Mopan. We selected a pair of episodes from one Yucatec and one Mopan story that dealt with various events taking place in the course of a hunting-trip, another pair of episodes that had a trickster theme, and a third pair of episodes that told a get-rich-quick story.

Since the stories are mythical, the gestures are not a response to any externally given spatial array. Rather, they create a virtual space in front of the speaker. For example, the pointing gestures in the stories do not point to any real location or direction. They establish a location or a direction in the gesturally created story-space (they are gestures of what has been called "abstract deixis" in McNeill, Cassell & Levy (1993) and McNeill (to appear)). The structure of this virtual space reveals how space is spontaneously used for representation, given a "blank slate."

Gestures about Spatial Concepts

Quantitative analysis of directionality of gestures   The goal of this section is to demonstrate the difference between Yucatec and Mopan with regard to the treatment of to-the-right-of and to-the-left-of relations in their gestural representation of spatial concepts. Among spatial concepts, we focused on motion and location in the story world. A motion in the story world can be gesturally represented by a sweep of a hand, and a location in the story world can be represented by indexing a seemingly empty space near the speaker. "Indexing" refers to a broad range of body movements, in which a location near the speaker's body is singled out. Pointing with an extended index finger or an open hand is one way, and the movement of a hand as if it places an object is another way.

If to-the-right-of and to-the-left-of relations are distinct in the conceptual handling of space, then the two points along the projected lateral axis can represent two different conceptual entities. For example, a particular instance of motion, which involves a source and a goal, can be gesturally represented along the projected lateral axis. Similarly, if the projected lateral axis is representationally distinctive, then gestures representing location can be performed with a predominantly lateral orientation, and the location indicated can be in contrast with another location (which is indicated by another gesture) along the projected lateral axis. The same holds for a particular narrative instance of caused motion (e.g., a story character puts something somewhere). If the projected lateral axis is distinctive, the gestural representation of caused motion can have a predominantly lateral component, for example, with one point representing the source and the other the goal of the caused motion.

Thus, we expect that compared to Mopan gestures, Yucatec gestures representing motion, location, and caused motion are more likely to be performed with a predominantly lateral orientation.

In order to maximize the match in the representational content of the gestures from the two cultures, a subset of gestures in the recordings were selected, in the following manner. Pairs of cognate lexemes (i.e., historically related lexemes) in Yucatec and in Mopan denoting location, motion, and caused motion that were used in at least one story in each language were listed (only cognate pairs that still retain substantial meaning overlap between the two languages are included in the list). Note that the two languages are genetically closely related, and thus it is relatively straight forward to identify cognate lexemes. The list of selected lexemes is in Table 5.1.

Since co-expressive gesture and speech typically overlap in time (McNeill, 1992), gestures that are synchronized with these lexemes are likely to represent location, motion, and caused motion. We analyzed only those gestures that temporally overlap with the breath group that contained one of the lexemes in Table 5.1 (a breath group was delineated by a pause, or a break in pitch contour, or an abrupt shift in speech rate).

The spatial form of this subset of gestures was coded for either "lateral" or "non-lateral" vector. If a gesture was performed with one hand, and the gestural movement has a predominantly lateral component (as opposed to vertical or sagittal (i.e. front-back) directions), then it was coded as a lateral gesture. If a one-handed gesture had a predominantly vertical or sagittal component, the gesture was coded as non-lateral. If the gesture was performed with two hands and the movement of the two hands was laterally symmetrical (e.g., one hand went to the right and the other went to the left), then it was coded as a non-lateral gesture (because such a gesture used the lateral axis symmetrically). If a two-handed gesture was not laterally symmetrical, but the main movement component was vertical or sagittal (e.g., one arm goes up, and the other arm goes

Table 5.1
The list of cognate location/motion lexemes that appear in at least one Yucatec story and one Mopan story

Cognate label*	Form class	Gloss
Location		
ALAN	preposition	"under"
ICHI	preposition	"in"
YOK	preposition	"over/on top of"
NAACH	stative predicate	"far"
KUCH	nominal	"place/niche"
TU	pronoun	"where" (a relative and a question pronoun)
Motion		
BIN	unaccusative verb	"go"
HOK	unaccusative verb	"exit"
KOCH	unaccusative verb	"arrive not-here"
MAAN	unaccusative verb	"travel/pass by"
NAK	unaccusative verb	"ascend"
OK	unaccusative verb	"enter"
TAAL	unaccusative verb	"come"
Caused motion		
CHA	transitive verb	"take"
CHIN	transitive verb	"throw stones at"
MACH	transitive verb	"grab/grasp"
PUL	transitive verb	"throw away"
TSA	transitive verb	"give/put"

* These labels are given in as notational shorthand, which conflates phonological elements of both Yucatec and Mopan.

down), then the gesture was again coded as non-lateral. If a two-handed gesture was not laterally symmetrical and the main movement component was lateral (e.g., two arms stretched together to the right), then the gesture was coded as lateral.

The proportions of lateral gestures (among the gestures that temporally overlap a breath group containing a spatial lexeme listed in Table 5.1) are shown in Table 5.2. Yucatec gestures are more likely to be lateral than Mopan gestures (one-tailed T-test, df $= 2$, T $= 11.1$, $p = .01$).

Table 5.2
The proportion of lateral gestures that are synchronized with a breath group containing one of the spatial lexemes listed in Table 5.1

	n	Proportion of lateral gestures
Yucatec		
Story 1	96	.40
Story 2	44	.43
Story 3	46	.39
Mean		.41
Mopan		
Story 1	90	.14
Story 2	20	.10
Story 3	80	.18
Mean		.14

Yucatec and Mopan gestures that express spatial content have different form characteristics. Yucatec gestures tend to be lateral, while Mopan gestures tend not to be. This is consistent with the idea that to-the-right-of and to-the-left-of relations play a role in the conceptual handling of space for Yucatec Mayans, but not for Mopan Mayans. In other words, the two points along the projected lateral axis can represent two distinct conceptual entities, for Yucatec Mayans, but not for Mopan Mayans.

Lateral deployment of non-lateral gestures   The above result on the laterality of gestures in fact underestimates the difference between the two cultures. This is because a gesture, which itself may not be lateral, can still be part of a sequential lateral deployment of multiple gestures. That is, a sequence of gestures can discursively establish multiple points with distinct interpretations along the projected lateral axis. Yucatec gesture sequences are often of this type, while Mopan sequences are not.

The following excerpt from a Yucatec story exemplifies the sequential deployment of multiple gestures. In this story, a lazy boy becomes wealthy by the information that he accidentally gets. Because of the laziness of the boy, his father has refused to serve food to him. When his hunger and desperation are at their peak, he happens to see a merchant hide a treasure-trove. (See the Appendix for the speech and gesture transcripts.)

Frontal View   Estimated Top View

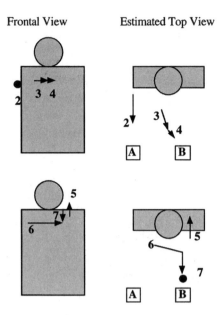

Figure 5.2
Spatial arrangement of gestures in Example 1.

Example 1: Yucatec Motion Scene (Lazy Boy Story)
"Where the boy sleeps," (Gesture 1, 2)
"not far from there," (Gesture 3)
"there he (the merchant) went to hide his money." (Gesture 4)
"So the man (the merchant) had left then," (Gesture 5)
"and so the boy went in order to see" (Gesture 6)
"what was dug in at the trunk of the tree." (Gesture 7)

The description of these events is accompanied by a sequence of gestures that establish two important story locations along the projected lateral axis. Gesture 1 seems to iconically represent a boy who is lying. Gesture 2 points to a location in front of the right edge of the speaker's torso, which represents the location where the boy sleeps. Gestures 3 and 4 point to a location on the speakers left side, which represents the location where the money is hidden (see Figures 5.2 and 5.3). These two locations are connected by Gesture 6, which points to the location A (Figure 5.2) at the beginning, and then traces a path to the location B. This gesture is synchronized with the speech expressing the boy's motion

Gesture 2
stroke offset

Gesture 4
stroke offset

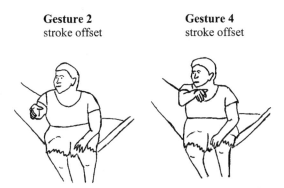

Figure 5.3
Yucatec motion scene: Gesture 2 and 4 in Example 1.

from where he sleeps to where the money is. Gesture 7 taps on the location B with the pointing hand shape. Note that in Gestures 2, 3, 4, and 7, the hand movement is predominantly non-lateral (i.e., forward). Nevertheless they, together with Gesture 6, make up a sequence in which spatial locations are contrastively indicated along the projected lateral axis. This structuring of the gestural representation is consistent with the quantitative analysis of the laterality of single gestures and the pattern-matching task, involving lateral mirror images. Namely, for Yucatec Mayans, to-the-right-of and to-the-let-of relations are conceptually distinct.

In the Yucatec stories, there is an abundance of cases like the above example, in which a sequence of gestures establish multiple story locations along the projected lateral axis. However, there were very few equivalent Mopan cases. The following Mopan example, which involves multiple landmarks, is the most complex motion scene in the three Mopan stories. This kind of case, involving multiple locations, has the best chance for the use of the projected lateral axis through a sequence of gestures. Yet, the gestures in the description of this scene have a non-lateral form, and even when taken as a sequence they do not set up any laterally distinctive locations.

In this Mopan story, a man marries a woman, with whom he has met during his hunting trip. This woman is from a community of "wild people." And, the woman's parents make an elaborate plan to cook and eat the couple. The woman realizes this plan. She outsmarts her parents, and escapes the plot. In the following excerpt, having escaped the plot, the couple is running away from the woman's parents.

Example 2: Mopan Complex Motion Scene (Wild Woman Story)
"They went again." (Gesture 1)
"You see, there were twelve mountains" (Gesture 2)
"that they passed through inside the core." (Gesture 3)
"There were twelve." (Gesture 4)
"And as for the water, it was the same way. There were twelve lakes."
(Gesture 5)
"They traveled inside the water." (Gesture 6, 7)
"So they went there." (Gesture 8)
"They went to come out at a village." (Gesture 9)

Gestures 1, 3, 5, 6, and 7 (Figures 5.4 and 5.5) represent the motion of the
couple (Gestures 2 and 4 represent the number 12). When the gestures
represent motion, the finger orientation and often the movement of the
hand indicate a direction straight away from the body. The mountains,
the lakes, and the village are gesturally localized roughly straight away
from the body. More importantly, these locations are not put into a lateral relationship with each other. This type of gestural representation
of motion and location are typical for all of the Mopan stories. This is
again consistent with the results of the pattern-matching task, and of the
quantitative analysis of the directionality of single gestures. For Mopan
Mayans, to-the-right-of and to-the-left of relations are not conceptual
distinct.

To summarize, Yucatec and Mopan gestural representations of spatial
concepts such as location and (caused or spontaneous) motion differ in
the use of the projected lateral axis. The gestural difference between the
two cultures is parallel to the differences in the pattern-matching task
involving lateral mirror images. Mopan Mayans do not use functional
equivalents of the to-the-right-of and to-the-left-of contrast in their spatial
conceptualization, whereas Yucatec Mayans do. In the next section, we
will show that the same difference holds between Yucatec and Mopan
Mayans in their gestural spatialization of non-spatial concepts.

Gestural Spatialization of Non-spatial Concepts

The six stories analyzed above are reviewed for cases of gestural spatialization of abstract concepts. We find two domains of non-spatial concepts
that are spatialized in both Yucatec and Mopan gestures: flow of time and
plot development, and paradigmatic contrast.

Frontal View   Estimated Top View

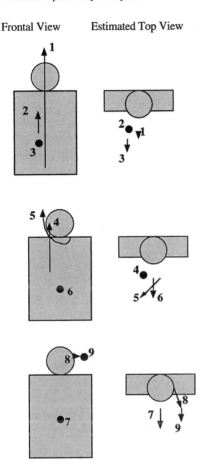

Figure 5.4
Spatial arrangement of gestures in Example 2.

Flow of time and plot development   In Yucatec gestures, flow of time and plot development can be represented along the projected lateral axis. In five cases out of a total of six cases from two Yucatec stories, the time flow or plot development is represented by a lateral movement from the speaker's right to left (the last case involves a vertical gesture). It is worth noting that in American Sign Language the time-flow is represented in the opposite direction along the projected lateral axis (Emmorey, this volume). Note also that it has been found that when people are asked to spatially depict temporal increase, the direction of writing determines the

Gesture 3   **Gesture 9**
stroke onset   stroke onset

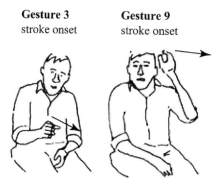

Figure 5.5
Mopan motion scene: Gesture 3 and 9 in Example 2.

direction of increase (Tversky, this volume). The Yucatec consultants
have limited literacy in Spanish.

The following excerpt is from a Yucatec story that involves two
brothers: an honest hunter, and an evil intellectual. The hunter is puzzled
by the fact that he finds a couple of gold coins under the hammock of
his children every morning. He visits the intellectual to ask about this
mysterious phenomenon. The intellectual suspects that the children have
stolen the gizzard of a magical bird, which he has intended to eat. Without giving any answer, he sends the hunter back home. The intellectual
interrogates his wife, who has cooked the magical bird, and she admits
that the gizzard has been stolen. Immediately after this interrogation
scene, the next excerpt follows. The following morning, the hunter goes to
the intellectual to get an answer about the mysterious gold coins.

Example 3: Yucatec Time-flow and Plot Development (Golden Bird Story)

"And it dawned again the following day" (Gesture 1)
"and the man went. He says . . ." (Gesture 2)

In Gesture 1 (Figures 5.6 and 5.7) the hand sweeps from the speaker's
right to left, and this movement along the projected lateral axis represents
time-flow. The relative location of Gestures 1 and 2 also laterally represents the plot development and the passage of time from the breaking of
the dawn to the departure of the man. Note that the left hand starts to
perform Gesture 2 from the point where the right hand finishes its gesture

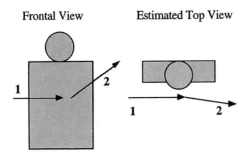

Figure 5.6
Spatial arrangement of Gestures 1 and 2 in Example 3.

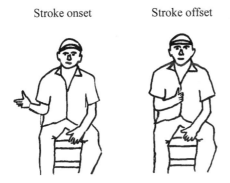

Figure 5.7
Yucatec time-flow and plot development: Gesture 1 in Example 3.

stroke. This suggests that the relative location of the two gestures may be meaningful.

In contrast, in the single example from a Mopan story, time flow and plot development are represented along the sagittal (i.e. front-back) axis. There is no Mopan example in which the projected lateral axis is used to represent time-flow or plot development.

The following example comes from a story, in which a poor man becomes rich by eavesdropping. The poor man has overheard that a certain bush has a special medical potency. In the following excerpt, the pivotal event in the story is described. The poor man, who is unemployed, is staying at an old woman's house. He learns that the king is in a critical condition. The poor man will eventually cure the king with the leaves from the magical bush, which makes him rich.

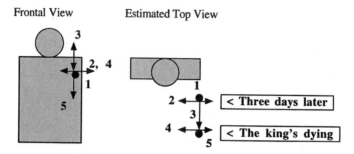

Figure 5.8
Spatial arrangement of Gestures 1–5 in Example 4.

Example 4: Mopan Time-flow and Plot Development (Poor Man Story)
"He rested."
"But when three days had gone by" (Gesture 1)
"There was (still) no work for him." (Gesture 2)
"But what the old woman heard was," (Gesture 3)
"that there was something that—" (Gesture 4)
"that was happening to the king." (Gesture 5)
"The king was dying."

In Gesture 1 (Figure 5.8) the open hand with the fingers upward faces straight away from the body. This may represent the passage of time as a direction away from the body. Gesture 2 is a conventionalized gesture for "nothing." Gestures 1 and 2 represent the state of the affairs before the king's death was mentioned. Gesture 3 (Figure 5.9) connects these gestures with Gestures 4 and 5, which represent an event concerning the king, namely his dying. This is the pivotal complication in this story. Thus, Gesture 3 with the sagittal movement can be interpreted as spatialization of the plot development.

Yucatec and Mopan gestural representations of time-flow and plot development differ in ways that are parallel to their gestural representation of motion and location. For Yucatec Mayans the projected lateral axis is contrastive, thus they can represent time-flow and plot development along the projected lateral axis. In contrast, for Mopan Mayans the projected lateral axis is not contrastive, and thus it cannot be used for representing time-flow and plot development. Instead, the sagittal axis is used for this purpose in the Mopan story. That is to say, the metaphorical spatialization of abstract concepts by gesture follows culture-specific patterns of conceptual structuring of concrete space, as revealed by the

Gesture 3

stroke onset   stroke offset

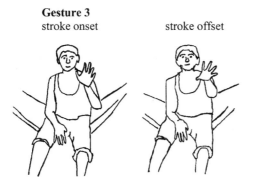

Figure 5.9
Mopan time-flow and plot development: Gesture 3 in Example 4.

gestural representation of spatial concepts and by the pattern-matching task.

Paradigmatic contrast   Also spatialized in both Yucatec and Mopan gesture arc cases of paradigmatic contrast, in which two things that are the same in some respects but are different in other respects are contrasted. Yucatec Mayans use the projected lateral axis to represent this contrast.

A Yucatec example comes from the story involving a hunting trip. In this story, an intellectual is asked to examine an unusual bird, which his hunter brother has shot. The intellectual finds out that it is a magical bird. If one eats its gizzard, one will get a golden coin under the hammock every morning. In this excerpt, the intellectual is wondering about the possibility of stealing the bird from his brother. The narrator introduces (Line 1) a monologue of the intellectual (Line 2–6) as a direct quote.

Example 5: Yucatec Paradigmatic Contrast (Golden Bird Story)
"And he (the intellectual) said like this:" (Gesture 1)
"I (the intellectual) must take it from my relative (the hunter)." (Gesture 2)
"If not," (Gesture 3)
"this man will become rich." (Gesture 4)
"Because if I get it from him," (Gesture 5)
"it is me who will eat it," (Gesture 6)
"it is me who will get the money." (Gesture 7)

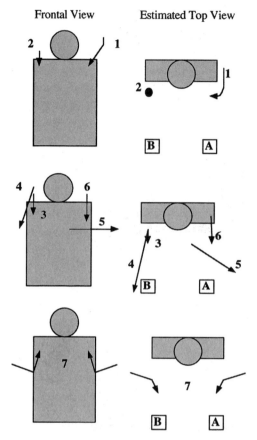

Figure 5.10
Spatial arrangement of gestures in Example 5.

Gestures 1, 2, 3 (Figure 5.10) are all pointing gestures, which indicate a location. Gesture 1, which points to the speaker's left, is synchronized with the utterance that frames the intellectual's monologue. Gesture 2, which points to the speaker's right, is in fact synchronized with the word "my relative" (see Appendix). Gesture 3 (Figure 5.11) is synchronized with the utterance "if not," which sets up a scenario of the hunter eating the bird. That is, these gestures localize the two protagonists and the two possible scenarios on the right and on the left. The speaker's right side represents the hunter and the possible scenario where the hunter eats the bird (the location B in Figure 5.10). The speaker's left side represents the

Gesture 3
stroke offset

Gesture 4
stroke offset

Gesture 5
stroke offset

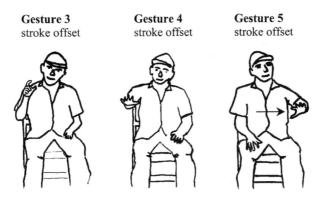

Figure 5.11
Yucatec paradigmatic contrast: Gestures 3, 4, and 5 in Example 5.

Gesture 7
stroke onset
                                                                stroke offset

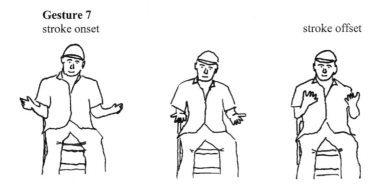

Figure 5.12
Yucatec paradigmatic contrast: Gesture 7 in Example 5.

intellectual and the possible scenario where the intellectual eats the bird (the location A in Figure 5.10). The two possible scenarios are similar, but different in one crucial respect, namely who eats the magical bird. Gesture 5 (Figure 5.11) seems to represent an action of pushing an object, presumably the magical bird, from the location B to the location A. This gesture is synchronized with the utterance, which sets up the second scenario. Gesture 7 (Figure 5.12) brings two hands together: one from the location A and the other from the location B. This may represent the resolution of the two possible scenarios as the intellectual sees it. This example shows that in Yucatec gestural spatialization of paradigmatic contrast, to-the-right-of and to-the-left-of relations play a crucial role, just like the cases above have shown. (We could not find any example of Yucatec gestures making paradigmatic contrast along the projected sagittal axis. However, because the projected sagittal axis is frequently used for the representation of concrete spatial concepts, we predict that Yucatec Mayans should also in principle be able to use both projected lateral and sagittal axes contrastively.)

In Mopan, paradigmatic contrast is made along the projected sagittal (front-back) axis as will be shown in Example 6. In the hunting trip story, the couple is trying to escape from the wife's parents who plan to eat them. The parents send the husband to cut wood, and the wife to get water. The parents plan to make fire and cook the couple with the wood and water that the couple brings back. The wife is telling the husband her idea to use a woodpecker as a substitute noise maker. Her plan is to run away from her parents while the woodpecker is making the noise of cutting wood. The narrator quotes the words of the wife.

Example 6: Mopan Paradigmatic Contrast (Wild Woman Story)
"You should make use of this bird, the woodpecker." (Gesture 1, 2, 3)
"That's what you will use." (Gesture 4, 5)
"That's your substitute." (Gesture 6)

Gestures 1–5 (Figure 5.13) are pointing gestures, which indicate the direction straight away from the speaker. They locate the woodpecker at the location A in Figure 5.13. Gesture 6 (Figure 5.14) makes an arc back toward the speaker's body to index two locations along the projected sagittal axis. This gesture connects the location A, which has been established as the location of the woodpecker in the preceding gestures, and a newly established location B, closer to the speaker's body, to represent the husband, for whom the woodpecker is a substitute. That is, the gesture spatializes paradigmatic contrast between the husband and the woodpecker, who are similar in one single respect critical to the story: the noise of the woodpecker sounds like a man chopping wood.

For gestural spatialization of paradigmatic contrast, we see again the same kind of difference between Yucatec and Mopan. We could not find any example of Mopan gestures depicting paradigmatic contrast along the projected lateral axis. This is consistent with the claim that the culture specific structuring of concrete space shapes the way in which abstract concepts are construed spatially.

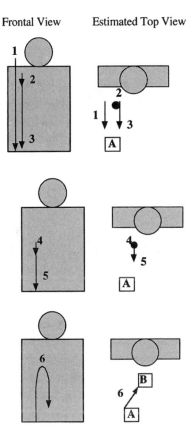

Figure 5.13
Spatial arrangement of gestures in Example 6.

5.3   Discussion

For Mopan Mayans, the projected lateral axis is not contrastive in the gestural representation of motion and location, whereas for Yucatec it is contrastive. When two distinct conceptual entities are to be represented gesturally (e.g., the source and the goal of motion, paradigmatic contrast), Yucatec Mayans, but not Mopan Mayans, use the projected lateral axis to lay out two entities. Mopan Mayans instead use the projected sagittal axis to do so. Note that this difference cannot be reduced to different motoric habits in the two cultures. That is, it is not the case that Mopan Mayans' body movement is restricted in general, nor is it the case

Gesture 6

stroke onset   highest point   stroke offset

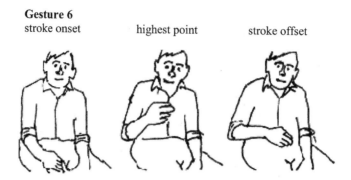

Figure 5.14
Mopan paradigmatic contrast: Gesture 6 in Example 6.

that they prefer to move their arms non-laterally regardless of the purpose of the body movement. Mopan Mayans freely move their arms laterally, like Yucatec Mayans, when the direction of their gesture is anchored to real-world locations (Danziger et al., in preparation). Another argument against motoric habit explanation is that in the Yucatec stories, a sequence of non-lateral gestures often represents laterally distinct points, whereas there are only very few cases of this in the Mopan stories. These facts support our interpretation that the cross-cultural gestural difference reflects a cross-cultural difference in how space is conceptually structured.

Since the stories analyzed in this paper do not involve any real-world locations, there is no extrinsic constraint on the directional characteristics of gestures that create virtual story space and that spatialize abstract concepts. Thus, these gestures provide a window into the 'default' conceptual structuring of space in the two cultures. For Mopan Mayans, the to-the-right-of and to-the-left-of relations are not distinctive in their habitual conceptualization pattern. For Yucatec Mayans, they are. The default status of these structures is also indicated by the reaction of Mopan Mayans and Yucatec Mayans to the pattern-matching task involving lateral mirror images. After the training session, where mirror-image counterparts are distinguished, Mopan Mayans in the experimental trials quickly adapt a different, presumably default, pattern of spatial conceptualization. They treat mirror-image counterparts as equivalent to one another. In contrast, Yucatec Mayans distinguish mirror-image counterparts also in the experimental trials. The converging evidence from the two different sets of observation substantiates the robustness of the finding of cultural specificity in the conceptual structuring of concrete space.

See also Danziger (1999), Danziger (to appear), Danziger et al. (in preparation) for other tasks in which Mopan Mayans behave consistently with these results.

Habitual patterns of spatial conceptualization manifested themselves in two very different behaviors: the pattern-matching task and the gestural representation of spatial concepts. The pattern-matching task involves the analysis of externally given stimuli in terms of what count as the same. In other words, the task involves the categorical analysis of the outside world. The gestural representation of spatial concepts involves building a virtual space in front of the speaker's body. Like the signing space for sign language (Emmorey, this volume), the space for gesture is not monolithic. There are constraints on how the gesture space is used to represent spatial concepts. The categorical structures used in the analysis of the outside world reappear as constraints on representational use of the gesture space. In other words, this structuring of concrete space (i.e., spatial schemas) is not confined to an input or output "module" (Fodor, 1983). The culture-specific spatial schemas are deeply rooted in the mind of Yucatec Mayans and Mopan Mayans.

This depth makes these spatial schemas good candidates to be employed in the metaphorical bridging between concrete space and abstract thought. We, indeed, observed that these culture-specific spatial schemas are used in the spatialization of abstract concepts such as time-flow, plot development, and paradigmatic contrast. For Yucatec Mayans, but not for Mopan Mayans, conceptually distinct entities can be located at different points along the projected lateral axis. Consequently, the "shape" of abstract thought is different in the two cultures: time flows and a plot develops along different axes, and contrasted entities are localized differently. To sum up, spatial schemas are culture-specific in very fundamental ways, and this leads to a concomitant cultural-specificity in the way abstract concepts are construed in terms of space.

Appendix: Speech and Gesture Transcripts

Speech-gesture synchronization is indicated in the following way. Square brackets indicate a single gestural excursion of hands ("Gesture Unit" in Kendon, 1980, "Movement Unit" in Kita et. al., 1998). An excursion can comprise more than one gesture, and gesture boundaries within an excursion are indicated by "|". The number beside "[" or "|" corresponds to the number in the gesture transcript and the diagram of gestural hand

Table 5.3
Abbreviations used in the examples

Abbr.	Term	Abbr.	Term
1	first person	MAN	manner
2	second person	MASC	masculine
3	third person	MD	medial deixis
CL	numeral classifier	NG	negation
CON	connective	OBL	obligation
CONJ	conjunction (clause subordinator)	PD	proximal deixis
D	deixis	PF	perfective aspect
DET	determiner	PL	plural
DUR	durative	PRC	processual
EMP	emphatic pronoun	PREP	preposition
EV	evidential	REL	relativizer
EU	euphonic glide	RES	resultative
EX	existential verb	SG	singular
FUT	future	SUB	subordinator
I	invisible or text/deixis	SBJ	subjunctive
IA	inanimate	TD	text deixis
IPF	imperfective aspect	TERM	terminative
LOC	locative	TRR	transitivizer

movements. The bold-faced portion of the speech is synchronized with the stroke phase of a gesture (the phase that is most forcefully performed), and the italicized portion of the speech is synchronized with a hold phase (the phase in which the limb is held in the air). A stroke and a hold are the phases that bear meaning. (See Kita et al. (1998) for more detailed definition of gesture phases). Abbreviations used in the examples are explained in Table 5.3.

Example 1: Yucatec Motion Scene (Lazy Boy Story)
X: story teller, Y: interlocutor

X: [₁ **Tu'x   k-u   wèen-el** |₂ **le   chan xib-e',**
       where IPF-3 sleep-IPF   DEF little male-CON
       "Where the boy sleeps,"

Gesture 1   Both hands sweep inwards and outwards in front of the chest. The palms are oriented downward and also facing each other, and the index fingers point away from the body.

Gloss (Possibly) a long horizontal object, namely, the boy lying on the ground.

Gesture 2 Right hand points straight away from the body. (See Figure 5.3).

Gloss The gesture indicates the location where the boy sleeps, located at A in Figure 5.2.

Y: *uh huuuh*

X: |₃ **ma' náach-il-e',**
     NG   far-REL-CON
     "not far from there"

te'l |₄ h **bin-∅** **u t***a'k u tàa*k'in-i'.]
there   PF go-3.PF 3 hide 3 money-TD
"there he (the merchant) went to hide his money."

Gesture 3 Right hand points forward and towards the midline of the torso.

Gloss The gesture indicates the location where the money is hidden (B in Figure 5.2).

Gesture 4 Right hand points further away, extending the vector defined by the previous gesture. (See Figure 5.3).

Gloss The gesture indicates the location where the money is hidden.

[₅ Ts'o'k u **lúuk'-ul** **túun le** **máak** *túun-o',*]
   TERM   3 leave-IPF then DEF person CON-MD
   "So the man (the merchant) had left then,"

Gesture 5 Left hand moves from the left side of the chest and points backward over the left shoulder.

Gloss The merchant leaves.

[₆ káa   túun h bin-∅   le   chan **xib-o',** *u-u y-il*
   and.then then PF go-3.SG.PF DET little male-MD 3-3 EU-see
   "and so the boy went in order to see"

Gesture 6 Left hand, with the index finger pointing away from the body, moves in front of the chest from right to left, and then straight away from the body.

Gloss The boy goes to where the money is hidden (B in Figure 5.2).

ba'x |₇ **túun** *muk-a'n-∅* t-u   *chùun le*   *che'-o'.*]
what   then dig.in-RES-3 PREP-3 start DET tree-MD
"what was dug in at the trunk of the tree."

Gesture 7   Left hand, with the index finger pointing away from the body, taps with a wrist movement.

Gloss   The boy investigates the location where the money is hidden (the location B in Figure 5.2).

Example 2: Mopan Complex Motion Scene (Wild Woman Story)

[₁ **Ka'   b'in-oo'** tukaye.]
    again go-3.PL again
    "They went again."

Gesture 1   Right hand moves up. The large vertical component may indicate great distance. The hand is in a loose open hand, with the palm oriented downward and the finger vector (i.e., wrist-to-knuckle vector) oriented forward.

Gloss   They go very far.

A-weel a   la   dose-kuul-∅   a   [₂ wit**z'**]
2-know DET D.1 twelve-round.thing-3 DET mountain
"You see, there were twelve mountains."

Gesture 2   Right hand moves up slightly. The hand is in the edge-wise orientation with the index and middle fingers pointing forward and slightly leftward.

Gloss   (Possibly) twelve.

[₃ a   man-oo'   **ich-il**   a   tz'u'.]
    DET travel-3.PL In-REL DET marrow
    "that they passed through inside the core."

Gesture 3   Right hand moves forward. The hand is in an edge-wise open hand and the fingers pointing forward (see Figure 5.5).

Gloss   They travel straight through the mountains.

[₄ **Dose-∅.**]
    twelve-3
    "There were twelve."

Gesture 4   Right hand moves up. The hand is in an edge-wise open hand with the index and middle fingers extended and oriented upward.

Gloss   Twelve.

Uxtun a   ja'-a,   [₅ *b'oob'e lik.*
as.for DET water-TOPIC,   D.MAN.I same
"And as for the water, it was the same way."

Dose-p'eel-∅ |₆ a   laguna
twelve-CL-3   DET lake
"There were twelve lakes."

Gesture 5   Right hand, with the index and middle fingers extended, makes an arc to the right and upward. At the beginning, the fingers point to the left. During the sweep, the fingers point forward and leftward most of the time, and at the end they point upward. (The opposite laterality of the hand movement and the finger direction neutralize each other to some extent, and the over all effect is that the direction roughly straight away from the body is indexed.)
Gloss   Twelve lakes ahead.
Gesture 6   Right hand moves straight forward through the C-shape formed by left hand's thumb and four other fingers (the palm upward). The right hand is in the edge-wise open hand with the fingers pointing forward.
Gloss   They travel inside the water.

Man-oo' |₇ **ich-il**   a   ja'.]
travel-3.PL   In-REL DET water
"They traveled inside the water."

Gesture 7   Right hand makes the same movement as 6 without the left hand. The hand is in the edge-wise orientation with the index and middle finger pointing forward.
Gloss   They travel inside the water.

[₈ Pues te'i   b'**in-oo'**,]
   SO   D.LOC.I   go-3.PL
   "So they went there."

Gesture 8   Left hand moves forward and slightly rightward. The height of the gesture may indicate the distance from the evil chasers. The hand is open hand with fingers pointing upward, and the palm faces right and slightly forward.
Gloss   They go to a village (which is very far).

[₉ (**gesture**) B'in-oo' ti   jok'-ol ich-il jun-p'eet   a   kaj]
          go-3.PL   PREP exit-IPF in-REL one-spread.out DET village
   "They went to come out at a village."
   N.B.: the gesture stroke was performed during silence.

Gesture 9   Left hand (the hand configuration the same as Gesture 9) moves forward (see Figure 5.5).
Gloss   They go to a village (which is very far).

Example 3: Yucatec Time-flow and Plot Development (Golden Bird Story)

[₁ Ka   tun bin **sáas**-chah-∅   bey] ka' t-u   he'l dia-e',
and.then then EV   light-PRC.PF-3.PF thus again PREP-3 other day-CON
"And it dawned again the following day."

Gesture 1   Right hand sweeps leftward (see Figure 5.7).
Gloss   It dawns.

[₂ ka   **bin**-∅ **le** **máak-e'**   **k-u**   y-a'l-ik bin-e']
and.then go-3.PF   DET   person-CON   IPF-3EU   say-IPF EV-CON
"and the man went. He says . . ."

Gesture 2   Left hand, in an open handshape, moves leftward, up, and slightly forward.
Gloss   And then, the man goes.

Example 4: Mopan Time-flow and Plot Development (Poor Man Story)

Kul-aj-i.
Stay-POS.PF-3
"He rested."

Pes [₁ ox   p'ee *k'in, k'och-ok*-∅,
So   three CL   day   arrive-SBJ-3
"But when three days had gone by"

Gesture 1   Left hand is held in front of the left side of the chest. The hand in an open handshape with the palm oriented forward and the fingers upward.
Gloss   Three days has pasted.

|₂ **Ma' yun-meyaj**.
NG   exist.3-work
"There was (still) no work for him."

Gesture 2   Left hand waves laterally (leftward, rightward, and then leftward). The hand is in an open handshape with the palm oriented forward and the fingers upward (a conventionalized gesture for "nothing").
Gloss   No work.

|₃ **Pere k'u   u-yub-aj**-∅ *a   nooch ch'up-u,*
but   what 3-hear-PF-3 DET old   woman
"But what the old woman heard was,"

Gesture 3 Left hand moves forward, making an arc (up and then down) (see Figure 5.9).
Gloss The plot develops.

|4 ka   yan-∅ **k'u** **a** ...
      CONJ exist-3 what DET
      "that there was something that ..."

Gesture 4 Left hand waves laterally (rightward and then leftward). The hand is in an open handshape with the palm oriented forward and the fingers upward.
Gloss (Possibly) something.

[5 **a**   **tun-yan-tal**   ti   a] rey-e.
      DET DUR.3-exist-PRC PREP DET king-TOPIC
      "that was happening to the king."

Gesture 5 Left hand moves straight down. The hand is in an open handshape with the palm oriented forward and the fingers upward.
Gloss ? To the king.

Tun-kim-il   a   rey.
DUR.3-die-IPF DET king
"The king was dying."

Example 5: Yucatec Paradigmatic Contrast (Golden Bird Story)

[1 Ka   tun bin **t-u** **y-a'l-ah**   **bey-a'**]
      and.then then EV PF-3 EU-say-PF thus-PD
      "And he said like this:"

Gesture 1 Left hand, with the index finger and the thumb extended, makes an arc downward and slightly to the right. At the end, index finger and the thumb point the space near the left shoulder.
Gloss The intellectual brother, localized at A in Figure 5.10.

[2 Yan in   ch'a'-ik-∅ ti'   in   **láak'-e'**
      OBL 1.SG take-IPF-3 PREP 1.SG relative-CON
      "I must take it from my relative."

Gesture 2 Right hand, with the index finger and the thumb loosely extended, moves straight downward. Through out the stroke, the index finger points forward and downward.
Gloss The hunter brother, localized at B in Figure 5.10.

|₃ wa **ma'-e'**
    if   NG-CON
    "If not,"

Gesture 3   Right hand moves downward and slightly forward (see Figure 5.11).
Gloss   A possible scenario, in which the hunter brother eats the bird. The scenario is localized at B in Figure 5.10.

|₄ le   máak-a'   yan u **ayik'al-tal**]
    DET person-PD OBL 3 rich-PRC.IPF
    "this man will become rich."

Gesture 4   Right hand moves forward and slightly rightward, by fully extending the elbow (see Figure 5.11).
Gloss   The wealth will go to the hunter brother, at B in Figure 5.10.

[₅ tumen   wa t-**in**   **man-ah ti'**-e'
    because if PF-1.SG pass-PF PREP-CON
    "because if I get it from him,"
    (The perfective aspect in this utterance indicates the hypothetical nature of the proposition.)

Gesture 5   Left hand moves leftward and forward, by extending the elbow almost fully. Through out the stroke, the hand is open and the palm is oriented roughly downward (see Figure 5.11).
Gloss   Another scenario, in which the bird is transferred from the hunter brother, at B, to the intellectual brother, at A in Figure 5.10.

|₆ **tèen**   **ken**   han-t-ik-e'|
    1.SG.EMP SUB.FUT eat-TRR-SBJ-CON
    "It is me who will eat it,"

Gesture 6   Left hand moves forward and downward, by swinging the forearm around the elbow. At the end, the hand is open with the fingers oriented forward, and the palm is oriented rightward.
Gloss   The intellectual brother, localized at A.

|₇ **tèen**   **kun**   yantal ten   tàak'in]
    1.SG.EMP SUB.FUT.3 become 1.SG.EMP money
    "It is me who will get the money."

Gesture 7   Both hands move symmetrically, coming closer to each other. And then, the hands move upwards, slightly coming close to each other (See Figure 5.12).

Gloss   The resolution of the two possible scenarios, localized at A and B in Figure 5.10, namely, the intellectual brother becoming rich.

Example 6: Mopan Paradigmatic Contrast (Wild Woman Story)

[₁ Pere **maant-e'**]   [₂ a   ch'iich' a |₃ la, aj   **kolonte'**].
   but borrow-SBJ.3   DET bird   DET   PD MASC woodpecker
"You should make use of this bird, the woodpecker."

Gesture 1   Right hand, with the index finger extended, moves downward. At the beginning, the index finger points upward and slightly forward. At the end, it points forward.
Gloss for Gestures 1–5   The woodpecker, localized at A of Figure 5.13.
Gesture 2   Right hand, with the index finger extended, moves downward. Throughout the stroke, the index finger points upward and forward.
Gesture 3   Right hand, with the index finger extended, moves down from the same starting point of Gesture 2 onto the lap. At the end, the index finger points forward.

[₄ Le'ek-∅ a   kaa |₅ **mant-e'**]
   EMP.3-3 DET FUT   borrow-SBJ.3
"That's what you will use."

Gesture 4   Right hand, with the index finger extended, slightly moves downward. Throughout the stroke, the index finger points forward and slightly upward.
Gesture 5   After a short pause, right hand, with the index finger extended, moves down from the end point of Gesture 4 down onto the lap. At the end, the index finger points forward.

[₆ Le'ek-∅ a **jel**.]
   EMP.3-3   2 substitute
"That's your substitute."

Gesture 6   Right hand makes an upward half circle backward slightly leftward. At the beginning, the palm is oriented leftward and the extended index finger points forward. At the end, all fingers are loosely curled toward the palm, and form a "bunch." The palm is oriented downward and backward, and the finger-tips point downward (Figure 5.14).
Gloss   The woodpecker and the husband are different individuals, but equivalent in that they would be making similar noise with trees.

Acknowledgments

This research was supported by the Cognitive Anthropology Research Group at the Max-Planck Institute for Psycholinguistics in Nijmegen, The Netherlands. We would like to acknowledge the reviewers, Merideth Gattis, and Mandana Seyfeddinipur for helpful comments. We would also like to thank all the consultants in the Yucatec and Mopan communities for their stories. Thanks are due to Carlien de Witte and Lisette Oliemuelen, who worked long and hard on gesture coding. The copyright of all the Figures and Table 1 in this article is held by Max-Planck Institute for Psycholinguistics, and they are re-printed here with permission.

Chapter 6

Space on Hand: The Exploitation of Signing Space to Illustrate Abstract Thought

Karen Emmorey

Signed languages are perceived visually, rather than auditorily, and produced by movements of the hands in space rather than by movements of the tongue and lips. As a result, signers have a rich spatial medium at their disposal to express both spatial and non-spatial information. *Signing space* is the term used for the three-dimensional space in front of the signer, extending from the waist to the forehead, where signs can be articulated. Signers schematize this space to represent physical space and to represent abstract conceptual structure. Section 6.1 of this chapter illustrates how locations in signing space are mapped isomorphically to locations in real space, and Section 6.2 explores how such an isomorphism may affect spatial reasoning in ASL. Sections 6.3 and 6.4 describe how signing space functions to convey more abstract information about time and order, and Section 6.5 explores the hypothesis that signing space can function "diagrammatically" to depict abstract concepts and mental models. As we will see, the research reviewed here indicates that the use of signing space to depict abstract schemas does not contradict or violate any of the principles or patterns described in this volume (see particularly the chapters by Gattis, Gentner, and Tversky).

6.1 Mapping Linguistic Form to Spatial Form: Classifier Constructions

We begin by examining how signers use space to talk about space; that is, how linguistic form is mapped to the spatial relations being described. For most locative expressions in ASL, there is a schematic correspondence between the location of the hands in signing space and the position of physical objects in the world. When describing spatial scenes in ASL, the identity of each object is indicated by a lexical sign (e.g., TABLE, T-V, CHAIR[1]). The location of the objects, their orientation, and their spa-

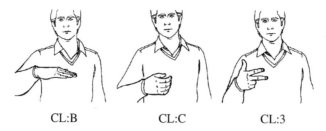

CL:B   CL:C   CL:3

Figure 6.1
Examples of ASL classifier handshapes. The illustrations are from *Basic Sign Communication* (Silver Spring, Md.: National Association of the Deaf, 1983).

tial relation vis-à-vis one another is indicated by where the appropriate "classifier" predicates are articulated. Classifier predicates express motion and location, and the handshape is a classificatory morpheme (see Figure 6.1). For example, the B handshape is the classifier handshape used for rectangular, flat-topped surface-prominent objects like beds or sheets of paper. The C handshape is the classifier handshape used for bulky box-like objects like televisions or cylindrical objects like cups, depending upon hand orientation. These handshapes occur in constructions that express the spatial relation of one object to another, or the manner and direction of motion. Where English uses prepositions to express spatial relations, ASL uses the visual layout displayed by classifier signs positioned in signing space.

Articulators **Map to Physical and Conceptual** *Elements*

Within classifier predicates, the hands represent physical objects, and various handshapes represent distinct types of objects. Such mapping follows a straightforward structural analogy in which physical elements (the hands) represent other physical elements (e.g., furniture, people, vehicles, etc.). Figure 6.1 illustrates the B and C classifier handshapes used for objects of particular shapes and sizes, i.e. flat surfaces or cylindrical objects. Also shown in Figure 6.1 is the 3 handshape used for vehicles (e.g., cars, boats, and bicycles).

However, the elements represented by classifier handshapes do not have to be concrete entities. Liddell (1995, 36) provides an example from a signer who describes the concept of culture using the C classifier handshape to represent "a container holding the linguistic and cultural behaviors that people carry with them as part of their culture." Wilcox

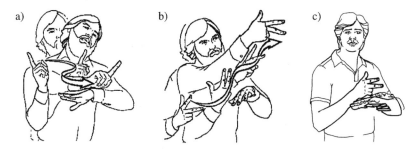

Figure 6.2
Illustration of ASL classifier predicates: (a) PERSON-WEAVE, (b) CAR-MEANDER, (c) SURFACE-PASS-UNDER-VEHICLE. Figures (a) and (b) are from Klima and Bellugi (1979), and (c) is from Lucas and Valli (1990).

(1993) provides another example in which the 1 handshape (index finger extended) is used to represent an idea and another example in which the mind is metaphorically represented by a classifier construction used for round containers. In these examples, there is a metaphorical mapping in which conceptual elements (e.g., culture, an idea) are mapped to the concrete domain (e.g., a container, a straight object) through the use of classifier handshapes.

Movements of the Articulators Map to the *Motion* of Elements

For classifier predicates referring to physical objects, the movement of the hand generally represents in schematic form the motion of the referent object. For example, a weaving motion of the hand can represent a person weaving back and forth while walking or a car meandering uphill (see Figure 6.2). Just as classifier handshapes do not have to represent physical objects, the movement within a classifier predicate is not required to represent true physical motion. For example, in an ASL lecture analyzed by Winston (1995), the signer describes his struggle to separate the art of poetry from the science of poetry. To express the separation of these two concepts, he uses a classifier predicate in which two C handshapes contact at the thumbs and then separate, moving laterally from the center. The movement of the hands represents the separation of two conceptions of ASL poetry, rather than the physical separation of two containers.

Another type of example in which the movement of the hands does not represent true object motion is when the movement represents *perceived* motion (Lucas & Valli, 1990), also termed *fictive motion* by Talmy (1996).

Room layout

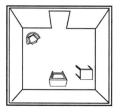

Description of layout using spatialized classifier constructions

| I-ENTER | TABLE | IS - THERE | TV | IS - THERE | CHAIR | IS - THERE |

Figure 6.3
Example of an ASL spatial description. An English translation of the ASL could be "I enter the room. There is a table to the left, a TV on the far side, and a chair to the right."

Figure 6.2 provides an example from Lucas and Valli (1990). The sign glossed as SURFACE-PASS-UNDER-VEHICLE is used to describe a car chase scene from a James Bond film. In this sign, the B handshape representing a surface moves rapidly back-and-forth under the 3 handshape representing a vehicle. Of course, the pavement surface is not actually moving, but would be perceived as moving if one were inside the car.

These few examples illustrate how the movements of the hands within classifier constructions can be schematized to represent the actual motion of objects, perceived motion, or abstract metaphorical motion.

Locations in Signing Space Map to *Locations* in Physical or Conceptual Space

As described above, there is an isomorphic relation between where the hands are placed in space and the physical locations being described. Figure 6.3 provides an example of a room description in which the position of the hands in signing space schematically represents locations of furniture within the room.

Spatial locations within signing space are not limited to representing the physical locations of objects or people. Data from ASL and other signed languages presented in Sections 6.3 to 6.5 will illustrate how abstract concepts can be associated with locations in signing space and how these locations can be structured within signing space to illustrate relations between concepts.

It is important to note that the mapping between signing space and physical space is not always straightforward and is constrained by language specific rules. For example, to indicate a cat on top of a car, it is ungrammatical in ASL to place the classifier handshape for small animals (a V handshape with hooked fingers) on top of the vehicle classifier (the 3 handshape), despite the fact that this configuration of the hands directly reflects the spatial configuration being described. The constraint arises from a morphological rule that prohibits any classifier handshape to be located on a "whole entity" classifier handshape (Valli & Lucas, 1995). Another example in which the spatial relation between classifier handshapes does not map neatly to the spatial relation between the two objects is the ASL description of a person getting into a car. Using a classifier construction, a signer locates the bent V handshape (also used for seated people) *next to* the vehicle classifier—the motion of the V handshape distinguishes between the meaning "in the car" (arc motion) versus "next to the car" (downward or "contact" motion). In this example, an *in* relation between objects in the physical world is mapped to a *next to* relation between the hands in signing space. Thus, while the mapping between signing space and physical space is generally isomorphic, it is constrained by linguistic factors.

Finally, the type of mapping described above is consistent with the constraints laid out in Gattis (this volume) for mapping between conceptual and spatial schemas. For example, the principle of iconicity constrains the mapping from the location and movement of the hands to the location and movement of objects described (whether abstract or concrete). Structural similarities constrain the mapping of relational structures, e.g., elements are mapped to elements (the hands to concepts) and relations are mapped to relations (the spatial relation of the hands is mapped to the relation of concepts, as in the poetry example).

6.2 Spatial Reasoning in ASL

Does the general isomorphism between signing space and physical space have consequences for spatial reasoning? One consequence appears to be that certain spatial reasoning tasks become trivial. For example, Johnson-Laird and colleagues (Johnson-Laird, 1996; Byrne & Johnson-Laird,

1989) asked hearing English speakers to make spatial inferences given the following type of discourse:

The knife is on the right of the plate.
The spoon is on the left of the plate.
The fork is in front of the spoon.
The cup is in front of the knife.
What's the relation between the fork and the cup?
Answer: The fork is to the left of the cup

A diagram makes explicit the spatial representations that are implicit in the English description:[2]

s   p   k
f   c

Figure 6.4 provides an illustration of an ASL version of the English text describing the spatial layout of the dinnerware.

As you can see from the figure, signing space can function like a diagram, schematically illustrating spatial relationships. However, signers must still build a mental model of the spatial relations from the signed description. Unlike the diagram, not all of the spatial relationships are expressed simultaneously, and each spatial relation must be maintained in working memory. Furthermore, if the signers are facing each other (as you, the reader, are facing the signer depicted in Figure 6.4), then the addressee must perform what amounts to a 180° mental rotation in order to understand the description from the signer's point of view. Sign addressees apparently have little difficulty with this process and prefer descriptions from the signer's perspective (see Emmorey, Klima & Hickok, 1998). What is unique about ASL is that space itself is used to express spatial relationships such that the mapping between the spatial relations within a mental model and within signing space is isomorphic and in the same modality. In this example, it is possible that the relation between the fork and the cup can be "read off" the linguistic representation in memory which encodes the locations in signing space associated with the two objects (see Emmorey, Corina & Bellugi, 1995, for evidence that topographic locations in signing space are well maintained in memory).

Another consequence of this spatial isomorphism is that spatial indeterminacy due to multiple models can be dramatically reduced. For example, the solution to the following problem is indeterminate because there are two spatial models consistent with the text (from Johnson-Laird, 1996):

"The knife is on the right of the plate."   "The spoon is on the left of the plate."

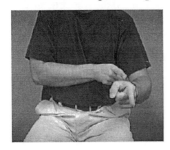 

"The fork is in front of the spoon."   "The cup is in front of the knife."

Figure 6.4
Illustration of the ASL translation of the English spatial description given in the text. The lexical signs PLATE, KNIFE, SPOON, FORK, and CUP are not shown. The English translation under each illustration indicates the relation depicted by the ASL classifier construction. The plate is represented by a 'bent L' handshape (thumb and index finger extended and bent). The knife, spoon, and fork are each indicated by a 1 handshape (in the bottom left example, the signer's right hand represents the fork, and his left hand represents the spoon). The cup is represented by a C handshape (thumb and fingers extended and curved).

The knife is on the right of the plate.
The spoon is on the left of the knife.
The fork is in front of the spoon.
The cup is in front of the plate.
What's the relation between the fork and the cup?

Model A			Model B		
s	p	k	p	s	k
f	c		c	f	

If a signer were to translate the English text into ASL using classifier constructions, he or she would have to be explicit about the spatial layout, choosing model A or model B. Now the question arises, is it possible for a signer to be more general and less explicit? The answer is yes. Signers could chose to describe spatial relations using lexical locatives such as BEHIND, FRONT, LEFT, RIGHT, ON, IN (see Emmorey, 1996, for a discussion of these forms). In particular, such expressions are used when signers want to label the spatial relation (e.g., for emphasis) or when they want to generalize across particular objects. However, classifier constructions are preferred in general over lexical locatives for spatial descriptions.

Another question that arises in the context of spatial reasoning is whether the mapping between signing space and physical space is always diagrammatic. Does signing space always have this type of format when spatial relations are described? The answer is no. In ASL, there are two types of spatial formats that signers use for describing environments, termed diagrammatic space and viewer space, which have the properties given in Table 6.1 (from Emmorey and Falgier, 1999).

The ASL examples that we have seen thus far have used diagrammatic space in which the vantage point is fixed and signing space has a map-like quality. In contrast, when signers use viewer space, the environment being described is conceptualized as present and observable. In this type of description, there is a more complex mapping between locations in signing space and the mental model that must be constructed from the signed discourse. Signing space does not map isomorphically to a mental model

Table 6.1

Properties of diagrammatic space versus viewer space

Diagrammatic space	Viewer space
Signing space represents a map-like model of the environment.	Signing space reflects an individual's view of the environment at a particular point in time and space.
Space can have either a 2-D "map" format or a 3-D "model" format.	Signing space is 3-D (normal-sized scale).
The vantage point does not change (generally a bird's eye view).	Vantage point can change (except for "gaze tour" descriptions) [a]
A relatively low horizontal signing space or a vertical plane	A relatively high horizontal signing space

a. A "gaze tour" description does not describe movement through space; rather, the environment is described from a fixed vantage point from which a signer or speaker views the environment.

of the entire spatial array. The following example illustrates the difference
between using diagrammatic versus viewer space for spatial reasoning:

English description of an office building
As you go in the entrance, you enter into a hallway. On your left is the
secretary's office. Go down the hall and turn right. The president's office
is near the end of the hall way on your left. Now turn right again and
walk a little way down the hall. The conference room is on your left, and
the exit is directly in front of you.

If you stand at the entrance, facing the building, is the conference room to
your right?
Answer: Yes.

   Figure 6.5 illustrates how landmarks (the rooms in the building) are
associated with locations in signing space when either diagrammatic or
viewer space is adopted. When viewer space is used, all of the rooms are
associated with a location on the signer's left, just as they are all described
as on the left in the English description. Both the English and the ASL
version using viewer space are route descriptions in which the reader/
viewer is taken on a tour of the environment (see Taylor and Tversky,
1992). The locations in signing space represent the relation between the
room and the signer as she imagines herself walking through the building.
To build a mental model of the office building from the viewer space

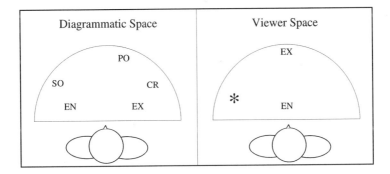

Figure 6.5
Illustration of diagrammatic and viewer space in ASL. The semi-circles represent
signing space. Each letter represents the location in signing space associated with
that particular landmark, where EN = entrance; SO = secretary's office; PO =
president's office; CR = conference room; and EX = exit. The asterisk in the
viewer space description indicates that the two offices and the conference room
were associated with that location in signing space.

discourse, ASL signers must infer the spatial relations between the rooms by transforming the "viewer-related" locations in signing space into a mental model representing relations between rooms. In contrast, when diagrammatic space is used, the spatial relationships between the rooms in the office building are schematically represented by locations in the plane of signing space. Thus, it may be much easier to build a spatial mental model from descriptions using diagrammatic space compared to viewer space, at least for environments of this type. Some support for this hypothesis stems from the finding that ASL signers strongly prefer to use diagrammatic space when describing the layout of a building similar to the one described above (see Emmorey and Falgier, 1999).

In sum, signing space can function like a diagram for expressing spatial relations, but it doesn't have to. The cognitive and linguistic factors that determine whether signers utilize diagrammatic or viewer space to describe spatial relations are not completely clear, but we may find that diagrammatic space is preferred when a spatial mental model must be created for an array of landmarks with a fixed viewpoint, i.e., the same circumstances for which a diagram enhances comprehension. When signing space does function like a diagram, spatial inferences are made explicit by the schematic mapping between locations in signing space and locations within the environment described. In addition, some types of spatial indeterminacy that are found in English do not appear to occur for ASL because if classifier constructions are used, many spatial relations must be made explicit within the signed description.

6.3   Space to Represent Time

Time is an abstract non-spatial construct, but humans often adapt spatial structures to convey temporal information (e.g., spatial metaphors, charts, and graphs; see Tversky, this volume). Similarly, signers adapt signing space to express temporal information both at the lexical level and at the discourse level (see also Kita, this volume, for a discussion of how the "gesture space" of speakers is used to represent temporal information).

Lexical Signs

In ASL, temporal signs utilize the "future is ahead" metaphor which is consistent with both the ego-moving metaphor in which the observer moves toward the future and the time-moving metaphor in which time is conceived of as a type of river that flows from the future toward the

Figure 6.6
(a) Lexical temporal signs. (b) Morphological variants of the sign WEEK indicating past and future time. The illustrations are from *Basic Sign Communication*, (1983), National Association of the Deaf: Silver Spring, MD.

observer (see Gentner, this volume). Within both types of metaphor, the future is conceptualized as ahead of the observer or ahead of the person signing in ASL (Taub, in press). Similarly, the past is conceptualized as behind the signer, and the present is co-located with signer. The deictic signs TOMORROW, NOW, and YESTERDAY illustrate this space-time metaphor (see Figure 6.6A). The sign TOMORROW moves ahead of the signer; the sign NOW is articulated at the body, and the sign YESTERDAY moves backward (i.e., toward the signer's back).

In addition, the spatial location of some temporal signs can be altered to indicate past and future (Cogen, 1977; Friedman, 1975). As shown in Figure 6.6B, when the sign for WEEK moves ahead of the signer, it means "next week" when it moves toward the signer's back, the sign means "last week." The sign YEAR also allows these form alternations. Certain temporal verbs and adverbs are also articulated with respect to the temporal structure associated with signing space. For example, the modal verb WILL moves outward from the signer's shoulder, and for the adverb glossed as PAST or BEFORE, the hand moves backward toward the signer's shoulder. For the sign POST-PONE, the dominant hand moves outward from the signer, and this sign is used when an event is moved to a future time (see Figure 6.8 below). If the dominant hand moves toward the signer, the form is sometimes glossed as PRE-PONE and means that an event is moved to an earlier time in the future. In this last example, the signer's body does not represent the temporal reference point; rather, the non-dominant hand represents the reference point, and the dominant hand begins its motion next to it and moves either forward to a future time (POST-PONE) or backward to an earlier time (PRE-PONE). Similarly, for the sign UNTIL, the non-dominant hand represents the temporal reference point and is held in central space while the dominant hand arcs from near the shoulder to the non-dominant hand (moving from "past space" to a point in "future space" represented by the non-dominant hand).

Finally, signs that do not reference time directly can also make use of the "future is ahead" metaphor (Taub, in press). For example, the dominant hand in the sign LOOK-BACK-ON ("reminisce") moves from near the eyes, around the head, and behind the signer. LOOK-FORWARD-TO is made with the same handshape but with movement upward and away from the signer. For both the signs CONTINUE and PREDICT, the hands move forward, ahead the signer.

These examples illustrate how the form of certain signs reflects a mapping between spatial structure and temporal structure. The mapping is based on the spatial metaphor in which future time is mapped to space ahead of a reference point, and the past is mapped to space behind this point. The temporal reference point can be represented either by the signer's body or by the non-dominant hand.

Time Lines

Time lines are spatial constructs within signing space that represent distinct types of temporal information. When a referent is associated with a location along a time line, the entire line is invested with specific referential potential, and non-temporal referents associated with the time line take on temporal meaning (Engberg-Pedersen, 1993). Time lines are always available, and they have a variety of meanings. Engberg-Pedersen (1993) first identified a deictic, anaphoric, and sequence time line for Danish Sign Language (DSL),[3] and Winston (1989) observed similar time lines in ASL (see Figure 6.7).

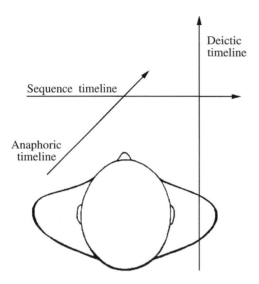

Figure 6.7
Time lines in ASL.

Deictic time line   The deictic time line extends forward from the dominant shoulder and is perpendicular to the body. The reference point for
the time line is the signer's body, and the default meaning is *deictic*, i.e.,
referring to the time of utterance. For both ASL and DSL, "after now" is
associated along the line outward from the signer, and "now" is associated with locations near the signer. For example, if the sign FRIDAY is
articulated with the arm extended, the form would mean "next Friday"
(see Figure 6.8). To indicate "this Friday," signers can point to a location
on the time line near the body and articulate the sign FRIDAY at this location (usually with an adverbial facial expression glossed as "cs" which
indicates recent time). However, DSL and ASL differ in how "before
now" is represented. In DSL, "before now" is behind the signer such that
a determiner can point to a location behind the signer to refer to a past
event (e.g., a conference held last January). In ASL, such deictic reference
to a location behind the signer cannot be temporal; it can only have spatial
meaning (i.e., referring to a location, person, or object that is actually behind the signer). In ASL, to refer to "last Friday," signers produce the
phrase PAST FRIDAY, and the sign FRIDAY is produced in its citation form
(i.e., roughly in the middle section of the time line). In ASL, it is not possible
to associate a referent with a location on the time line behind the signer.

Figure 6.8
Illustration of the deictic time line from the following ASL discourse (only the bolded signs are pictured): TUESDAY, MUST PASS OUT REVIEW PAPERS. WHY? NEXT-FRIDAY TEST. IF NOT-YET PASS-OUT, TEST POST-PONE. "On Tuesday, I must pass out the review papers because the test is on Friday. If I haven't yet passed them out, Friday's test will be postponed."

For both DSL and ASL, nominals that do not have inherent temporal meaning can be associated with the deictic time line and thereby take on temporal meaning. Figure 6.8 provides an example in which the sign TEST is associated with a location on the deictic time line. TEST is not a time expression, but it takes on temporal meaning ("next Friday's test") by virtue of its spatial location.

Anaphoric time line   The anaphoric time line extends diagonally across signing space (see Figure 6.7). The default meaning of this time line is not "now" (i.e., the time of the utterance); rather, the temporal reference point is determined within the discourse. The time line is *anaphoric* in the sense that temporal meaning is derived from the narrative, and there is no default temporal reference point.

Winston (1989) provides an example from an ASL lecture about sign poetry in which the signer actually shifts his body along the anaphoric time line. He signs the following centrally:[4] "Why were there deaf poets after the 1970's but not before? I doubt that is what really happened. I believe that before that no one had noticed their existence. Why? You're right." Then he steps left and backwards signing "Before, in the late 1960's, Stokoe recognized ASL as a language. He tried to tell people about this, but he was resisted at first. Then his ideas began to be accepted and . . ." The signer then moves back to the center while signing "over the years they spread, and now they have been widely accepted." He then moves backward and left again signing, "Before, maybe they had (ASL) poetry but no one noticed it. I believe that it existed but no one noticed it." In this example, the anaphoric time line was used to express changes in time frames within the discourse. Chunks of discourse, rather than single signs, were associated with locations along the time line.

Sequence time line   The sequence time line is parallel to the body and extends left to right, representing early to later periods or moments in time. Unlike lexical signs, the left-to-right direction of the sequence time line is not reversed in left handers. The directionality of the sequence time line may reflect language culture since the sequence time line in Jordanian Sign Language extends right to left (Dan Parvaz, personal communication, November, 1998; see Tversky, Kugelmass and Winter (1991) for evidence of left-to-right temporal mapping for English speakers and right-to-left temporal mapping for Arabic speakers).

Like the anaphoric time line, the temporal reference point is established within the discourse. Winston (1989) provides an example in which a signer associates 1960 with a location on the left and 1980 with a location on the right, tracing a line between the two locations. The signer then refers to specific events in time (e.g., marriage, divorce, and re-marriage) by articulating signs near the appropriate locations on the time line (e.g., closer to one of the locations associated with the endpoints, 1960 or 1980). As with the other time lines, non-temporal signs can take on temporal meaning when associated with the sequence time lime. For example, when the sign MARRY is articulated to the left (i.e., at or near the location associated with 1960), it indicates an earlier event compared to when MARRY is articulated to the right, near the location associated with 1980. The sequence time line is used when signers refer to ordered events that are not related to the utterance time.

The deictic, anaphoric, and sequence time lines all appear to have distinct temporal functions. In general, the deictic time line is used to refer to points in time related to the immediate context of an utterance (as in English "next Friday"). The sequence time line appears to be used when signers want to talk about the temporal order of events, and the reference

TUESDAY   FRIDAY

beginning   end   beginning   end
          TEST   MOVE-TO-THE-NEXT-WEEK

Figure 6.9
Illustration of the calendar plane from the following ASL discourse (only the bolded signs are pictured: TUESDAY, PASS OUT REVIEW PAPERS. **FRIDAY** TEST. IF NOT-YET PASS-OUT, **TEST MOVE-TO-THE-NEXT-WEEK**. "On Tuesday, I pass out review papers because tests are on Friday. If I haven't yet passed them out, the test is moved to the next week."

point is established within the discourse (as in English "the following Friday"). Finally, the anaphoric time line appears to be used to contrast or compare time periods related to the topic of discourse. Further research may reveal additional semantic characteristics associated with these timelines, as well as constraints on their use.

Calendar plane   The calendar plane is a two dimensional plane with the surface parallel to the body (Engberg-Pedersen, 1993). In Danish Sign Language, it is used primarily for the year, but in ASL it appears to be most often used for weeks within a month. As shown in Figure 6.9, the signs for the days of the week are associated with a relatively high location on the plane (as if "labeling" columns on a calendar page for a month), and like the sequence line, time moves from left to right. The example in Figure 6.9 is parallel to the example in Figure 6.8, which illustrated the deictic time line. However, the sign POST-PONE cannot be

used here, perhaps because its form, which requires forward motion, con-
flicts with the structure of the calendar plane. The calendar plane tends
to be used when signers are describing the general structure of events
within a week, whereas the deictic time line is used when describing
events with respect to particular time (by default, the time of the utterance). Thus, the example using the calendar plane (Figure 6.9) could be
interpreted as a description of events that occur every week, but the
example using the deictic time line (Figure 6.8) could not.

The mapping from space to time appears to be quite rich semantically
for both ASL and DSL. As in other cognitive domains, signers map time
to a line or plane in space. The mapping to a plane is based on how time
is represented on a Western calendar, and the mapping to a line may be
based on the conceptualization of time as a one dimensional construct
with a direction (see Gentner, this volume). The semantics of time lines
may differ for distinct sign languages, and not all sign languages utilize
time lines (Engberg-Pedersen, 1993). However, when time lines are used
by signers, they appear to preserve a basic structural mapping between
space and time in which a spatial direction (e.g., forward from the body)
is mapped to a temporal direction (e.g., toward the future), and a spatial
reference point (e.g., the signer's body) is mapped to a temporal reference
point (e.g., the time of speaking).

6.4   Space to Represent Order

Signing space can also represent serial order and simultaneity. It appears
that signers may use some type of spatial coding to represent serial order
within linguistic working memory (i.e., memory for sign language). This
spatial coding appears to function as a memory device distinct from any
of the structures available for spoken language. We are also finding that
signers can use signing space as a type of diagram to indicate serial
order as well as simultaneity within an abstract non-spatial domain (see
Tversky, this volume, for a discussion of how graphics perform these
same functions).

Spatial Coding of Serial Order in Working Memory

Working memory is traditionally divided into two major domains: verbal
and visuo-spatial. However, there is an ambiguity with respect to how
this division is characterized. It has been defined in terms of sensory
modality—auditory vs. visual-spatial representations, and it has also been

defined in terms of language—linguistic representations vs. non-linguistic imagistic/spatial representations. This ambiguity is challenged by signed languages that are both linguistic and visual-spatial. In a recent series of studies, Wilson and Emmorey (1997a, 1997b, 1998a) have shown that many of the properties characteristic of so-called "verbal" working memory can also be observed with ASL. For example, we observed a *phonological similarity effect* (lists of signs with similar handshapes yield poorer recall than lists of dissimilar signs), a *sign length effect* (lists of long signs yield poorer recall than lists of short signs), and an effect of *manual articulatory suppression* (poorer recall when nonsense hand motions are produced during presentation of to-be-remembered signs). The sign length effect, but not the phonological similarity effect, is eliminated under articulatory suppression. This pattern of results parallels results with speech and supports a model of working memory for ASL containing a sign-based phonological store and an articulatory loop that refreshes information within the store.

However, working memory for sign and for speech may not be completely parallel. Specifically, working memory for ASL may involve a type of spatial coding that is unavailable for spoken language. We were led to this hypothesis when we noticed that during serial recall, some of our deaf subjects spontaneously responded by signing each item at a separate spatial location from left-to-right, perhaps taking advantage of the sequence time line. This response pattern suggests that introducing a spatial component into the memory representation may assist performance, and that certain subjects spontaneously discovered a strategy of coding in this manner.

To investigate this hypothesis, Wilson and Emmorey (1998b) presented deaf subjects with a serial recall task comparing memory for signs with a *moveable location* (neutral space signs like MILK, LIBRARY) to signs with a *fixed body location* (body-anchored signs like BAR, LEMON). Figure 6.10 provides an illustration of some of the stimuli. We hypothesized that deaf subjects would be able to use spatial coding only for the signs with moveable locations because only these signs could be mentally "rehearsed" in diverse locations.

Our results supported this hypothesis: signs with a neutral space location were remembered more accurately than signs with a body-anchored location. In addition, several subjects were observed to articulate the neutral space signs in a sequence of distinct locations. These results demon-

A)

BATHROOM   ONE-DOLLAR

B)

TWINS   CANDY

Figure 6.10
Illustration of (A) signs with a moveable location (neutral space signs) and (B) signs with a fixed body location. The illustrations are from *Basic Sign Communication* (Silver Spring, MD.: National Association of the Deaf, 1983).

strate that spatial coding can be used as a memory device over and above mere repetition of the to-be-remembered material. Furthermore, we found that when signs were presented at distinct locations on the videoscreen (e.g., in one of four quadrants), serial recall was not improved compared to central presentation. This finding suggests that when the spatial coding is non-linguistic (i.e., the locations on the videoscreen are not part of ASL phonology), signers do not take advantage of spatial coding for recall. Since the spatial coding used by ASL signers is unavailable to speech-based working memory, these findings suggest that language modality can alter the structure of working memory. Our next step is to discover the nature of the spatial coding used to encode serial order. For example, is the coding articulatory (and thus eliminated by manual suppression) or is it associated with the phonological store (and thus unaffected by suppression)? Further research will help to uncover the nature of the mapping between signing space and serial order within working memory for sign language.

The Diagrammatic Function of Signing Space within Non-spatial Domains

Many studies have shown that diagrams can facilitate comprehension of written text. For example, Glenberg and Langston (1992) found that diagrammatic pictures help to build mental models of the text and reinforce critical inferences. It is possible that signers may similarly manipulate signing space within a discourse to facilitate comprehension and the construction of mental models of the situation described within the discourse. In Glenberg and Langston's study, subjects read texts describing a four-step procedure in which the middle steps were described as occurring at the same time, although the written description of the steps was sequential. Within a mental representation of the *procedure*, the two middle steps would be equally related to the preceding step because they are conducted simultaneously. In contrast, within a mental representation of the *text itself*, the middle step described first would be more strongly related to the preceding step than the middle step described second. Glenberg and Langston (1992) found that subjects who were presented with a picture diagramming the temporal relation of the steps (see Figure 6.11) tended to mentally represent the procedure. That is, these subjects were equally facile in judging the performance order of the middle steps relative to the initial step. In contrast, subjects who were only presented with the text tended to judge the middle step that was described second as occurring later in time (rather than simultaneously). Glenberg and Langston (1992) conclude that diagrams facilitate comprehension by encouraging subjects to represent information in the text in the form of a mental model. We are beginning to investigate whether manipulations within signing space can perform a similar function.

For example, it is possible in ASL to describe the four step procedures of Glenberg and Langston's study in two different ways. One way parallels the English text version in which the signer simply lists the procedures and their order. Such a description does not rely much on signing space, and it is not unusual. However, another way of describing the same procedure uses signing space to represent the temporal relations between the steps in a manner parallel to the pictorial diagrams. For example, the first step is described using a relatively high signing plane; the middle steps are described side-by-side using the center of signing space. The sign NEXT is produced with two hands moving down simultaneously from where the first step was described to the two locations that will be used to describe the middle steps. The "middle" descriptions are connected with the sign

Writing a paper
There are four steps to writing a paper. The first step is to *write a first draft*. To do this, you must follow an outline and disregard style. The nest two steps should be performed at the same time. One of these steps is to *consider the structure*. You must correct flaws in logic and gaps between main points. The other step is to *address the audience*. You should explain novel terms adequately and support bold statements. The final step is to *proof the paper* for grammar, punctuation, and style. It is a good idea to have someone else do this for you, since you may not notice such surface details.

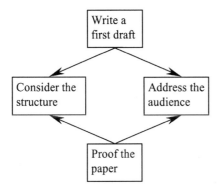

Figure 6.11
Illustration of the text and diagram used by Glenberg and Langston (1992).

SAME-TIME moving between the two locations. The signer then produces one description on the left and the other on the right of signing space (thus, there is more temporal influence in the signed description than in a diagram). The final step is signed slightly lower in signing space.

We are currently designing an experiment in which ASL signers will be presented with one of the two types of discourse describing four step procedures. We predict that subjects who receive the spatialized version of the discourse will be more accurate in their temporal order judgments because they will be more likely to build a mental model of the procedure than subjects who receive the non-spatial version. Such a finding would support the hypothesis that the structured use of signing space within a discourse can facilitate the construction of mental models of non-spatial information. Furthermore, this finding would also have important implications for how ASL can be used within an educational setting for the deaf to foster comprehension of complex information.

6.5 Space to Illustrate Abstract Concepts

Although the use of signing space to illustrate the temporal order of a set of procedures is quite natural, the example was created for experimental purposes, rather than observed in spontaneous signing. In this section, we examine how a deaf teacher who is a native ASL signer spontaneously uses signing space in her explanation of physical and chemical change during a lecture to her deaf third grade students.[5] Finally, we end with a brief discussion of how ASL signers use signing space to express conceptual metaphors in which abstract concepts and relations are mapped onto concrete schemas.

Mapping Conceptual Relations to Spatial Relations: Examples from an ASL Science Lecture

The teacher begins her lecture about physical change by writing the word "gas" on the chalkboard at about shoulder height. The sign G-A-S is fingerspelled at about this same height. During her lecture, she introduces the terms L-I-Q-U-I-D and SOLID, writing these words on the board, as shown in Figure 6.12. When discussing these physical forms, the teacher associates G-A-S with a location about shoulder height in signing space, L-I-Q-U-I-D with the middle of signing space, and she signs SOLID at a very low location in space. Thus, different locations within signing space are associated with different states of matter.

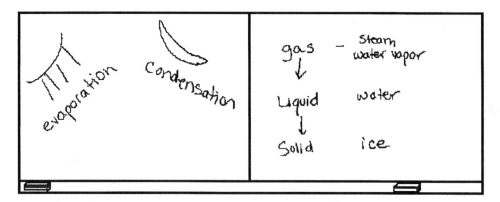

Figure 6.12
Illustration of chalkboard diagrams and text from an ASL science lecture.

Furthermore, verbs can be articulated such that they move between these locations, illustrating changes in state. For example, the signs EVAPORATE (see Figure 6.13) and STEAM move upward from the location associated with a liquid state to the higher location associated with a gas state. The teacher also uses the sign B-A-C-K to indicate changing from a gas state back to a liquid state by moving the sign downward from the spatial location associated with gas to the location associated with liquid. The phonological and morphological structure of these verbs allows the teacher to map them onto the model of physical change she has created in signing space. However, the phonological structure of the sign MELT does not match this model because the movement of the sign is downward, rather than upward (see Figure 6.13). This form is iconically motivated by the visual perception of the height of a solid decreasing as it melts. However, within the model created in signing space by the teacher, the liquid state is above the solid state, but it is ungrammatical to articulate MELT with upward motion to illustrate change from a solid to a liquid. None-

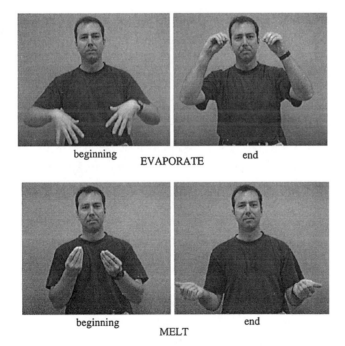

beginning   EVAPORATE   end

beginning   MELT   end

Figure 6.13
Illustration of the signs EVAPORATE and MELT.

theless, the teacher uses the sign MELT in its grammatical form, and it does not create confusion or conflict. Thus, the teacher refers to the spatial model within signing space only to the extent allowed by linguistic constraints, and the spatial model does not override these constraints.

Integration of Written Text and Diagrams with Signing

Like speaking teachers, signing teachers often point to words or pictures drawn on the chalk board while they are lecturing. For speaking teachers this communication occurs in two modalities: sound and vision. For signing teachers, the communication is purely visual: one hand points to the relevant information on the blackboard while the other hand signs. For example, the teacher points to the word *solid* on the blackboard with her left hand while signing "What does water do?" with her right hand, meaning "What does water become when it is a solid?" Pointing and signing can also alternate; e.g., the teacher points to the word *evaporation* and then describes the process of evaporation. Deictic pointing is easily integrated with signing, in a manner quite similar to the way deictic pointing is integrated with speech.

In addition, signers can also integrate non-pointing signs with written diagrams and text. Figure 6.12 shows the chalkboard illustrations that the teacher used during her lecture. In addition to pointing to various words and illustrations, she produced several signs on or near the chalkboard during her lecture. For example, she produced the sign EVAPORATE on the chalkboard, moving upward and toward the written word *evaporation*. In another example, she pointed to the word *gas* and asked a child, "If it gets cold, what happens?" When the child answered incorrectly, she signed NO B-A-C-K. The verb B-A-C-K moved from the word *gas* on the blackboard to the word *liquid*. In another example, the teacher is explaining that the physical form of matter changes (but the matter itself does not). She points to each of the words *steam*, *water*, and *ice* written on the board. She then signs THREE A-L-L LOOK-SAME? SAME? ("Do all three look the same? Are they the same?"). The bolded signs were articulated near the chalkboard. The sign A-L-L moved from the word *steam* downward to *ice*, and she articulated the sign SAME (Y handshape) over the words *steam*, *water*, and *ice*. In these examples, the teacher takes advantage of the ability of neutral space signs to change their location. However, rather than manipulating locations within signing space, she articulates signs at locations outside normal signings space, i.e., on the chalkboard.

The teacher integrates the chalkboard text with signing for several purposes. By producing the sign EVAPORATE toward both the drawing of the sun and the English word *evaporation*, she links the ASL sign to the written English term and illustrates the process as well. By articulating the signs A-L-L and SAME over words on the chalkboard, she groups together the words (and the concepts they stand for). She integrates locations in signing space with locations on the blackboard by articulating the sign B-A-C-K on the chalkboard in a way that is similar to how it would be articulated in signing space to convey a change in state from gas to liquid. Furthermore, because the words *gas* and *liquid* remain on the chalkboard (unlike in signing space), the students can see all three elements of the process at the same time: the initial and end states (the written words) and the sign B-A-C-K describing the state change.

Conceptual Metaphors: A Double Mapping

In conceptual metaphors, an abstract domain is consistently described in terms of a concrete domain (e.g., Lakoff & Johnson, 1980; Lakoff & Turner, 1989). For example, the abstract domain of communicating is often mapped to the concrete domain of sending objects, e.g., "We tossed some ideas back and forth" or "That went right by me." In this metaphorical mapping, *ideas* correspond to *objects*, and the act of *communicating* corresponds to *sending*. In recent work, Taub (in press) has shown that conceptual metaphors in ASL involve a double mapping: (1) a metaphorical mapping from an abstract target domain to a concrete source domain (e.g., concepts are mapped to objects) and (2) an iconic mapping from the concrete domain to the linguistic form (e.g., cylindrical objects map to cylindrical handshapes). For example, ASL signers also use the "communicating as sending" metaphor, but there is an additional iconic mapping between the concrete domain (objects) and the articulators (the hands). For instance, the sign glossed as THINK-BOUNCE indicates a failure to communicate and consists of an iconic depiction of a projectile bouncing off a wall (the 1 handshape moves from the head and bounces off the non-dominant hand). The sign is roughly equivalent to the English "I didn't get through to him," but in English there is no iconic mapping between the form of the words and the concrete domain they express, unlike in ASL (Taub, in press).

Such double mapping occurs for signing space as well. For example, the metaphorical mapping between power and height ("power is up") has an additional iconic mapping between height and signing space. Thus, authority figures are often associated with higher locations in signing space, and conversely, less powerful people are associated with lower locations. Similarly, signers use the "intimacy is proximity" metaphor and associate known or preferred objects/people with locations near their body and less preferred objects/people with locations away from their body. We have already seen how spatial-temporal metaphors are mapped onto signing space. Thus, spoken and signed languages appear to share many of the same schematic mappings between abstract conceptual domains and concrete spatial domains. However, Taub's (in press) research indicates that sign languages exhibit an additional mapping between the concrete domain and the linguistic form itself.

6.6   Summary and Conclusion

ASL signers exploit signing space to schematically represent spatial relations, time, order, and aspects of conceptual structure. When signers describe spatial relations, there is a structural analogy between the form of a classifier construction and aspects of the described scene. Specifically, physical elements in ASL (the hands) map to physical elements within the scene (objects); movement of the hands maps to the motion of referent objects; and locations in signing space map to physical locations within the scene. Through metaphorical mapping, signers can extend the use of classifier constructions and signing space to describe abstract concepts and relations.

In addition, signers can create spatial models within signing space to represent both abstract and concrete information. Such models make certain types of spatial reasoning very efficient because of the schematic mapping between the spatial relations of the hands in signing space and the spatial relations of objects within the spatial mental model that must be constructed from the signed discourse. Within the abstract domain, signers associate conceptual elements with locations in signing space and manipulate the form of signs to indicate relations between these elements. Individual signers can create such spatial models for specific purposes within a discourse; for example, to illustrate the temporal order of procedures or to help explain physical change and states of matter. However, in some instances, the mapping between signing space and an abstract domain becomes conventionalized. Time lines are not invented by individual signers but are always available for use. Signers can evoke a time line by articulating a temporal sign at a particular location in signing space, and each time line has a particular temporal semantics associated with it. Finally, the use of signing space to represent order information appears to influence the architecture of working memory for ASL signers. Spatial coding for order is not available for speech-based working memory (e.g., Li and Lewandowsky, 1995), but signers appear to use signing space to represent serial order for immediate recall. Sign-based working memory appears to allow an additional resource for coding serial order: signing space.

To conclude, ASL signers do not appear to violate or contradict any of the principles discussed in this volume regarding how space is co-opted to represent abstract relations and concepts. Signers exploit the same type of analogical mapping between space and abstract concepts found to be used for temporal reasoning (Gentner, this volume), for reasoning about conceptual relations (Gattis, this volume), and to depict non-spatial information (Tversky, this volume). In addition, language modality appears to have cognitive consequences with respect to these domains. The availability of signing space as a cognitive resource for coding both spatial and abstract information may influence the ease of spatial reasoning, affect the coding within linguistic working memory, and may encourage the conceptualization of abstract information via spatial metaphor and analogical mapping.

Acknowledgments

This work was supported by the National Science Foundation (Linguistics Program, SBR-9510963) and the National Institute for Child Health and Human Development (HD-13249). I thank Steve McCullough for help with the illustrations, and I thank Ed Klima for many discussions of issues presented in this paper.

Notes

1. Words in small capital letters represent English glosses for ASL signs. Multiword glosses connected by hyphens are used when more than one English word is required to translate a single sign. Hyphens between letters (e.g., G-A-S) indicate a fingerspelled word. English translations are given in quotes.

2. Some ASL signers may be surprised to see the diagram as drawn here (the drawing follows Johnson-Laird, 1996). We are finding that ASL signers interpret the English words *in front of* and *behind* differently than monolingual English speakers with respect to a spatial layout of this sort (where there is no occlusion of objects). Given the English description, ASL signers tend to draw a diagram that looks like this:

f   c
s   p   k

3. Engberg-Pedersen (1993) also observed a *mixed time line* for Danish Sign Language which is a mixture of the deictic, anaphoric, and sequencing lines. The mixed time line is used when "expressing a sequence of moments in time or a period of time seen from a point before its start (p. 88)." However, whether this time line exists for ASL is not clear.

4. The verbs in this English translation are marked for tense, but the ASL verbs were not. Also, if the discourse described here were produced by a seated signer, the signer's upper body would lean along the anaphoric time line, and signs would be articulated at appropriate locations along this time line, but the location of the signer's body would not change.

5. I thank Carol Padden for providing me with the videotape of this lecture, and I thank Claire Ramsey for bringing some of the examples of signing on the chalkboard to my attention.

Chapter 7

Children's Mathematics: Lost and Found in Space

Peter Bryant and Sarah Squire

The first mathematical experiences that children have are with concrete objects. They count the buses going by or the steps that they are climbing (Nunes and Bryant, 1996). They share sweets, more or less fairly, between themselves (Frydman and Bryant, 1988; Miller, 1984). They add toys to their collections of toys—one more doll, two more toy cars.

These concrete objects—the objects of the child's first mathematical manipulations—are out there in space and inevitably there is a close connection between many of the child's manipulations and the spatial arrangement of the objects that he or she is manipulating. The higher the step that the child has reached, the greater its number will be (at any rate when the child is going upstairs): the more friends the child has to share the sweets with, the smaller will be each of their portions. The greater the new addition to the pile of toys, the higher that pile becomes.

For a long time now psychologists have recognized the possibility of a connection between the way that children think about space and their understanding of mathematics, but they have usually done so in a negative way. Space, for them, is part of the problem in children's mathematics, not part of the solution. Piaget, for example, and before him Binet, demonstrated that young children often confuse spatial extent with number. Young children stubbornly maintain that the longer of two rows of objects is the more numerous, when the two rows are equal in number and even when the shorter one actually contains more members. They often stick to this judgement even when one-to-one correspondence lines, drawn between individual members of the two rows, show that each member of one row has its equivalent member in the other and therefore that the two are equal. Their belief that "longer is more numerous" is hard to shake.

The evidence that spatial factors can get in the way of children's mathematical judgements is incontrovertible, but it need not be just that.

It is quite conceivable that a child's understanding of space can help as well as hinder his or her mathematical prowess. Even the attention that young children give to length when making judgements about number may be an integral and important part of their mathematical development. The longer of two rows is the more numerous when their relative density is the same. Young children, of course, tend to ignore differences in density, when they should be attending to density as well as to length, but this may be an essential part of development. First they recognize length, and then they learn to qualify it by attending to density as well. It may not be a question of them learning to ignore length as Piaget and many others claim. They may begin by using one of these important spatial cues and then progress to using both.

There is a good reason for pursuing the strangely neglected possibility of a connection in children's development between their spatial and their mathematical understanding. It is the relational nature of children's spatial ideas. That mathematical understanding is about relations goes without saying. But it is just as true to say that children's grasp of space is relational too. Young children can tell and remember whether one thing is above or behind or at the side of another (Bryant, 1974; Pears and Bryant, 1990): they can judge whether two lines are parallel or not. They have no difficulty in realising that one pile of bricks is higher than another or further away than another (Bryant, 1974). They can even co-ordinate spatial and temporal relations with great skill. If you're on a walk and can't find a camera, and you work out that you last saw it at the white gate and realised that you no longer had it when you were on the bridge, you can conclude that the critical area to look for it is between the gate and the bridge. So can a four-year-old child (Wellman, Somerville & Haake, 1979).

In this chapter we shall make the case that the spatial relations which children use so proficiently make a powerful impact on their mathematical thinking. We shall argue that many of their mathematical successes and some of their difficulties too can be explained in terms of the spatial cues that they are using to help them solve various mathematical problems.

7.1   Children's Understanding of Spatial Relations

The theoretical framework that we start with rests on a distinction between relative and absolute values. In space relative values like "further away than," "parallel to," "in line with," "more dense (in texture) than," "higher than," "along that trajectory" are important, and so are absolute values like "6 meters away," "an oblique with a 30° slope," "12 centimetres long." Our thesis is that from the start children are rather good at taking in and remembering spatial relations, but have immense and lasting difficulties when it comes to absolute spatial values. How then do they remember anything about an object's actual position, its height or its orientation? How do they compare an object which they saw before with another object which they see now along these dimensions if they can't remember their absolute values? They cope with these demands, we claim, by making deductive inferences about space.

These spatial inferences are based on stable features of the environment—the floor, the table top, the kitchen door, the cot's bars—which are always there and pretty invariant from the point of view of spatial dimensions. They are usually in the same place and their size and the orientation of their different bits, barring the occasional earthquake, is always the same. Children recognize and come to rely on these stabilities, so our theory goes, and begin to match them with less common and often less reliable perceptual experiences. They notice if something matches a stable feature along some spatial dimension or other—if it is in line with the stable feature or not, for example, or if it is parallel to this feature or not (see also the chapter by Liben in this volume which does refer to the importance of landmarks in spatial tasks). Then they use transitive inferences to compare successive percepts through these comparisons. If the principal axis of object A is always parallel to the door frame and if object B's principal axis is also always parallel to the door frame, then the child can work out that all three are always in the same orientation even though he or she hasn't ever seen A and B together. If he or she sees that A is parallel to the door frame and that B is not, then he or she can deduce that A and B have different orientations. These two inferences can be expressed as (1) $A = D$, $B = D$, therefore $A = B$; and (2) $A = D$, $B \neq D$, therefore $A \neq B$.

The relative judgements that are put together in these spatial inferences are either dichotomous or trichotomous. In the examples that we have given, they are dichotomous: either two lines are parallel or they are not, either two dots are in line or they are not. In other cases there are three possible relations: for example nearer than, at the same distance as, further away than. Inferences based on dichotomous relations therefore can pick up regularities when either one or two percepts produce a match signal (i.e. are the same along a spatial dimension as the stable feature) but they are less help when both percepts produce a mismatch signal. In this case the child cannot tell whether the two percepts are the same or not. He or she needs at least one match to make an informative perceptual inference. In much the same way the inferences based on three possible relations are informative when $A = B$ and $B = C$, when $A > B$ and $B > C$, when $A = B$ and $B > C$ and when $A > B$ and $B = C$. In all these cases the children can make a legitimate transitive inference to decide whether A and C are the same or one is larger than the other. However, the child, and anyone else, will have nothing to conclude about A versus C when $A > B$ and $B < C$ and when $A < B$ and $B > C$ (see also the chapter in this volume by McGonigle and Chalmers on the abilities of children to draw transitive inferences).

We should like to review, very briefly, some of the early work which led to this idea. One set of results came from experiments on the perception and memory of the orientation of straight lines (Bryant, 1974). It had been known for a long time that children have some difficulty in discriminating oblique lines from each other, even though they can tell apart horizontal from vertical lines and horizontal and vertical lines from any oblique. Two assumptions had dominated discussion of this rather specific difficulty. One was that the difficulty is a problem of immediate perception: children simply could not see that there were two oblique lines, pointing in different directions. The second assumption reflected psychologists' obsession with the symmetry of the central nervous system: it was always assumed that the difficulty was something to do with mirror-image perception and so strong was this assumption that it was never actually tested: children were simply asked to discriminate mirror image obliques and if they could not, well that must be a mirror-image problem—no question about it.

Both assumptions turned out to be quite wrong and their disproof led to the theory that we are presenting now. The children's difficulty with obliques is not one of immediate perception since they discriminate simultaneously presented obliques perfectly well even at the age of 4 years (Bryant, 1974; Over and Over, 1967). But they do have problems in successive discriminations in which the standard is presented on its own and then the child is given two choices after a short interval, one of which is in the same orientation as the standard line and the other not. In these they remember and discriminate horizontals from verticals, and horizontals and verticals from obliques with hardly a mistake, but not obliques from obliques. Secondly this difficulty with obliques has hardly anything to do with symmetry: young children have as much difficulty in discriminating a left pointing oblique with a 20° slope from a right pointing oblique with a 50° slope as they do two opposite pointing obliques both with a 45° slope. It makes no difference that the first pair of lines are not mirror images of each other and the second are (Bryant, 1974).

These clear results suggest that children can remember verticals and horizontals and obliques differently, since they can discriminate all three from each other, but they do not remember the slope, or even the direction, of obliques. The reason for the apparently specific memory for horizontals and obliques and the rather gross categorisation of obliques could be a matter of stable environmental features. In these studies the lines were drawn on square cards and so the vertical lines paralleled the sides of the cards and the horizontals the top and bottom (two different match signals) while the obliques were not parallel to any side (a consistent mis-match signal). Thus transitive inferences using these match mismatch signals would lead to a horizontal-vertical discrimination (two different match signals), discriminations between horizontals or verticals and obliques (a match-mismatch difference) but not between two obliques (two identical mismatch signals).

The way to test this is to provide stable cues for oblique lines, which we did by providing cards which always had a distinctive red oblique line, present in all the cards and always in the same orientation. In some oblique-oblique discriminations (always successive ones) one of the choice obliques was parallel to the stable oblique line and in others neither was. When one of the oblique lines was parallel to the stable feature the children could make the successive discrimination between obliques perfectly well. When neither paralleled this framework feature they were in trouble again. In match-mismatch terms the easy discriminations were between match and mismatch signals and the difficult—usually impossible—ones between two mismatch signals.

Another of our studies (Bryant, 1974) which took much the same form was about position—in this case about the position of a dot on a card. The dots were either to the left or the right of the card and either in the top half or in the bottom half, and the child had to tell us in which of two choice cards the dot was in the same position as in the standard card. When all three cards were side by side in simultaneous discriminations, the left-right discriminations were very hard for the young children but the up down discriminations were very easy. But when they were lined up vertically the left-right discriminations were easy and the up-down ones

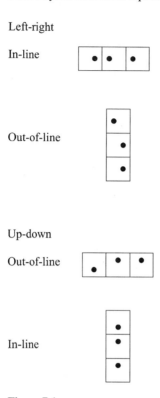

Figure 7.1
Left-right and up-down discriminations.

very hard (Figure 7.1). This was not a mirror image problem because the difficult left right discriminations were as hard when the two cards were not symmetrical around the vertical axis as when they were and the difficult up-down discriminations were as difficult when they were not symmetrical around the horizontal axis as when they were.

Our explanation is simple and we cannot see any alternative to it. When one choice dot is in line with the standard and the other not the children can manage: when all three are in line with each other the children are completely at sea. Therefore, the cue that they use to plot the dots' positions in the cards is whether or not they are in line. In line is a match signal: out of line is a mismatch signal.

When we added a vertical or a horizontal dot as a stable framework feature in all three cards the difficult discriminations immediately became easy whenever one of the choice card dots lined up with this stable feature and the other did not (match vs. mismatch). But the children's difficulties stubbornly persisted whenever neither choice dot lined up with this stable feature (two mismatches).

The evidence that the children were actually making transitive inferences about space in these tasks was indirect, but the idea was bolstered by some other work (Bryant & Trabasso, 1971), done in a completely different context, on transitive inferences. We made the controversial claim that we had shown that pre-school children can make transitive inferences about quantity provided that they could remember the premises that they had to put together to make the inference.

It was several years before we got around to demonstrating that children can make transitive inferences about a more obviously spatial continuum. We (Pears & Bryant, 1990) gave children a tower building task. The children had to build a tower of coloured bricks arranged in a certain order (e.g. red at the top, green next below it and so on). The children had to work out the order by looking at pairs of bricks: so if the order from the top down was A, B, C, D, E we gave them A/B, B/C, C/D, and D/E pairs of bricks (where "/" means above). Our interest was not actually in how well the children constructed the towers (which they did quite proficiently) but in their answers to some questions that we asked them before they did their building (Figure 7.2). We asked them, for example, which would be higher in the tower that they were going to put together, B or D? This is an inferential question. B and D are not together in any of the pairs that they can see: their relative position can only be worked out through their relations to C (B will be above it, D below). We found that four-year-old French children (naturally we did this work in Paris because that was where Piaget (1929) first tried out transitivity problems on young children) made these inferences quite successfully when working with 4, 5 and 6 brick towers. We think that this demonstrates that children do make transitive inferences about this spatial dimension at least. It could be argued that inferences about space do not satisfy the rather stringent criteria for transitivity set by Piaget or by Halford, both of whom require that children should be able to combine relational judgements about quantity without the help of concrete cues. However, the children had to be able to put two relational premises about a continuum together in order to succeed in our task, and that seems to us to be the essence of a transitive inference.

1. The arrangement of the premise towers

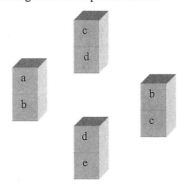

2. The material given to the child

3. The inferential question: which is the higher (lower)?
    A?C   B?D   C?E

4. The tower that the child is asked to build

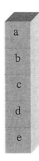

Figure 7.2
The four steps in the Pears and Bryant spatial transitivity task with 5 values. The
letters on the blocks represent different colours.

7.2   Number: Spatial and Temporal One-to-One Correspondence

The theory that children rely on relational judgements whose power they extend with the use of inferences is in the end a theory about their understanding not just of space but also of a lot of their cognitive activities and particularly those in which spatial information plays a part (see also the chapter by McGonigle and Chalmers in this volume for a similar point). To make this point we want to start with children's understanding of number and the way that they set about comparing the number of objects in different sets. The most straightforward way of showing that children rely on relations rather than on absolute information with number as well as with spatial continua would be to show that children are able to say whether there are more objects in one set than in another long before they can decide how many there actually are in each set. But the story about children's comparisons of number is more complex and more interesting than that.

It is certainly true that children of five and even six years apparently have difficulty in making absolute judgements about number. Children who have known how to count small numbers for some years nevertheless are remarkably reluctant to count the number of objects in each of two sets that they are asked to compare (Frye, Braisby, Lowe, Maroudas & Nicholls, 1989; Saxe, 1979; Sophian, 1988).

However, at first sight, their relational judgements are just as suspect. To make a reliable judgement about the relative number of two sets you have to use one-to-one correspondence: in other words you have to see whether each item in one set can be paired off with an equivalent item in the other. If each item in one set can be paired with one in the other and none is unpaired in either set, the two are equal in number. If not, the one which contains unmatched items has more. This use of one-to-one correspondence is a genuinely relational comparison: you know whether the two numbers are the same or not but this does not tell you how many items there are in either set.

The trouble for a simple relational hypothesis is that children are just as reluctant to use one-to-one correspondence as they are to count when comparing the number in two sets of objects. Piaget (1952), for example, showed that five and six-year-olds who are given one row of objects and asked to set up another row with the same number of items in it, usually match the two rows in length and ignore one-to-one correspondence. The fatal attraction of the treacherous length cue is as strong when the child is given two rows side by side and asked to compare them. If the rows are equal in length and unequal in number young children say they have the same number of items as each other: if they are unequal in length but equal in number, the child says that the longer one is more. As we have already noted, Piaget and Inhelder (1966) showed, and Cowan and Daniels (1989) confirmed, that children continue to make this mistake when one-to-one correspondence is emphasised by lines being drawn between individual items in each set. Still they ignore this correct cue and use the inappropriate length cue instead. It's the sort of thing that gives space a bad name.

One might feel compelled to abandon the relational hypothesis about number comparisons if it were not for the obvious fact that children do use one-to-one correspondence with conspicuous success, but in another context. They share, and when they share they do so on a one-to-one basis—one for you, one for me—until the entire set of items is shared out. This is a matter of common observation, but several studies have confirmed that it is true of 4- and 5-year-old children (Desforges & Desforges, 1980; Frydman & Bryant, 1988; Miller, 1984). The reason why children take so easily to temporal correspondence (one-to-one sharing) when they have such difficulty with spatial one-to-one correspondence is not known at the moment but it may have something to do with social conventions which children adopt at an early age. But if this is the case they seem nevertheless to have a reasonable understanding of what they are doing: they do not seem just to be blindly adopting a procedure which they have learned in a rote manner.

We (Frydman & Bryant, 1988) gave children a variant of the sharing task in which we asked children to share out chocolate (actually plastic bricks) to two recipients, but with the rider that one of the recipients (A) preferred the chocolate in units (one piece at a time) while the other (B) liked them in two piece nuggets. Then we gave the child a set of single and of double bricks, asking him or her to make sure that the two recipients ended up with exactly the same amount of chocolate as each other. We did this because we argued that if the child is blindly using a procedure, learned from others, he or she would give one single to A and one double to B, another single to A and another double to B and so on. On the other hand, if the child understands the underlying nature of sharing, he or she should be able to adjust the procedure by giving two singles to A and one double to B at each sharing round.

Many four-year-olds but very few of the five-year-olds fell into this trap. Even the four-year-olds learned to escape the trap very quickly when we helped them to do so with a colour cue. We gave some of them the same task but this time some of the singles were yellow and some blue, and all the doubles were made out of one yellow and one blue. Without further encouragement nearly all of these children began to put out two singles (one blue, and one yellow) for A and one double (consisting perforce of one blue and one yellow) in each sharing round. (Another group who were given yellow and blue bricks, but for whom the doubles were either two yellows or two blues made no such change.) More importantly, the group who learned from the colour cues also transferred their newly acquired knowledge to a subsequent task in which all the bricks were the same colour. Evidently they could learn about one-to-one correspondence very quickly.

This research on sharing suggests two things. One is that children do use relational cues even for as sophisticated a continuum as number. The other is that, almost ironically, their sensitivity to spatial cues can sometimes divert them away from the right relational comparisons and towards the wrong ones.

7.3   Space and Division

Sharing is a form of dividing. In fact, the connection between sharing and division is such a common-place that "sharing" is the term that teachers use at first when they introduce children to division in UK schools: the "division" word comes later. Yet, even though children's sharing seems at first to be based on temporal rather than on spatial one-to-one correspondence, it seems quite plausible to us that children's ideas about space must play part in their learn about division. The most tangible examples of division in a child's life (dividing a cake, a room, a play area) are bound to involve space.

This semantic connection is a useful starting point for thinking about children's ideas about division, because it is easy to see that though sharing is dividing, dividing is a great deal more than just sharing. In one sense sharing and division are truly synonymous: in another they are not. When someone shares out sweets to two or more recipients he or she is certainly dividing the original set—the dividend, and he or she can be sure that the recipients will end up with equal quantities. But that is as far as sharing per se will go. The sharer knows the relation between each recipient set of sweets (they are equal), but nothing more about the amount in each set—the quotient.

This is not a distinction between relative and absolute quantities. In fact, we are distinguishing a simple from a more complex relation, and here the complex relation is the relation between the divisor and the quotient. *It is a fundamental principle of division, and one which is essential to the proper understanding of division, that with the dividend held constant there is an inverse relation between the divisor and the quotient.* If we start with two sets of 12 sweets and share one set to 3 recipients and the other to 4 recipients, each recipient in the first group (smaller divisor) will get more sweets (bigger quotient) than each recipient in the second group. This seems obvious to any adult, but we cannot assume that the successful sharer will understand this crucial relationship. The successful sharer will know that all the recipients within each group have the same amount as each other (the simple relation in sharing), but he or she may not understand that the recipients in the larger group will each get less than the recipients in the smaller group.

We (Correa, Nunes & Bryant, 1998) have established that 5- and 6-year-old children, who have absolutely no problem about sharing correctly, nevertheless often fail completely to grasp the inverse divisor-quotient principle. Our measure of this form of understanding was a task in which we established that we had two absolutely equal dividends A and B: these were sets of sweets (Figure 7.3) and in different trials there were either 12 or 24 sweets. In one version of the task (partitive division) we showed the child the two equal dividends (A and B) and then we explained that we would share out A to one group of rabbits and B to another. The rabbits were assembled so that the child could see how many there were in each group. On half the trials the number of rabbits in the two groups was the same: in the other there were more rabbits in one group than in the other.

We wanted to know whether the child would realise that each rabbit in the more numerous group would end up with a smaller number of sweets than each rabbit in the less numerous group, and to find this out we actually shared out the sweets putting them in baskets which were attached to the rabbits' backs. Then we removed the screen and asked the children whether the rabbits in one group had as many or more or less sweets than the rabbits in the other.

Will each rabbit in A get the same as each rabbit in B, or will the rabbits in one group get more than the rabbits in the other?

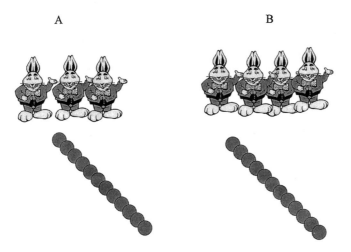

Figure 7.3
Partitive division.

Most of the 5-year-old children, about half of the 6-year-old children, and a minority of the 7-year-old children appeared to have no idea of the inverse divisor-quotient relationship. Among the five-year-olds a frequent mistake was to say that the rabbits in each group would get as much as each other when the groups were unequal in number and therefore the quotient differed between the two groups. The older children, in contrast, tended to make a different kind of mistake: in trials when the two groups were unequal in number, they asserted that the rabbits in the more numerous group would each receive more sweets than those in the less numerous group. We think that this change means that the younger children for the most part did not realise that the size of the divisor had any effect on the quotient, whereas some of the older children realised that the divisor does have an effect but got the relationship the wrong way round. The greater the divisor, the greater the quotient—seemed to be the principle that they were following.

Will the same number or a different number of rabbits in
the two groups get a portion of sweets?

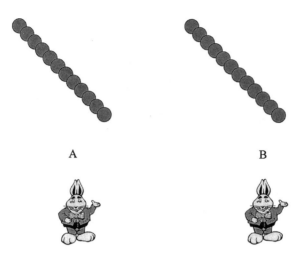

Figure 7.4
Quotitive division.

In the partitive task that we have just described the number of recipients is the divisor and the portion of sweets is the quotient. It is the other way round in another kind of task which is called a quotitive task. Quotitive tasks are portion control tasks. In a quotitive task you decide that each recipient will get, say, 3 sweets and you go on doling out 3-sweet portions until you run out of sweets. So the greater the allotted portion of sweets the smaller will be the number of recipients fortunate enough to receive a portion. So the size of the portion is the divisor, and the number of recipients the quotient.

We (Correa et al., 1998) also gave young children a quotitive task (Figure 7.4) in which again there were two equal dividends. We told the children that each dividend was for a different group of rabbits and that a particular portion would be allotted for each group. Sometimes the portion was the same for each group and sometimes it was different. In either case we would share out these portions among the rabbits until the dividend was exhausted, and we asked the child to think about how many rabbits in each group would receive portions. Then we actually did this sharing behind a screen and asked the child whether the same number of rabbits in each group were given sweets or whether more rabbits were fortunate in one group than in the other.

This was a harder question than the partitive one, but nevertheless we found much the same pattern of results. Most of the children in each of the three age groups (5-, 6- and 7-years) showed no sign of understanding the inverse divisor-quotient rule, but the number of children who did consistently well increased with age (3/20, 5 years; 8/20, 6 years; 9/20, 7 years). Looking at the types of errors we found that the proportion of mistakes which took the form of saying that the number of recipients was the same in each group, when it wasn't, was high in the youngest group. The proportion of mistakes which took the form of saying that more rabbits were given sweets in the group with the larger portion than in the group with the smaller one increased with age: 95.6% of the 6-year-olds' mistakes and 100% of the 7-year-olds' took this form. Thus again children seem to change from a stage at which they think that the size of the divisor has no bearing on the size of the quotient to one in which they think that the larger the divisor is the larger the quotient will be as well.

So, we have to draw a line between being able to divide by sharing and understanding the relations between dividend, divisor and quotient in division. One is no guarantee of the other, and it is clear that children have a great deal to learn about divisors and quotients. How do they learn about these more complex relationships? In our view spatial experiences play a part. Certainly we have evidence now that the way in which objects are grouped or children group objects for themselves can have a considerable effect on children's judgements about the divisor and the quotient in a division problem. This evidence comes from a recent series of experiments by Sarah Squire on children's ability to distinguish the quotient from the divisor.

In these experiments she allocated some items to recipients, and then asked the child how many items each recipient would get. The recipients were dolls and when she did her allocations, she put the items in boxes. There were two kinds of allocation. In one, which we call *grouping by the divisor*, each doll had her own box and when the sharing was done there was the same amount in each box: so, with 12 items and 4 dolls there were 4 boxes each of which contained 3 items (Figure 7.5a). The quotient was the number of items in each box and the divisor corresponded to the number of boxes. Therefore in the *grouping by the divisor* condition the spatial groupings—the number of containers—coincided with the divisor.

(a) Grouping by the divisor

(b) Grouping by the quotient

Figure 7.5
Two ways of grouping the objects to be shared (for the result of 12 ÷ 4).

In the other condition, which we call *grouping by the quotient*, Sarah Squire also put the items in boxes but this time put an item for each doll in each box. So, if there were 12 sweets and 4 dolls, there were 3 boxes each of which held 4 items (Figure 7.5b). Here the quotient was the number of boxes and the divisor corresponded to the number of items in each box. Thus, in the *grouping by the quotient* condition the spatial groupings corresponded with the quotient, not with the divisor.

Notice that the spatial relationships between the items and the recipients were the same in both conditions, but the spatial boundaries (in fact the gestalts) were different. So were the results: in this, as in several other experiments with concrete material, the children did a great deal better in the *grouping by the divisor* condition than in the *grouping by the quotient* condition. These differences were very great but also diminished with age: there was a gentle improvement with age in the *grouping by the divisor* condition, but a much more marked one in the *grouping by the quotient* condition.

Many of the mistakes that the children made in the *grouping by the quotient* condition took the form of failing to distinguish the divisor from the quotient and giving the divisor as the quotient. So, when there were 4 recipients, and 3 boxes (the quotient) each with 4 items (the divisor), a common error was to state that each recipient would be given 4 items.

This result is highly reliable. It happened again, for example, in another experiment where the tasks were presented on paper, using pictures of the dolls, the boxes and the sweets. In one part of this experiment neither the boxes nor the items were lined up with the recipients, as they had been in the previous experiments. This time the alignment of the boxes was perpendicular to that of the recipients (Figure 7.6). Again the *grouping by the quotient* condition was much the harder one, again the children identified the divisor as the quotient very frequently in that condition, and again there was quite a sharp improvement with age in the more difficult *grouping by the quotient* condition. So we found the same effect in the original spatial arrangement and in the spatial arrangement where the alignment of the boxes was perpendicular to that of the recipients (Figure 7.7).

What are we to make of this difference between the conditions and the evident difficulty that young children have in distinguishing the divisor from the quotient? One explanation, and the one that we favor, is that young children base their judgements on the two sets of spatially defined entities, which in these tasks were the *recipients* and the *containers*. When the number of recipients and the number of containers co-incide the children have no difficulty in working out that the number of items in each container is the quotient. On the other hand when the number of containers and the number of recipients are different, the children have to break up the gestalt by working out that one item in each container corresponds to one recipient and also to continue to treat the containers as entities, since the number of containers is actually the quotient. In spatial terms the *grouping by the quotient* condition is much more complex than the *grouping by the divisor* one. Another way of putting this is that in the easier condition the initial grouping coincides with what will be the final grouping when the sweets are divided between the recipients.

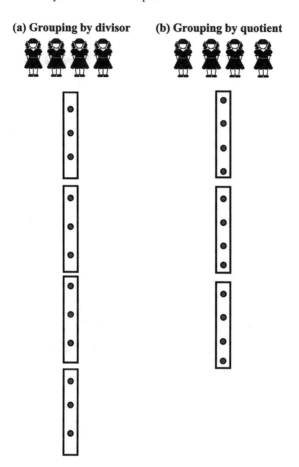

Figure 7.6
Tasks where the alignment of the groups is perpendicular to that of the dolls.

In the more difficult condition the initial grouping does not co-incide with the final grouping because the groups coincide with the quotient and not with the divisor.

The test of this hypothesis, it seemed to us, was to compare partitive with quotitive division again. Quotitive tasks provide the crucial test because here the *recipients* co-incide with the quotient not with the divisor. This means that the number of the final groups co-incides with the quotient and therefore that children will find the task easier if the initial grouping is by the quotient and not by the divisor.

Five-year-olds

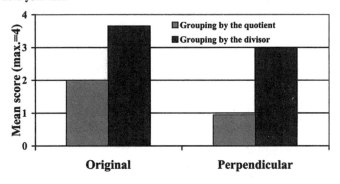

Six-year-olds

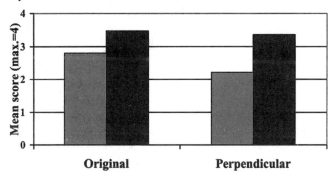

Seven-year-olds

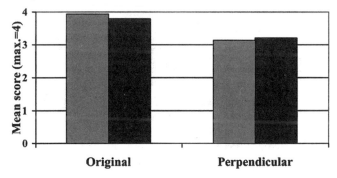

Figure 7.7
Children's performance in tasks in the original spatial arrangement and when the alignment of boxes was perpendicular to that of the recipients.

To make this point concretely, we will describe our partitive and quotitive tasks in Sarah Squire's next experiment. These tasks were about seating a class of girls at tables for the school dinner. In both tasks the dividend was the number of girls to be seated. In the partitive task the divisor was the number of tables available and the quotient which the child had to identify was therefore the number of girls who would have to sit at each table. For example, for the sum $12 \div 4$, the problem would involve twelve girls sitting around four tables. So the final grouping is by tables and the number of tables is the divisor.

In the quotitive task the children were told that each table took a certain number of girls (that number was therefore the divisor) and the question was the number of tables that would be needed to seat all the girls. The equivalent problem for $12 \div 4$ in this case would involve twelve girls who had to sit so that there were 4 girls on each table. The number of tables was the quotient here and the groups of girls were the *recipients*. So the final grouping is again by tables and the number of tables is the quotient.

If our idea is right that the children find it easiest when the original grouping co-incides with what will be the final grouping after the division has taken place, then in both tasks the children should do better when the number of original groups of girls co-incides with the number of tables in the final grouping. This means that in the partitive tasks the children will do better in the grouping by divisor condition and in the quotitive task they will do better in the grouping by quotient condition. In both of these cases the children can match the groups of children to the final arrangement of tables without having to make any mental re-arrangement to get the correct answer.

In both tasks we ran the same two conditions as in the earlier experiments (Figures 7.8 and 7.9). We presented pictures of the girls (the dividend) in groups. In the *grouping by the divisor condition* the number of groups co-incides with the divisor (the number of tables in the partitive condition, and the number of children at each table in the quotitive task). In the *grouping by the quotient condition* the number of groups co-incides with the quotient (the number of children at each table in the partitive task, and the number of tables in the quotitive task).

The results were as we predicted. When the children were given the partitive task they did much better in the *grouping by the divisor* than in the grouping by the quotient condition: when they were given the quotitive task they did much better in the *grouping by the quotient* than in the group-

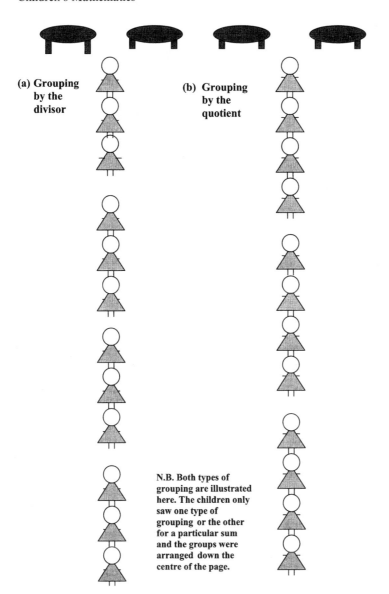

(a) Grouping by the divisor

(b) Grouping by the quotient

N.B. Both types of grouping are illustrated here. The children only saw one type of grouping or the other for a particular sum and the groups were arranged down the centre of the page.

Figure 7.8
Partitive division for the result of 12 ÷ 4.

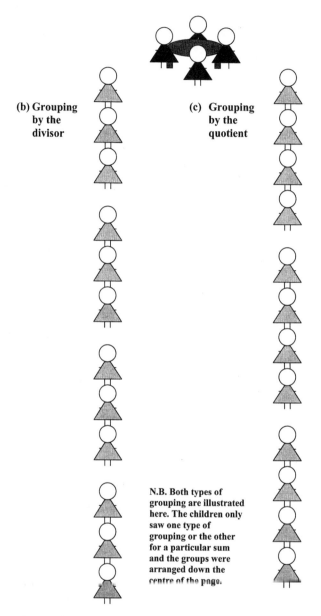

(b) Grouping by the divisor

(c) Grouping by the quotient

N.B. Both types of grouping are illustrated here. The children only saw one type of grouping or the other for a particular sum and the groups were arranged down the centre of the page.

Figure 7.9
Quotitive division for the result of 12 ÷ 4.

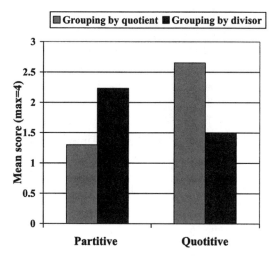

Figure 7.10
Children's scores in the partitive and quotitive tasks with the different ways of grouping the girls.

ing by the divisor condition (Figure 7.10). To put it another way—our way—they prospered when the original spatial arrangement co-incided with the number of tables, and they made mistakes when this was not so.

Children start with simple relations and acquire the ability to work with more complex ones. In this development spatial thinking is of very great importance. To understand the more complex relation—the relation between the divisor and the quotient—the child must transcend spatial groupings and re-arrange his or her spatial representations.

7.4   Space and Proportions

Another distinction between simple and complex relations is the distinction between all-or-none relations, like bigger and smaller, and ratios and proportions. It is one thing to know that A is bigger than B and quite another to work out that A is twice as big as B. Nothing in what we have presented so far suggests that children can manage the second, more formidable, kind of comparison. But some of our work (Spinillo & Bryant, 1991) suggests that on the basis of relational codes children can take in some ratios but not others. We started with the argument that, with size, children can take in and act on the relations *same as, larger than* or *smaller than*. We then deduced that, in a quantity which is divided into two parts, children should be able to work out whether the two parts are equal, or whether one part takes up more space, and is therefore bigger, than the other. This led us to the idea that children might be able to act on the distinction between *half, more than half* and *less than half*.

An illustration of the task that we gave 6-, 7- and 8-year-old children is the best way to show why we concentrated on the half-boundary. We gave the children a small picture of a box divided into a blue and a white section (Figure 7.11). In the example we are using here the left half was white and the right half blue. At the same time we showed the children two quite large boxes consisting of many blue and white bricks. In these boxes the top part was white and the bottom part blue.

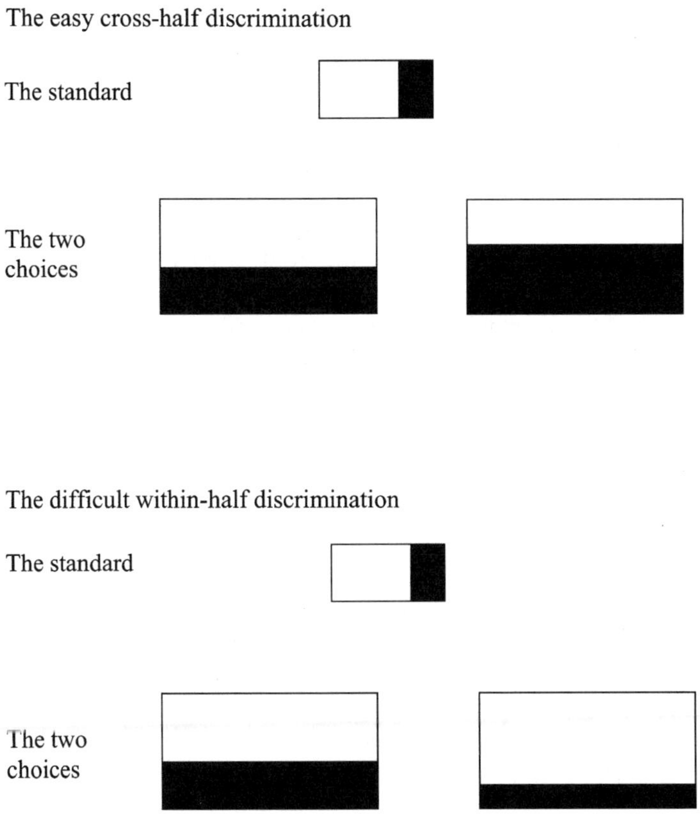

The easy cross-half discrimination

The standard

The two choices

The difficult within-half discrimination

The standard

The two choices

Figure 7.11
The cross-half (easy) and within-half (difficult) discriminations in a size ratio task (Spinillo & Bryant, 1991).

We explained to each child that the picture was a picture of one of these two boxes, but that since the time when the picture was taken the spatial arrangement of the bricks in the box had been changed so that whereas it was divided into left-right sections at the time of the picture, now it was divided into up-down sections (or vice versa).

The task that we gave the children was to say which box was represented in the picture, and we argued that this was a genuine ratio task since the child could only solve it on the basis of the blue-white size ratio. We had eliminated other cues like shape and absolute size.

In some trials the discriminations that the children had to make either involved the half-boundary directly or they crossed it, and we argued that these trials should be quite easy for young children. When the trials involved the half-boundary (*half trials*) the blue-white ratio was equal in one of the two choice boxes (either the correct or the incorrect choice) and not, of course, in the other. We argued that this should be easy for the children because they would see that the blue white relation was the same in one box and different in the other box, and work out that the correct box had the same blue-white relation (same or different) as the one in the picture.

Similarly, when there was more blue than white in one box and more white than blue in the other (*cross-half trials*) , the children, we thought,

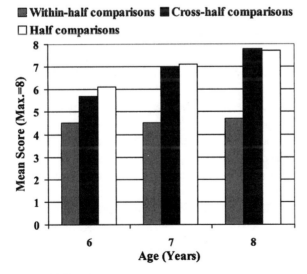

Figure 7.12
Mean scores in Spinillo and Bryant's Proportional Judgement tasks (1991).

should again have no difficulty. Again the blue-white relation was palpably different in the two boxes.

However in a third set of trials the blue-white ratio was different in the two boxes, but the blue-white relation was the same (*within-half trials*): there was always more blue than white or more white than blue. Here, we argued, the children should be in difficulty: when the discrimination did not cross the half-boundary, the children's relational codes would be no help.

We found that the *within-half* trials were indeed a great deal harder than the *cross-half* and the *half* trials (Figure 7.12), which means that the half-boundary is crucial in children's proportional judgements. Some spatial arrangements allow young children to use a relational code to distinguish proportions: others prevent them from doing so.

7.5   Summary

The experiments that we have described show that some spatial arrangements help and others hinder children's solution to various mathematical problems. Young children are adept at using simple, all-or-none spatial relations, and the principles of gestalt psychology provide a good account of the way that they do so. Add to this their evident ability to combine relationships in deductive and transitive inferences and you have already a formidable set of mechanisms for learning about the environment.

This menu of simple relations-plus-inferences, however, is plainly not enough for learning about mathematics. In every aspect of learning about number, and about additive and multiplicative reasoning, children need to transcend and to extend their existing relational strategies. What they have at the start gives them a toe-hold in mathematical problems (they manage temporal but not spatial one-to-one correspondence, they identify the quotient when the dividend is grouped by recipients, they distinguish ratios which cross the half boundary). The new, and more complex, relations which they have to struggle with and learn about, in order to make any progress in mathematics, can also be expressed in spatial terms. Our developmental data show that most children do indeed make steady progress with these new relations in the early school years. How they do so, and to what extent this new learning is based on spatial experiences, are questions that we still have to answer.

Part III

Adapting Space for Abstract Thought

Chapter 8

Spatial Metaphors in Temporal Reasoning

Dedre Gentner

We often talk about time in terms of space: of looking *forward* to a brighter tomorrow, of troubles that lie *behind* us, or of music that played all *through* the night. The language of spatial motion also seems to be imported into time, as when we say that the holidays are *approaching*, or that a theory was proposed *ahead* of its time. Many researchers have noted an orderly and systematic correspondence between the domains of *time* and *space* in language (Bennett, 1975; Bierswisch, 1967; Clark, 1973; Fillmore, 1971; Lehrer, 1990; Traugott, 1978). The following examples illustrate the parallel use of static spatial and temporal expressions:

at the corner → *at* noon

from here *to* there → *from* two o'clock *to* four o'clock

through the tunnel → *through* the night

There appear to be some universal properties in importing language about space to describe time (Clark, 1973; Traugott, 1978). First, since time is usually conceived as one-dimensional, the spatial terms that are borrowed are uni-dimensional terms (e.g., *front/back, up/down*) rather than terms that suggest two or three dimensions (e.g., *narrow/wide, shallow/ deep*). Second, to capture temporal sequencing, directionally ordered terms such as *front/back* and *before/after* are used, rather than symmetric terms such as *right/left*. Overall, spatial terms referring to *front/back* relations are the ones most widely borrowed into the *time* domain cross-linguistically (Traugott, 1978).

There are two distinct space-time metaphoric systems in English and many other languages (see Bierwisch, 1967; Clark, 1973; Traugott, 1978): the *ego-moving* metaphor, wherein the speaker is moving along the time-line towards the future, and the *time-moving* metaphor, wherein the

Ego-Moving Metaphor

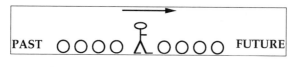

Time-Moving Metaphor

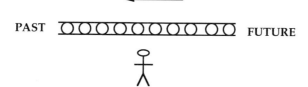

Figure 8.1
Time-moving and ego-moving metaphors.

speaker stands still and time—conceived of as a river or conveyor belt—flows by from future to past. The two systems appear based on two different spatial schemas (see Figure 8.1). Examples of the ego-moving metaphor are the following:

- I am going to do that.
- We are fast approaching the holidays.
- We must go forward with this plan.
- The Present is a Point just passed. (David Russell)

Examples of the time-moving metaphor are these:

- The years to come/the years gone by
- The holidays are coming fast.
- Night follows day.
- Time is a circus always packing up and moving away. (Ben Hecht)

The two systems lead to different assignments of *front/back* to the time-line (Clark, 1973; Fillmore, 1971; Lakoff & Johnson, 1980; Lakoff & Turner, 1989; Lehrer, 1990; Traugott, 1978). In the ego-moving system, the future is normally conceived of as in *front* and the past as *behind*. In the time-moving system, the reverse is true: time moves from the future to the past, so that past (earlier) events are in *front* and future (later) events are *behind*.

The apparent systematicity of the ego-moving and time-moving systems in language suggests that space provides a framework that is mapped into time to facilitate temporal reasoning. Such a view would be consistent with evidence that spatial representations are carried into abstract arenas such as interpretations of graphs (Gattis, in preparation; Gattis & Holyoak, 1996; Huttenlocher, 1968; Tversky, Kugelmass & Winter, 1991), and more generally with evidence that analogies from concrete domains are used in reasoning about abstract domains (Bassok & Holyoak, 1989; Gentner & Gentner, 1983; Holyoak & Thagard, 1995). Moreover, indirect evidence that space-time mappings serve conceptual functions can be found in the pervasive use of spatial representations of time across cultures in artifacts such as clocks, timelines, drawings, and musical notation (Friedman, 1990). Thus it is tempting to think of these metaphoric systems as a means of *spatial or visual reasoning*—"the use of ordered space to organize non-spatial information and generate new knowledge," as Gattis and Holyoak (1996) put it—about event sequences.

Despite the intuitive appeal of the idea of a conceptual mapping from space to time, there is good reason to be cautious here. The perils of relying on intuition in interpreting metaphorical language are delineated in Keysar and Bly's (1995) study of the illusory transparency of idioms. They gave people archaic English idioms (for which the meanings are no longer current) in different contexts. People who heard "The goose hangs high" in the context of a sad story considered that it expressed sadness (a dead goose); those who heard it in a happy story thought it expressed happiness (a plentiful larder). More tellingly, both groups were confident that they would have arrived at the same interpretations without the story; they felt that the interpretation could be derived simply from the idiom. Keysar and Bly found that the perceived transparency of an idiomatic expression (the perceived connection between the expression and its meaning) increases with repeated use of an expression, and is largely independent of whether such a connection is conceptually motivated.

Thus the mere presence of metaphorical language does not by itself tell us whether the space-time metaphor is a psychologically real conceptual mapping. For example, the temporal and spatial meanings could be represented as alternate meaning senses or even as separate homophonic lexical entries. The apparent systematicity would then be illusory, the result of post hoc regularization.

In order to establish the conceptual role of space-time mappings, we first lay out a set of possibilities, including skeptical alternatives. There are at least four broad possibilities. The strongest possibility is *system-mapping*: the abstract domain of time is organized and structured in terms of systems borrowed from the more and readily observable domain of space. That is, people actively use spatial mappings to think about time. In this case, the ego-moving and time-moving systems would constitute two distinct globally consistent systems that are metaphorically mapped from space to time and used on-line to process temporal expressions. The second possibility is *cognitive archaeology*: there are indeed two separate space-time conceptual systems, but although these systems were originally borrowed from space, they now exist as independent temporal systems. In this case the existence of two spatial-temporal systems may testify to the importance of spatial representation in the history of language. However, recourse to spatial knowledge is no longer needed during temporal reasoning.

The third possibility is *structural parallelism* in the domain representations. As Murphy (1996) suggests, it is possible that, due to inherent similarities in the referent domains of *space* and *time*, parallel relational systems evolved independently in the two domains. The common language then reflects structural alignment (Gentner & Markman, 1997; Medin, Goldstone & Gentner, 1993) between the two parallel domain representations. In this case space and time share conceptual systems, but neither is derived from the other. If either the second or third possibility holds, the ego-moving and time-moving systems could function as coherent systems within time. However, there would be no online processing asymmetry between time and space. The fourth and weakest possibility is *local lexical relations*. There are no large-scale systematic mappings; space-time metaphors consist simply of individual polysemies and/or homophonies. For example, a term like "before" would have spatial word senses, such as "spatially in front of," and also temporal word senses, such as "temporally prior to." A related possibility is that the spatial and temporal senses are stored as separate homophonic lexical entries. Either way the phenomenon would involve local lexical processes such as word-level priming and would not entail conceptual mapping.

The goal of the chapter is to evaluate these possibilities. More specifically, three experiments are discussed that use the metaphor consistency effect to discount the local lexical relations possibility. Then, other literature is reviewed that contrasts the remaining three alternatives.

1   Evidence for Conceptual Metaphors: The Metaphor Consistency Effect

How could one test for large-scale conceptual metaphoric systems? Gentner and Boronat (1992, in preparation; Gentner, 1992) devised a *mixed mapping* paradigm. This technique is based on the 'boggle' reaction that occurs when one reads mixed metaphors, such as these examples from the *New Yorker*:

• The ship of state is sailing towards a volcano.
• The U.S. and the Middle East are on parallel but nonconverging paths.

In both cases, the individual phrases are locally interpretable, yet the combination is arresting. This boggle response suggests the clash of two inconsistent metaphoric mappings.

This mixed mapping phenomenon formed the basic idea for the Gentner and Boronat technique. Our method was to set up a metaphoric mapping and then present a further statement either from the same metaphor system or a different one. If subjects are processing the metaphors as a systematic domain mapping, then the inconsistent metaphor should take longer to comprehend.

To establish a global mapping, we asked subjects to read vignettes containing a series of conceptual metaphors from a single coherent domain. The passages were presented one sentence at a time; subjects pressed a key to see the next sentence. The final test sentence was either consistent, in that the same metaphor was maintained throughout, e.g.,

Anna was boiling mad when you saw her.
Later she was doing a slow simmer.

or inconsistent, in that there was a shift of metaphor between the initial passage and the final sentence, e.g.,

Anna was a raging beast when you saw her.
Later she was doing a slow simmer.

The dependent measure was the time to read the last (metaphorical) sentence. To ensure comparability, this final test sentence was always the same; the initial setting passage was varied between conditions. In all cases the same meaning in the target domain was conveyed in the two passages.

Using this technique, Gentner and Boronat (1991, in preparation) found that subjects' reading time for the final sentence was longer following a shift between metaphoric systems. This cost in comprehension time for mixed mappings suggests that the metaphors were processed as part of global on-line mappings. Interestingly, we found this mixed mapping cost only for novel metaphors, not for highly conventional metaphors. This finding is consistent with other evidence that highly familiar metaphorical meanings are stored and processed at a lexical level (Cacciari & Tabossi, 1988; Swinney & Cutler, 1979). More broadly, it is consistent with the *career of metaphor* claim, that metaphors start as generative mappings and with increasing conventionalization come to have their metaphorical meanings stored as alternative senses of the base term (Bowdle & Gentner, 1995, 1999, in press; Gentner & Wolff, 1997, in press; Wolff & Gentner, 1992, 2000).

We interpret the mixed mapping cost as indicative of metaphors that are processed as large-scale conceptual systems. Other evidence for the existence of such global conceptual metaphors comes from studies by Allbritton, McKoon and Gerrig (1995) who found that large-scale conceptual metaphor schemas facilitated recognition judgments for schema-related sentences in text (see also Allbritton, 1995; Gattis & Holyoak, 1996; and Gibbs, 1990, 1994; but see Glucksberg, Brown & McGlone, 1993, for contradictory evidence).

We now return to *space* → *time* metaphors and to the question of their psychological status. Are *space* → *time* sequencing expressions processed as part of global conceptual systems? There is reason to doubt this possibility. As just discussed, Gentner and Boronat obtained evidence for domain mappings only when conceptual metaphors were relatively novel; tests using highly conventional metaphors (such as "get this topic across") did not reveal a significant cost for re-mapping. Glucksberg, Brown and McGlone (1993), whose metaphors were highly conventional, also found no evidence that global metaphoric systems are accessed during metaphor comprehension. Our findings suggest that their conclusion—that domain mappings are not involved in metaphoric processing—should be restricted to conventional metaphors; novel metaphors are processed as system mappings. But even so, *space* → *time* metaphors are highly conventional. Indeed, these metaphors are almost invisible: people are generally surprised to find that they use two different space-time mappings in everyday language. It therefore seems quite likely that, even if the two mapping metaphors were once active in the dim history of language, they now are stored simply as alternate word-senses of the spatial terms. If this is the case, we would not expect to see a mixed metaphor effect when space-time metaphors are used.

A second reason for caution is that the contrast between metaphors here is quite subtle, since both apply between the same two domains of *space* and *time*. In the materials used by Gentner and Boronat, two metaphors from different base domains (e.g., *heat* and *dangerous animal*) were applied to the same target (*anger*). In the present case, however, there are two conceptual systems from the same base domain, *space*, to the same target domain, *time*. For this reason, we will call these mappings *system mappings* rather than *domain mappings*. Evidence that these two space-time metaphors are psychologically distinct in online processing would be particularly interesting because it would suggest considerable representational specificity in metaphoric systems.

To test for the use of the two space-time metaphors in online processing, Gentner and Imai (1992) employed a reaction-time comprehension task similar to that used by Gentner and Boronat (1991; in preparation). A test sentence describing a temporal relation between one event (E1) and a second event (E2) was preceded by three setting sentences. In the Consistent mapping condition, the setting sentences and the test sentence used the same metaphoric system—either ego-moving or time-moving. In the Inconsistent mapping condition, the setting sentences used a different mapping system from that of the test sentence. According to the domain-mapping hypothesis, there should be a Mixed Mapping effect. Processing should be slower in the Inconsistent mapping condition than in the Consistent mapping condition. This is because in the Consistent condition, subjects can continue to build on the same systematic mapping as they progress from the setting sentences to the test sentence, but in the Inconsistent condition, to understand the test sentence subjects must discard their existing mapping and set up a new one.

To ensure that subjects really processed the stimulus sentences, we required them to place the events on a timeline. Figure 8.2 shows how the experimental materials were presented. Sentences were presented one at a

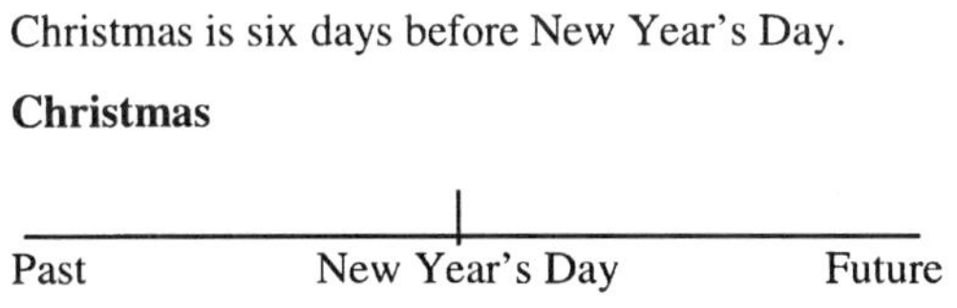

Christmas is six days before New Year's Day.

Christmas

Past   New Year's Day   Future

Figure 8.2
Stimulus presentation for Experiment 1.

time on the top of a CRT screen, with a timeline below. The reference event (which was always the second event mentioned (E2)) was located on the timeline. Subjects pressed one of two keys to indicate whether the first-mentioned event (E1) was located in the PAST or FUTURE of E2. Responses were scored for response time and accuracy.

There were 30 setting sentences—half using the time-moving metaphor and half using the ego-moving metaphor. These were presented in sets of three, followed by a test sentence, which was either in the time-moving or the ego-moving metaphor. Thus there were 10 test sentences, five from each metaphor. Subjects saw five blocks of three setting sentences, each set followed a test sentence. For all sentences their job was to press the past or future key to locate E1 relative to E2. Using the four possible combinations of setting and test sentence, we obtained a 2 (Metaphor Type) $\times$ 2 (Consistency) design with four between-subject conditions. A sample set of materials appears in Table 8.1.

The results showed an overall accuracy rate of 93.0%, with errors evenly distributed across the four conditions. In accord with the global mapping hypothesis, subjects in the Consistent conditions responded significantly faster ($M = 4228$ ms) than those in the Inconsistent conditions ($M = 4799$ ms). There was a marginal effect of Metaphor type: responses for the time-moving metaphor ($M = 4934$ ms) tended to take longer than

Table 8.1
Sample stimuli for experiment 1

Consistent

Setting sentences, time-moving
  I will take the Math exam before the English exam.
  My birthday is ahead of John's birthday.
  I will take two months vacation after graduation.
Test sentence, time-moving
  Dinner will be served preceding the session.

Inconsistent

Setting sentences, ego-moving
  I am looking forward to the concert.
  In the weeks ahead of him, he wanted to finish this project.
  We are coming into troubled times.
Test sentence, time-moving
  Dinner will be served preceding the session.

responses for the ego-moving metaphor ($M = 4093$ ms) (I return to this effect later in the discussion). There was no interaction between Consistency and Metaphor Type.

The mixed mapping cost—the fact that subjects were disrupted in making inferences when the test sentences shifted the metaphoric system of the setting sentences—is consistent with the system mapping hypothesis. This pattern suggests that at a minimum, the two metaphoric systems are coherent systems within the temporal domain. The results are consistent with the strong possibility that people understand these metaphorical terms via a systematic mapping from the domain of *space* to the domain of *time* (as well as with some related accounts discussed later). However, because the combinations of setting and test sentences were randomized, it is also possibility that a much more prosaic phenomenon—local lexical interactions of synonymous and otherwise related words—contributed to the results.

We conducted a second study to guard against the possibility that local lexical associations led to the Consistency effect. In this experiment we took advantage of a small set of spatio-temporal terms that can be used in both the ego-moving and time-moving metaphors, but which convey the *opposite* temporal order in the two systems. This set includes *before, ahead* and *behind*. This sequence reversal is exemplified in the following two sentences.

(1) Christmas comes before New Year's Day.

(2) The holiday season is before us.

In sentence (1) (time-moving), the E1 event (Christmas) is located in the *past* of E2 (New Year's). In sentence (2) (ego-moving), E1 (the holiday season) is located to the *future* of the referent E2 (U.S. nation).

The test sentences utilized the three terms *ahead, before* and *behind*; all are common to both the space $\rightarrow$ time mapping systems. By doing so, we could explicitly control and test for possible local effects. We manipulated the setting sentences so that the test sentences were preceded equally often by setting sentences of the following three types: the *same* term (e.g., *before* in Setting $\rightarrow$ *before* in test); the *opposite* term (e.g., *after* $\rightarrow$ *before*); or a *neutral* term (e.g., *coming* $\rightarrow$ *before*). If the advantage for the Consistent conditions obtained in Experiment 1 was merely due to local lexical priming and response bias effects, no overall advantage should be found for the Consistent mapping conditions in Experiment 2. More generally, if the effects are chiefly at the lexical level, we might expect an

Table 8.2

Sample stimulus set for experiment 2: six *ahead*-time-moving blocks

	Consistent	Inconsistent
Same	*S3:* Christmas is six days *ahead of* New Years.	*S3:* The final exam lies *ahead of* us.
	Test: Transistors came *ahead of* microprocessors.	*Test:* The parade is *ahead of* the festival.
Opposite	*S3:* Adulthood falls *behind* puberty.	*S3:* We are happy that the war is *behind* us.
	Test: The physics exam is *ahead of* the English exam.	*Test:* The news cast is *ahead of* the late night movie.
Neutral	*S3:* The most productive years are still *to come*.	*S3:* We met each other ten years *back*.
	Test: I will arrive in Tokyo three days *ahead of* you.	*Test:* John's graduation is *ahead of* my graduation.

"S3" is the setting sentence that directly preceded the test sentence. The italics are for explication and did not appear in the actual experiment.

advantage for same-word priming and possibly a disadvantage for opposite word priming, and little or no effect for the neutral term. Consistency should either have no effect or an effect only in the same-word case.

Experiment 2 used methods similar to the first study: subjects again responded 'past' or 'future' to indicate the position of Event 1 relative to Event 2. Each subject saw twelve blocks of three setting sentences plus a test sentence—a total of 48 sentences. Of the twelve test sentences, six expressed the ego-moving metaphor; and six, the time-moving metaphor. Within each metaphor type, half the blocks were in the Consistent condition (i.e., the setting and test sentences were in the same metaphor system) and half were in the Inconsistent condition. The setting sentences appearing prior to a test sentence could either contain the same (e.g., *before/ before*), opposite (e.g., *after/before*), or neutral (e.g., *preceding/before*) terms. Thus, each of the 12 blocks contained all combinations of two Metaphor types, two Metaphor Consistency conditions and three Lexical relations (See Gentner, Imai & Boroditsky, in preparation, for further details.) A sample stimulus set can be found in Table 8.2.

The results are summarized in Table 8.3. As predicted by the global mapping hypothesis, people were faster to process Consistent ($M = 4525.3$ ms.) than Inconsistent ($M = 4769.1$) metaphors.[1] As in the previous study, people were also significantly faster to process statements that used the

Table 8.3
Experiment 2: mean response times (msecs) for consistent and inconsistent metaphors for same, opposite, and neutral lexical relations

	Consistent	Inconsistent
Same	4369.6	4986.9
Opposite	4609.0	4670.5
Neutral	4597.2	4650.2
Total	4525.3	4769.1

ego-moving metaphor ($M = 3639.3$) than statements that used the time-moving metaphor ($M = 5655.2$).

Further, the Metaphor Consistency effect did not depend on lexical priming relations. Subjects were faster in the Consistent Condition than in the Inconsistent Condition in all three Lexical conditions (same, opposite, and neutral). This means that the Metaphorical Consistency effect was not an artifact of local lexical associations. We also found no evidence for a response-priming effect: item sets that required the same response in the test sentence (e.g., *future-future*) as in the setting sentence were no faster on average than those that required different responses. Thus the Mixed Mapping cost does not appear to result from local effects, but rather from a system-level facilitation. These results suggest that spatio-temporal metaphorical expressions are processed as part of large-scale conceptual systems, and not as lexical fragments. That is, the ego-moving and time-moving systems function as coherent conceptual frames.

So far these findings indicate that the ego-moving and time-moving spatial systems are used as global systems when people make temporal inferences. That is, they allow us to rule out the fourth and least interesting of the four possibilities laid out earlier, namely, that these metaphors are processed as purely local lexical relations. With this invitation to consider stronger possibilities, we turn to the larger question of whether *space → time* metaphoric systems have force in real life. Do people use these spatial metaphoric frameworks in natural temporal processing? To address this concern, we designed a third experiment that was a purely temporal task in a natural setting (Gentner, Imai & Boroditsky, in preparation, Experiment 3).

In Experiment 3, an experimenter went to O'Hare airport and asked people the kind of temporal questions that naturally come up in travel. The key manipulation was whether the questions maintained the same spatial metaphor throughout or shifted from one metaphor to the other. Experiment 3 was based on the same Mixed-mapping rationale as Experiments 1 and 2: If space-time event-sequencing statements are processed as coherent domain-mappings, then switching between the ego-moving and the time-moving metaphors should lead to increased processing time.

Passengers at Chicago's O'Hare airport (40 in all, balanced for gender across conditions) were approached individually by an experimenter with a digital watch (actually a stop watch) and engaged in a dialogue like the following:

E   "Hello, I'm on my way to Boston." (Intro) "Is Boston *ahead* or behind us time-wise?" (EM setting question)
S   "It's later there."
E   "So should I turn my watch forward or back?" (Test question) (EM)
S   "Forward."
E   "Great. Thank you!"

In the Consistent condition (as shown), the setting question used the ego-moving metaphor like the test question. In the Inconsistent condition, the setting question ("Is it later or earlier in Boston than it is here?"[2]) used the time-moving metaphor and the test question used the ego-moving metaphor. We used the same (ego-moving) test question throughout. At the end of the test question, the experimenter surreptitiously started the stop watch. Timing terminated when the subject responded to the test question. As the questions dealt with adjusting a watch to match a time-zone change, the participants did not suspect that they were being timed.

Within the setting question, half the subjects heard the incorrect possibility first (e.g., "earlier or later"), and half heard the correct possibility first (e.g., "later or earlier"). Thus there were four possible setting questions (two ego-moving and two time-moving), and one test question (ego-moving). All responses were written down by the experimenter immediately following the exchange.

The results were as predicted: subjects in the Consistent condition ($M = 1445$ ms) responded significantly faster than subjects in the Inconsistent condition ($M = 2722$ ms), $t(38) = 2.449$, $p < .05$. Most people answered correctly; three erroneous responses were excluded from the analyses. Neither order of presentation nor gender had any significant effect on response times. These results demonstrate a sizable cost for shifting between metaphorical systems in ordinary commonsense reasoning about time. This is evidence for the psychological reality of the two metaphorical systems.

Interestingly, we found that many (60%) subjects in the Inconsistent condition (i.e., given the time-moving setting question) converted the question to an ego-moving framework. Responses to the setting question in the Inconsistent condition could be either Direct or Converted:

E   "Is it earlier or later in Boston than it is here?"
S   *Direct*: "It is later."
     Converted: "Well, they are ahead of us, so it is later."

No subjects in the ego-moving (Consistent) condition converted to the time-moving metaphor: in contrast, as noted above, 60% of the time-moving subjects spontaneously converted to the ego-moving metaphor. This is concordant with the findings in Experiments 1 and 2 that the time-moving metaphor was more difficult (in terms of requiring longer response times) than the ego-moving metaphor.

Not surprisingly, subjects who converted to the ego-moving frame ($M = 1912$ ms) were much faster on the test question (in the Inconsistent condition) than those who did not convert ($M = 3938$ ms) $t(18) = 4$, $p < .01$. Subjects who converted had already adopted an ego-moving framework; when presented with the (ego-moving) test question they had no need to re-map and could respond quickly. In contrast, subjects who did not convert needed to abandon their old time-moving structure and set up a new ego-moving structure to answer the test question.

The results of the airport study also address a concern raised by McGlone and Harding (1998), namely, that the use of a timeline in Experiments 1 and 2 may have accentuated, or even created, a reliance on spatial representations in this task. It is clearly possible that subjects in the first two studies were influenced by the explicit timeline task to transfer temporal information into a spatial format. However, the persistence of the metaphor consistency effect at O'Hare is testament to the psychological reality of these spatio-temporal metaphoric systems.

Across all three studies, we found that processing took longer in the Inconsistent mapping condition than in the Consistent condition. This is evidence that large-scale conceptual systems underlie the processing of spatio-temporal metaphors on-line. This conclusion is further buttressed by a study by McGlone and Harding (1998). Participants answered blocks of questions phrased in either the ego-moving or the time-moving metaphor. The ego-moving blocks were composed of statements like "We passed the deadline yesterday." The time-moving blocks were composed of statements like "The deadline was passed yesterday." For each statement participants were asked to indicate the day of the week that the events in the statement had occurred or will occur. After each block, participants were presented with an ambiguous temporal statement, which could be interpreted using either metaphor (yielding different answers)—e.g., "Friday's game has been moved forward a day"—and were asked to perform the same task. McGlone and Harding found that participants in the ego-moving condition tended to respond according to the metaphoric system they had seen in the previous block: Following ego-moving metaphors, they responded that the game was on Saturday, and following time-moving metaphors they responded that the game was on Thursday.

Taken together, these results suggest that the ego-moving and time-moving systems function as coherent systems of relations. People reason in these temporal systems using relational structure parallel to that in the spatial base domain. The results obtained from the three experiments are evidence for two distinct psychological systems used in processing event-sequencing statements. The two metaphoric systems discussed in this paper are highly conventional and are rarely noticed in everyday language. Yet our experiments showed that when people make inferences about temporal relations in text, they process more fluently if the sequence of metaphors belongs to the same global metaphor system. Further, we observed the same effect in a purely temporal, oral task conducted in a natural setting. These findings make it very unlikely that spatio-temporal metaphors are processed simply by lexical look-up of local secondary meanings in the lexicon. Rather, they suggest the existence of two psychologically distinct, globally consistent schemas for sequencing events in time.

We can set aside the alternative of local lexical processing (alternative 4). But can we conclude that time is (partly or wholly) structured by spatial analogies? Not yet. There are still three possible mechanisms, as noted earlier. The first is the *system-mapping* account, which indeed postulates that time is (partly) structured by space, by means of analogical mappings from spatial frames to temporal frames. In such a system-mapping, the representational structures of the domains of space and time are aligned, and further relations connected to the base system are projected as candidate inferences from the base domain (*space*) to the target domain (*time*) (Gentner & Markman, 1997). Thus, parallels between space and time are partly discovered and partly imported.

On this account, an existing domain-mapping can facilitate future consistent mappings via a process of incremental mapping. In incremental mapping, an existing system of correspondences is extended by introducing new structure into the base and computing new correspondences and new candidate inferences consistent with the existing mapping. Such incremental mapping has been shown to be computationally feasible in such models as Keane and Brayshaw's (1988) Incremental Analogy Machine (IAM), and Forbus, Ferguson and Gentner's (1994) Incremental Structure-Mapping Engine (I-SME).

However, the second possibility, *cognitive archaeology*, is also consistent with our findings. On this account, space-time metaphors were originally analogical mappings, but have over time become entrenched in relational systems within the temporal domain. (Note that this possibility differs from possibility 4, the *local lexical processing* account, in postulating two connected systems of temporal relations parallel to (and borrowed from) the corresponding spatial systems.) Such a view would be consistent with the contention that abstract domains such as time are structured by metaphorical mappings from more concrete experiential domains such as space (Fauconnier, 1990; Gibbs, 1994; Lakoff & Johnson, 1980). We must also consider the third possibility, *structural parallelism* (Murphy, 1996). On the structural parallelism account, time and space can be structurally aligned by virtue of their parallel relational systems. The perception of aligned structure led historically to the use of the same terms, but there is no directional mapping from space to time. These last two accounts differ in their linguistic history assumptions but lead to the same current state. The *cognitive archaeology* account holds that the metaphors were originally directional mappings from space to time, but how simply express relational systems that are now entrenched in both domains. The *structural parallelism* account holds that the metaphors were never directional, but rather expressed an inherent parallelism in the relational systems for space and time. On both accounts, there is no current reliance on spatial representation in temporal reasoning. Thus space may have had a special role in deriving temporal representations (as in the cognitive archaeology view) or not (as in the structural parallelism view), but there is no current directionality between space and time.

Although our findings and those of McGlone and Harding are compatible with these last two accounts, recent research by Boroditsky (in preparation) argues for the stronger account of *system mapping* (alternative 1). Boroditsky found evidence for an asymmetry: People appear to understand time in terms of space, but not space in terms of time. Participants were slowed in their processing of temporal statements when they were primed with an inconsistent spatial schema, relative to a consistent spatial schema. This consistency effect occurred for transfer from space to time, but not for transfer from time to space, indicating that there is a directional structure-mapping between these two domains. A further finding was that people were influenced by spatial perspective when reasoning about events in time. These results lend support to the metaphorical mapping claim. Together with the present results, they suggest that our representation of time is structured in part by online structural analogies with the more concrete experiential domain of space.

It should be noted that the metaphorical mapping account does not entail the extreme position that spatial mappings *create* temporal representations—that is, it does not imply that the structure of space is imposed on time as on a *tabula rasa*. Murphy (1996) persuasively argues against this extreme interpretation of metaphorical processing, maintaining instead that metaphors typically express a structural alignment between the two relational systems (e.g., Gentner & Markman, 1997; Medin, Goldstone & Gentner, 1993). However, in structure-mapping the most typical case is that an initial structural alignment leads to further mapping of inferences from the base domain to the less coherent domain. Thus the system-mapping account overlaps with the structural parallelism account; in both cases, the metaphorical insight begins with structural alignment. The evidence here suggests that spatial and temporal sequencing are perceived as partly parallel, but that space, as the richer and more elaborated relational system, is used as a further source of inferences about time.

2   Why Are Time-Moving Metaphors More Difficult Than Ego-Moving Metaphors?

In Experiments 1 and 2, ego-moving metaphors were processed faster than time-moving metaphors, overall. In Experiment 3 we observed spontaneous conversion from the time-moving to the ego-moving metaphor. Such conversions never occurred in the reverse direction, despite an equal number of opportunities. It seems that the O'Hare participants preferred to reason with the ego-moving metaphor. This observation, together with the finding in Experiments 1 and 2 that subjects took longer to respond to time-moving metaphors than to ego-moving metaphors suggests that the ego-moving metaphor is somehow easier or more natural for English speakers.

The most obvious advantage of the ego-moving framework is that it requires fewer distinct conceptual points. Statements in the ego-moving metaphor express the temporal relationship between an event and an observer (e.g., "We are approaching the holidays") and therefore can be represented as two points on a time-line:

[Past ... us/(observer) ... holidays ... Future]

Statements using the time-moving metaphor, in contrast, typically express the temporal relationship between two events from the point of view of an observer (e.g., "Spring will come after winter"). In this case, three time points must be represented, one each for event 1, event 2 and the observer:

[Past ... winter ... (observer) ... spring ... Future]

The fact that the time-moving metaphor is typically a three-term relation whereas the ego-moving metaphor is typically a two-term relation probably contributes to the greater processing difficulty of time-moving metaphors.

We can draw a second explanation for the apparent relative difficulty of time-moving metaphors from recent work on temporal reasoning by Schaeken, Johnson-Laird and d'Ydewalle (in press). Because, as discussed above, the relative temporal location of an observer is not specified in the time-moving metaphor, the observer can occur as a third point anywhere on the timeline. For example, the statement "John arrives ahead of Mary" can produce the following three timelines:

[Past ... Obs ... John ... Mary ... Future]
[Past ... John ... Obs ... Mary ... Future]
[Past ... John ... Mary ... Obs ... Future]

Schaeken et al. (in press) found that subjects take longer to reason about temporal sequences when more than one sequence can be constructed from the available information (as in the example above). Therefore, if subjects in our experiments were trying to place an observer on a time-moving timeline, they would incur a processing time cost that may give rise to the main effects for metaphor type found in Experiments 1 and 2. Such effects of multiple mental models might contribute to the greater difficulty of time-moving metaphors.[3]

3   Beyond Two Systems

We have suggested that spatial mappings influence the processing of temporal sequences. But we stop short of suggesting that "space structures time." The event sequencing studied here is only one facet of temporal representation and reasoning. Further, the ego-moving and time-moving metaphors are only two of a larger set of temporal metaphors, many of which are far less obviously spatial. Lakoff and his colleagues have reported several metaphors for *time* in English (Lakoff & Johnson, 1980; Lakoff & Turner, 1989); and Fraser (1987) and Alverson (1994) note that many different time metaphors have occurred across history and across languages. However, Alverson reports that the space-time ego-moving and time-moving metaphors are among those that occur repeatedly cross-linguistically.

I speculate that when sufficient cross-linguistic data are gathered, we will find that although the ego-moving and time-moving metaphors are not the only ways to structure time, they will be widespread in the world's languages. Our experiences of space and time are such that the two domains are perceived as partly parallel structures (as Murphy suggests). But this parallel structure is only the beginning. Our representations of space are so exceptionally coherent and well-structured that (I suggest) we go beyond the initial parallel structure to import further relations. We use spatial language to talk about order of precedence among events (which might be simple parallelism), but we go on to apply notions like an event receding into the past or looming over our future. This is typical of analogical mapping. An initial alignment between common relational structures invites the mapping of further inferences from the more systematic domain to the less systematic domain. Thus, candidate inferences are projected from the highly structured domain of *space* to the more ephemeral domain of *time* (Bowdle & Gentner, 1997; Clement & Gentner, 1991; Gentner, Falkenhainer & Skorstad, 1988; Gentner & Markman, 1997; Markman, 1997).

4   Global Consistency and Conventionality

A striking aspect of this research is that we found system-level consistency effects for space-time metaphors that are highly conventional. This runs contrary to the findings of Gentner and Boronat (1991, in preparation; See also Gentner, 1992, in press; Gentner & Wolff, 2000) who found consistency effects for novel but not conventional metaphors, and of Glucksberg, Brown and McGlone (1993), who failed to find any consistency effects for conventional metaphors. Indeed, we and others have suggested that conventional metaphors and idioms may be encoded and processed simply as alternate lexical entries, and not as part of large-scale mappings (Bowdle & Gentner, 1995, 1999, in preparation; Cacciari & Tabossi, 1988; Gentner, Bowdle, Wolff & Boronat, in press; Gentner & Wolff, 1997, 2000; Swinney & Cutler, 1979; Wolff & Gentner, 1992, 2000, in preparation).

Why should space-time metaphors continue to act as domain mappings, unlike other conventional metaphors? One possibility, as noted above, is that these space-time metaphors may in part be constitutive of temporal representational structure (Langacker, 1986; Talmy, 1985, 1987). By highlighting particular relations, the use of concrete spatial models may be illuminating for articulating the structure of time. A second consideration is that, unlike many conventional metaphors—e.g., "Anger is a raging beast" or "Music is food for the soul"—that convey some sensory attributive properties, these spatio-temporal sequencing metaphors are entirely relational. The spatial terms derive their meanings from their positions within their respective relational systems. Thus they may more naturally retain their system-level interpretations and resist congealing into local lexical associations.

A final point is the conceptual utility of the space-time metaphor. The two space-time systems exhibit three characteristics that facilitate reasoning, as laid out by Gattis (in preparation). They use ordered space to represent elements (here, events) and their relations (sequential ordering); they use spatial dimensions (here, a single linear dimension, which is placed in correspondence with time's single dimension); and they appear to form non-arbitrary analogs for abstract concepts. Temporal reasoning is non-trivial, as any traveler can attest. Perhaps these metaphors retain their systematicity because they do serious work for us.

Acknowledgments

This work was supported by NSF/LIS grant SBR-9720313/5-27481, NSF grant SBR-9511757 and ONR grant N00014-92-J-1098. This research was conducted jointly with Mutsumi Imai and Lera Boroditsky. Philip Wolff wrote the reaction time programs and aided in the analysis of the results. The writing was carried out in part during a sabbatical fellowship at the Center for Advanced Study in the Behavioral Sciences, with support provided by the William T. Grant Foundation, award no. 95167795. I thank Philip Wolff, Brian Bowdle and Matthew McGlone for insightful comments on earlier drafts of this paper and Kathleen Braun for help with data analysis and interpretation.

Notes

1. In a 3 (Group) $\times$ 2 (Consistency) $\times$ 2 (Metaphor type) $\times$ 3 (Context Word type) mixed-measures ANOVA effect of Consistency was marginally significant, $F(1, 69) = 3.74$, $p = 0.057$. Further, the effect of Consistency was significant when the *same* condition was removed and the analysis performed over only the opposite and neutral conditions.

2. Although this phrase preserves the sense of one event preceding another, it is admittedly at best a rather poor example of a time-moving metaphor.

3. Another possibility that should be investigated is whether the ego-moving metaphor simply occurs more frequently in discourse than the time-moving metaphor. But even if it does, it would not be clear whether such a frequency differential was cause or effect of the greater processing ease.

Chapter 9

Reading Pictures: Constraints on Mapping Conceptual and Spatial Schemas

Merideth Gattis

9.1 Reading Pictures

In the fifth century a monastery was built for a man known to us now as St. Nilus in return for his dedication to the Christian faith. St. Nilus suggested that the church in the monastery be painted with scenes from the old and new testaments, turning the building into a book to be read by the unschooled (Manguel, 1997). In doing so he began a tradition of communicating Christian teachings through highly symbolic and carefully juxtaposed pictures—a tradition continued not only in paintings but also in stained glass windows and picture bibles, known as *bibliae pauperum*, or bibles of the poor. The reason that picture reading was so popular, not only within Christianity but also in preceding and coinciding cultures, is that written language is largely arbitrary, requiring instruction to master, and for many centuries after the invention of writing, few people other than scribes and clerics were taught to read. The reliance of illiterate cultures on pictorial media for communicating belief and history suggests an interesting possibility—that unlike reading words, reading pictures does not rely on specific training. This wouldn't be surprising if reading pictures was simply a matter of perceiving and recognizing objects and scenes. But in fact early pictorial media such as painted churches, stained glass, and picture bibles were highly symbolic, using certain elements to represent abstract concepts (for example a bird to represent the Holy Spirit) and using spatial arrangement of multiple objects and multiple scenes as a meaningful communicative tool (for example the juxtaposition of a scene depicting Abraham preparing to sacrifice Isaac and a scene depicting the crucifixion of Christ to convey an analogy between the two). Similarly, in modern times people use calendars, charts, diagrams, and graphs to reason about conceptual information with remarkable ease, adroitly interpreting diagrams of beliefs, evidence, and other elaborate conceptual structures, despite the fact that these representations are highly variable and often novel, making specific literacy nigh impossible. How is it then that people without specific training can decipher and reason about conceptual meanings expressed in visuospatial representations?

9.2   Constraints on Mapping Conceptual and Spatial Schemas

Reading pictorial media involves attaching meaning to them, a process that is achieved by establishing correspondences between abstract concepts and spatial representations, or in other words, mapping conceptual and spatial schemas. In this sense reading pictures is *not* like reading written language, in which the mapping between meaning and script is mediated by sound. Reading pictures, or more specifically reasoning with spatial representations, is more direct and easier to acquire. Research in linguistics, semiotics, and cognitive and developmental psychology suggests three cognitive constraints governing the process of mapping concepts to spatial representations: iconicity, associations, and polarity. Each of these constraints leads to an identifiable category of mapping patterns defined by a certain type of similarity between the represented concept and the spatial representation in which it is communicated. In the following sections, I will describe each of these constraints in detail and present evidence that a fourth and much deeper form of similarity—structural similarity—also constrains the mapping process.

Iconicity

Iconicity constrains the interpretation of spatial representations when a spatial representation preserves some perceptual characteristics of what it represents, either by maintaining similar perceptual features, or similar perceptual relations. The simplest example of iconicity constraining a representation is when a drawing of an object is used to represent that object. Such symbols were common in pre-writing systems, which used pictograms, or pictures resembling the object represented, rather than alphabetic characters representing sounds (Fromkin & Rodman, 1998; Hung & Tzeng, 1981). Pictograms can still be found in some languages, including a few Chinese characters (for instance, the characters for *mountain*, *tree*, and *net*), and in international signs posted along roads or in tourist destinations (see Tversky, this volume, for further examples).

Some of the most familiar and diverse examples of iconicity constraining representation are found in maps, including such diverse forms as world maps, wayfinding maps, and room plans (see Liben, this volume). The diversity of maps underscores the point that iconicity allows not only the representation of individual objects but also sets of objects, and the relations between objects. While maps may and sometimes do represent objects (think of a city map in which each house and building is drawn in outline), the most common maps represent relations—particularly relations between locations and routes of travel, such as streets, paths, and transportation networks. Compare a street map of a city with an underground transportation map of the same city and you will immediately see that any given map is designed to represent particular relations, and to omit other relations. Iconicity is thus a selective constraint: it does not imply total but partial isomorphism, and that partial isomorphism (or in simpler language, resemblance) may facilitate the representation of objects, sets of objects, or relations between objects.

The advantages of using iconicity-constrained representations in reasoning are related to our abilities to process and remember pictures (Hung & Tzeng, 1981; Shepard, 1967). Representations based on iconicity can be used to remember a set of objects, to compare attributes of different objects, or to compare different relations between objects, for example alternative routes of travel, or size differences between two different pairs of objects. The picture-like qualities of iconic representations also have, however, significant limitations. The most important of these limitations for representations used in reasoning is that it is difficult for iconic representations to represent abstract attributes or relations, such as brightness, temperature, or conjunctive and disjunctive relations. The same difficulties limited pictographic pre-writing systems, and led to an important development in representation.

Associations

As pictographic pre-writing systems evolved, many signs became ideographs, representing attributes associated with objects rather than objects alone (Fromkin & Rodman, 1998; Hung & Tzeng, 1981). For example, in Chinese, brightness is represented by the characters for sun and moon (Fazzioli, 1986), and in Egyptian hieroglyphics, cool is represented by a picture of water pouring from a vase (Fromkin & Rodman, 1998). The evolution toward representing associations rather than just objects allowed writing and graphic systems to represent concepts, attributes, and other abstractions. Many contemporary spatial representations convey concepts, attributes, and other abstractions by following the same principle of meaning-by-association as these ideographic writing systems. For example, Leach (1976) has pointed out that the association of actions or events with particular locations in space can lead to maps of social space. For example, a picture of a temple or church may represent the activity of prayer. Such representations exploit an association between a physical space and an action to signify the action or event itself. Werner (1978a) also noted that using or interpreting objects to represent abstract ideas is common in children. Children frequently interpret line drawings as representing tactual and kinaesthetic qualities, for instance interpreting angular figures to represent things that prick (Muchow, 1926, as cited in Werner, 1978a). In other studies described by Werner, adults drew or interpreted lines to represent abstractions such as emotions, basic metals (iron, silver, and gold), or actions (i.e., "He catches a fly" and "He catches a criminal") with remarkable consistency (Krauss, 1930, as cited in Werner, 1978a; Werner & Kaplan, 1978). Such interpretive consistencies are often surprising to us, perhaps because the notational system most familiar to us, our writing system, is largely arbitrary. Consistent interpretations of abstract concepts conveyed by novel spatial representations are possible because the representation contains properties associated with the concept or attribute being represented. Thus perceptual properties can convey meaning despite a lack of literal resemblance.

Associations are so common in spatial and graphic representations that we sometimes fail to notice that our interpretations or readings are dependent on previously acquired associations, and not only on properties of the representation itself. For example, graphs and other diagrams often follow the convention of using *bigger* to represent *more* suggested by Willard Brinton near the beginning of this century (Brinton, 1914, as cited in Modley & Lowenstein, 1952). This principle is easily followed by anyone who has experienced that for most solids, *more* is indeed characterized by greater physical extent (see Bryant & Squire, this volume). Thus, like mappings based on iconicity, mappings based on associations are also rooted in perceptual experience—experience with the object, relation, or attribute being represented and with the medium of representation. Likewise, psychological research suggests that conventions such as using *bigger* to represent *more* and *up* to represent *more* are not arbitrary rules, but reflect associations acquired through experience. When Tversky, Kugelmass and Winter (1991) asked people to place stickers on a piece of paper to represent increases, both children and adults did so in a way that was consistent with an association between *up* and *more*: Not only adults but also children as young as five represented quantitative increases in a vertical direction by placing the lowest level (i.e., "a small amount") at the bottom of the page and the highest level (i.e., "a really big amount") at the top of the page (see also Tversky's chapter in this volume). Similarly, when Handel, DeSoto and London (1968) asked adults asked to map comparative relational terms to vertical or horizontal lines, they mapped *above* and *below*, *better* and *worse*, and *more* and *less* to vertical lines, placing the first term of each pair at the top and the latter term at the bottom.

Once we've noted that meaningful associations constrain the construction and interpretation of many spatial representations of conceptual information, it is easy to assume that all interpretations of spatial representations are based on prior learning or experience, in the form of either iconicity or associations. In fact, meaning-by-association becomes the parsimonious default hypothesis against which other explanations of consistencies in spatial representations are evaluated. Werner (1978b) argued, for instance, that the tendency to pair *louder* with *higher* is also the result of an association acquired through experience—the association between singing loudly and lifting the body upwards. Recent linguistic and psychological research suggests, however, that we should be careful about explaining mappings of concepts and space with examples of situations where one might have learned to associate one quality with another. Polarity, a subtle but powerful form of similarity, may be the source of some surprising mappings, including the mapping between *louder* and *higher*.

Polarity

Unlike iconicity and associations, mappings of conceptual and spatial schemas based on polarity do not rely on perceptual resemblance, nor on previously experienced pairings between attributes and objects. Instead, polarity is based on the organizational structure underlying many perceptual and conceptual dimensions. Polarity constrains mappings of spatial and conceptual schemas when a spatial representation shares oppositional structure or directionality of dimension with the concept being represented. A simple way to envision this oppositional structure is as a continuum with asymmetrically weighted ends.

The oppositional or asymmetrical structure of dimensions is perhaps best known through the linguistic phenomenon of polar grading (Sapir, 1944) or marking (Clark, 1969; Greenberg, 1966). When two adjectives describe opposite characteristics along some dimension, for instance *good* and *bad*, one of these terms usually refers to the entire dimension, in this case *goodness*, as well as to a specific end of the dimension. This term is called the unmarked term. The second term refers only to a specific end of the dimension (*badness*, for example, does not refer to a dimension including *good* and *bad*, but refers only to various degrees of *bad*) and is called the marked term, because it is understood by reference to the first term. The asymmetric semantic structure conveyed by marking is exemplified by the fact that only the unmarked term can be used to formulate an unbiased nominal question, such as "How good is it?" In addition to being more general, the unmarked term is usually the older and more common of the two words (see Hamilton & Deese, 1971, for word histories and frequencies of many common unmarked and marked word pairs). To the layperson, the most noticeable characteristic of polar terms is their valence: an unmarked term usually has a positive connotation or value (or a neutral value), while the marked term has a negative value. Polarity refers to these asymmetric positive and negative valences. Polarity is characteristic of unmarked and marked adjectives and many other linguistic items, for not only are constructions involving dimensional adjectives sensitive to valence, but also many constructions involving determiners, adverbs, verbs and conjunctions (Israel, 1996).

Clark (1969, 1973) and others (Lakoff & Johnson, 1980; see also Tversky, this volume) maintain that this asymmetry of linguistic structure is rooted in the asymmetries of perceptual space. The clearest form of this argument was given by Clark, who pointed out that the structure of our bodies and our movements in the world define three reference planes, two of which are asymmetrical. The only plane characterized by perceptual symmetry is the right-left plane. Two reference planes are asymmetrical: the front-back plane, and the top-bottom (or head-feet) plane. Clark claimed that the front end of the front-back plane is positive because it is the direction of movement and the side toward which most of our perceptual receptors are oriented. Similarly, he reasoned that the top end of the top-bottom plane is positive because up-down is the canonical orientation of the body as well as the primary direction of observed movement (objects fall from up to down but never in the opposite direction). The asymmetric structure of perceptual space has since been confirmed by psychological experiments. For example, when Bryant, Tversky and Franklin (1992) asked adults to read a short narrative and then identify the locations of objects described in the narrative, people were faster at identifying objects in front of their bodies than in back of their bodies.

Sensitivity to the polar organization of both perceptual and linguistic dimensions is present very early in development. In several experiments, Smith and Sera (1992) asked 2-to-5-year-olds and adults to perform a percept-to-percept cross-dimension matching task, or a word-to-percept matching task. In one experiment, for example, the percept-to-percept task involved selecting one of two toy mice who was "very much like" an exemplar mouse. The mice varied along three dimensions—size, achromatic color (shade of grey), and loudness (a tone emitted from a box under the mouse). For each judgment, the exemplar mouse differed from the choice mice along one dimension (for instance, the color of the exemplar might be dark grey) while the two choice mice were constant along that dimension (the color of both choice mice being medium grey) and differed from one another along another dimension (for instance, one choice mouse was bigger than both the other choice mouse and the exemplar). When two year old children were asked to make a size-darkness comparison such as the one described here, they consistently paired big with dark, and little with light, indicating that for very young children, the dimensions of size and achromatic color are similarly organized into positive and negative ends occupied by big and dark, and little and light, respectively. Interestingly, linguistically neither *dark* nor *light* is marked with respect to the other. The results indicate that for young children, the dimension of achromatic color is perceptually organized despite the fact that it is not linguistically organized. Older children who demonstrated an understanding of the words *dark* and *light* (and other relevant dimensional adjectives) did not exhibit the same polar organization of the perceptual dimensions as younger children: older children consistently paired big and loud, and little and quiet, but not big and dark and little and light. *Loud* and *quiet* are an unmarked-marked pair, unlike *dark* and *light*, indicating that as children acquire language, linguistic organization plays an important role in cross-dimensional matching, while pre-linguistic children exhibit consistent cross-dimensional matches that appear to reflect a different, and perceptually-based organization.

What Smith and Sera's (1992) results show us is that not all matching of representations is based on associations acquired through experience. The finding that very young children paired mice according to perceptual polar organization, whereas older children and adults paired mice according to linguistic polar organization indicates that similarity of organizational structures, whether perceptual or linguistic, may be the basis for cross-dimensional mappings. This finding is particularly relevant for reasoning with spatial representations such as pictures, graphs, and diagrams, which often involves mapping non-spatial dimensions to spatial dimensions. Smith and Sera's results suggest that the mappings involved in interpreting spatial representations may be based on the polar organization of dimensions, and not only on iconicity and associations (see Gattis & Molyneaux, 1999; Gattis, 2000a).

The influence of polar organization on reasoning is well-established: drawing inferences about pairwise relations from premises containing related pairs is more difficult when premises use the marked comparative, such as *worse*, than when premises use the unmarked comparative, such as *better* (Clark, 1969). As Hummel and Holyoak's simulation with the LISA model (this volume) demonstrates, this may be because using the marked comparative leads to an assumption that the object has a smaller-than-average value, and to the assignment of the stated elements to a restricted range in a mental spatial array. Polar organization and the related spatial array assumptions built into the LISA model may also be able to explain a recent finding about the Semantic Congruity Effect. The Semantic Congruity Effect is a facilitation in performance on pairwise comparisons when the comparative term used coincides with the relative value of the objects with respect to that comparative, and a corresponding decrement in performance when it does not. For example, people are faster at judging the higher of two balloons than judging the lower of two balloons, and faster at judging the lower of two yo-yos than judging the higher of two yo-yos (Banks, Clark & Lucy, 1975). Ryalls, Winslow and Smith (1998) recently reported a Semantic Congruity Effect on children's judgments involving dimensional terms such as *higher* and *lower* or *bigger* and *smaller*, but not for simple relational comparatives like *over* and *under*. This result suggests that the influence of polar organization is restricted to comparatives suitable to an array representation, or to use language introduced at the beginning of this section, judgments involving a perceptual or linguistic continuum.

While powerful, these three constraints—iconicity, associations, and polarity—do not fully account for the diverse mappings of conceptual and spatial schemas reported in studies of reasoning and interpretation of spatial representations. As Werner (1978) argued, we are able to construct and reason with novel spatial representations in many situations, and these representations assist rather than confuse our conceptual understanding, despite their novelty.

In addition, in any given representation, multiple mappings of conceptual and spatial schemas may exist, and may even conflict. When multiple mappings conflict, judgment patterns indicate that some mappings take priority over others. Gattis and Holyoak (1996) gave adults graphs which compared two natural mappings: graphs contrasted the iconic mapping of up, representing "up" in the atmosphere as "up" on a vertical line, with a non-iconic mapping of rate, representing a faster rate of change with a steeper slope. When adults were asked to make rate judgments, the latter mapping exerted a stronger influence on reasoning performance.

Finally, the direction and strength of some mapping patterns are not easily explained by iconicity, associations, or polarity, as for instance the tendency of both young children and adults to use slope as an indicator of rate in judgments made from graphs (Gattis & Holyoak, 1996; Gattis, 2000c). These and other findings suggest that some other aspect of representation may also constrain the mapping of conceptual and spatial schemas, and indeed, recent research indicates that a fourth and much deeper form of similarity—structural similarity—also constrains the mapping process.

Structural Similarity

In the previous three sections, I have argued that iconicity, associations, and polarity constrain the mapping of conceptual and spatial schemas based on different types of similarity between a concept and the spatial representation in which it is communicated. Iconicity constrains mappings based on perceptual similarity (or resemblance), associations constrain mapping based on attribute or property similarity (without actual resemblance), and polarity constrains mappings based on similarity in valence or directionality. *Structural similarity*, in contrast, constrains mappings when the representation shares relational structure with the represented (see Gentner, 1983, for a description of structural similarity in the context of analogy). Mappings constrained by structural similarities are based on similarity of relational structures, and lead to a pairing of elements to elements, relations to relations, and higher-order relations to higher order-relations.

This hand means MONKEY.   This hand means ELEPHANT.

Figure 9.1
In the first phase, text accompanying these drawings assigned a specific meaning
to each hand.

Structural similarity in adults' reasoning with novel signs   In several recent
experiments, I used an artificial sign language representing very simple
relational structures—elements and relations between elements—to explore whether relational structure constrains the mapping of verbal statements to spatial schemas (Gattis, 2000b). In each experiment, adults
were given diagrams of hand gestures paired with simple statements,
and asked to judge the meaning of new gestures. In one experiment,
adults were given signs paired with active declarative statements. In the
first phase, drawings of a man extending each hand (see Figure 9.1) were
paired with statements assigning an animal to each hand, such as "This
hand means Monkey" and "This hand means Elephant." In the second
phase, two drawings (see Figure 9.2) were paired with statements involving the animal previously assigned to the right hand, for example
Monkey. The drawings paired with these statements depicted the man
touching his right ear with his right hand, and touching his left ear with
his right hand. In the accompanying statements, the subject, the object,
or the predicate relation varied between the two statements. Examples
of statements in which the subject varied are "Mouse visits Monkey"
and "Bear visits Monkey." Note that this example introduces two new

Subject varying	This means <u>MOUSE</u> VISITS MONKEY.	This means <u>BEAR</u> VISITS MONKEY.
Object varying	This means MONKEY VISITS <u>MOUSE</u>.	This means MONKEY VISITS <u>BEAR</u>.
Relation varying	This means MONKEY <u>VISITS</u> MOUSE.	This means MONKEY <u>BITES</u> BEAR.

Figure 9.2
In the second phase, two signs made with the right hand were accompanied by active declarative statements or conjunctive and disjunctive statements.

animals, Mouse and Bear, both of whom perform the same action: they visit Monkey. When the object varied, the statements took the form, "Monkey visits Mouse" and "Monkey visits Bear." In this example, the same two animals and the same relation as is the previous example are introduced, but the two new animals are the objects of the action, rather than the subjects of the action. When the relation varied, the statements took the form, "Monkey visits Mouse" and "Monkey bites Mouse." Relation-varying statements introduced only one new animal, in this example, Mouse, who could perform two different actions, visiting or biting. Note that in all three conditions (varying subject, varying object, and varying predicate relation), the sign-statement pairs were ambiguous: the assignment of one statement to each sign leaves open whether it is the object touched by the hand (right ear, left ear) or the relation of the hand to body (ipsilateral, contralateral) that carries meaning.

The third phase used drawings of complementary signs made with the left hand (touching the left ear with the left hand and touching the right ear with the left hand, as seen in Figure 9.3) to probe how people mapped

What does this mean?

Subject varying
MOUSE VISITS ELEPHANT   or   BEAR VISITS ELEPHANT

Object varying
ELEPHANT VISITS MOUSE   or   ELEPHANT VISITS BEAR

Relation varying
ELEPHANT VISITS MOUSE   or   ELEPHANT BITES MOUSE

Figure 9.3
In the third phase, two signs made with the left hand, complementary to those previously shown with the right hand, were used to probe conceptual-spatial mappings.

meaning to the two signs. People were asked to judge which of two statements, similar to the statements given in the second phase but this time involving the meaning assigned to the left hand, was represented by each sign. To continue the example described above, in the subject-varying condition, the probe statements took the form, "Mouse visits Elephant" and "Bear visits Elephant." In the object-varying condition, the probe statements took the form, "Elephant visits Mouse" and "Elephant visits Bear." In the relation-varying condition, the probe statements took the form, "Elephant visits Mouse" and "Elephant bites Mouse."

For each of those conditions, the assignments given in Phase 2 combined with the choices made in Phase 3 was the indicator of how the varying and unassigned portion of the statement in both phases was mapped to the artificial sign. For example, in the varying-subject condi-

MOUSE VISITS MONKEY   BEAR VISITS MONKEY

What does this mean?

MOUSE VISITS ELEPHANT   or   BEAR VISITS ELEPHANT ✓

Figure 9.4
An object-mapping.

tion, if a person chose "Mouse visits Elephant" as the meaning of the left-hand-touching-right-ear sign, and "Bear visits Elephant" as the meaning of the left-hand-touching-left-ear sign, comparing that choice with the sign-statement pairs given in Phase 2 allows the inference that Mouse was assigned to the right ear, and Bear to the left ear, or in other words, that the unassigned and varying portion of the statements (Mouse and Bear) was mapped to the object touched by the hand (right ear, left ear) (Figure 9.4 illustrates this point). I call this pattern of meaning assignment an object-mapping, because it is an object in the drawing, namely an ear, that carries meaning. If the choices were reversed, and people chose "Bear

MOUSE VISITS MONKEY   BEAR VISITS MONKEY

What does this mean?

✓ MOUSE VISITS ELEPHANT   or   BEAR VISITS ELEPHANT

Figure 9.5
A relation-mapping.

visits Elephant" as the meaning of the left-hand-touching-right-ear sign,
and "Mouse visits Elephant" as the meaning of the left-hand-touching-
left-ear sign, comparing that choice with the sign-statement pairs in Phase
2 allows the inference that Mouse was mapped to the the ipsilateral relation of the hand to body, and Bear to the contralateral relation of the
hand to the body (Figure 9.5 illustrates this point). I call this pattern of
meaning assignment a relation-mapping, because it is the relation of the
hand to the body that carries meaning.

If structural similarity constrains the mapping of simple statements to
spatial schemas, people would be expected to map the unassigned and

varying portion of a statement to a structurally similar aspect of an accompanying sign. Structural similarity thus predicts that varying subjects and objects would be mapped to the ears, similar because they are both objects or elements. Varying semantic relations, on the other hand, would be mapped to the ipsilateral and contralateral spatial relations according to structural similarity. These predictions can be tested by comparing the occurrence of object-mappings and relation-mappings in the three conditions: the theory predicts more frequent object-mappings in the varying-subject and varying-object conditions, and more frequent relation-mappings in the varying-relation condition. If structural similarity does not constrain the mapping of conceptual and spatial schemas however, mappings would be expected to vary across individuals or across conditions in a random pattern.

Judgment patterns were consistent with the predictions of structural similarity. In the subject-varying and object-varying conditions, object-mappings were more prevalent than relation-mappings. In contrast, in the relation-varying condition, relation-mappings were more common than object-mappings. In other words, varying subjects and objects were consistently assigned to the ears and varying semantic relations were assigned to the bodily relations. This pattern of results indicates that mappings of active declarative statements to novel signs are constrained by the similarity of relational structures.

In another experiment, people were given the same series of artificial signs paired with conjunctive and disjunctive statements, such as "Monkey and Mouse," and "Monkey or Mouse." As in the previous experiment, the hands always signified two animals, assigned during the first phase of the experiment, and different types of relational structure were contrasted by varying which aspect of the statement was ambiguously mapped. In the second and third phases of the experiment, either the first animal, the second animal, or the relation between them varied. When the first animal varied, two new animals were paired with the animal previously assigned to the right hand, by either a conjunctive relation (*and*) or a disjunctive relation (*or*). For example, similar to the subject-varying condition described above, in the second phase a person might have received the statements, "Mouse and Monkey" and "Bear and Monkey," each paired with a diagram of a sign made with the right hand (see Figure 9.2). When the second animal varied, the statements were similar with the difference that the animals assigned to the hands occupied the first position in the statements and the two new animals occupied the second position in the statements. For example, similar to the object-varying condition described above, a person might have received the statements, "Monkey and Mouse" and "Monkey and Bear," each paired with a right-hand sign. When the relation varied, both conjunctive (*and*) and disjunctive (*or*) relations were introduced. For example, similar to the relation-varying condition described above, a person might have received the statements, "Monkey and Mouse" and "Monkey or Mouse," each paired with the right-hand signs.

As in the previous experiment, mappings constrained by structural similarity would be expected to lead to assignment of the varying portion of a statement to a structurally similar aspect of an accompanying sign, revealed in judgments made in the probe phase, in which two left-hand signs were paired with appropriately varying statements. And again, this was so. As predicted by structural similarity, varying animals, whether in the first position or the second position of the statements, were mapped to the ears, and varying conjunctive and disjunctive relations were mapped to the ipsilateral and contralateral spatial relations.

The results of these and other experiments (see Gattis, 2000b, for more detail) indicate that when asked to interpret novel spatial schemas, adults choose physical objects to represent conceptual elements and physical relations to represent conceptual relations. These results are also compatible with previous research with signed languages indicating that in signing space, objects or actors are assigned to a spatial locus, while verbs may involve movement between loci to highlight the relation between objects or actors (see Emmorey, this volume), and observations of graphic depictions indicating that graphics use elements to represent elements, and relations to represent relations (see Tversky, this volume).

Structural similarity in children's reasoning with graphs   The experiments described above and the patterns noted by Emmorey and Tversky (see chapters from each in this volume) lend support to the hypothesis that structural similarity constrains the mapping of simple relational structures—elements and the relations between elements—in conceptual and spatial schemas. Structural similarity also predicts, however, that similarity of more complex relational structures can influence mappings of conceptual and spatial schemas. Specifically, structural similarity claims that conceptual elements are mapped to spatial elements, conceptual relations are mapped to spatial relations, and higher-order conceptual relations are mapped to higher-order spatial relations, each according to the level of relational structure.

One indicator that higher-order relational structure does play a role in the mapping process is the rate judgment patterns mentioned earlier, reported by Gattis and Holyoak (1996). We gave adults graphs of atmospheric temperatures which either maintained a correspondence between rate of change and the slope of the line, so that steeper lines represented faster rates of change, or which violated that correspondence, so that steeper lines represented slower rates of change. When asked to judge the rate of change in atmospheric temperature represented by one of two function lines, adults' judgments corresponded to the slope of the the probed line in a manner that was both polarity-consistent (steeper = faster) and structurally consistent (slope = rate).

In recent experiments, I have explored the hypothesis that this tendency to map rate to slope during rate judgments reflects a differentiation between relations between elements and higher-order relations during the mapping process. To investigate this hypothesis, I asked young children with no experience with graphs or related representations to reason about conceptual variables using graph-like diagrams (Gattis, 2000c). In these experiments, children were shown an L-shaped diagram (much like the frame for Cartesian graphs, but without any labels, unitization, or numerical marking) and taught to map abstract variables such as time, age, quantity, size, or rate to the vertical and horizontal lines of the L-shape. Children were either taught to map increases along the vertical line in an upward direction or in a downward direction (the reason for this manipulation will be apparent shortly). In the second phase, children were shown an L-shaped frame containing a "story line," a function line which told a story integrating the values of the two variables mapped to the horizontal and vertical lines. Children who had been taught to map increases in an upward direction saw an upward-sloping function line, and children who had been taught to map increases in a downward direction saw a downward-sloping function line. In the final phase of the experiments, children were shown a similar diagram, but this time with two story lines, and asked to make a judgment about a conceptual value, as represented by one of the lines. Children who had been taught to map increases in an upward direction were shown a diagram with two upward-sloping function lines of equal length (see Figure 9.6). Note that in this diagram, the higher of the two lines is also the steeper of the two lines.

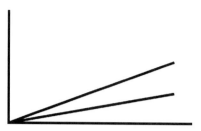

Figure 9.6
Children taught to map increases in an upward direction were shown a diagram
with two upward-sloping function lines of equal length.

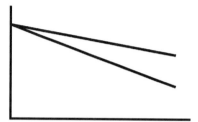

Figure 9.7
Children taught to map increases in a downward direction were shown a diagram
with two downward-sloping function lines of equal length.

Children who had been taught to map increases in a downward direction
were shown a diagram with two downward-sloping function lines of equal
length (see Figure 9.7). In this diagram, in contrast to the other, the lower
of the two lines is the steeper of the two. My assumption was that because
these children did not have prior experience with graphs, their judgments
from these diagrams would either be random, or correspond to a particular spatial cue, such as height or slope. The diagrams (and the
manipulation of direction of increase along the vertical) were designed to
distinguish between judgments corresponding to the height of the line and
judgments corresponding to the slope of the line. If judgments correspond
to height, for instance, probing the upper line in either diagram should
yield the same response, whereas if judgments correspond to slope, probing the upper line in each diagram should yield different (but predictable)
responses (see Figures 9.6 and 9.7).

In one set of experiments, children were taught to map time and quantity to the horizontal and vertical lines. In the second phase of the experi-

ment, the children were taught to integrate time and quantity to form a story line representing changes in both quantity and time. In the final phase of the experiments, children were asked to judge either the quantity represented by a particular story line, or the rate represented by a particular story line (see Gattis, 2000c, for complete details). Children asked to judge the quantity represented by a line responded in a way that corresponded to the height of the line: regardless of the diagram studied, children judged the higher of two lines as representing greater quantity, and the lower of two lines as representing lesser quantity. In contrast, children asked to judge the rate represented by a line responded in a way that corresponded to the slope of the line. Regardless of the relative heights of the lines, children reported that the steeper line represented a faster rate, and the shallower line represented a slower rate. Note that in these experiments, the initial mapping procedure and the integration process encouraged children to conceive of rate as a second-order relation composed of changes in both time and quantity. In this context, young children mapped quantity to height (structurally similar because they are both relations between elements) and rate to slope (structurally similar because they are both relations between relations).

In another set of experiments, children were encouraged to conceive of rate as a first-order relation, the speed of travel of a particular animal. In the first phase of the experiments, children were taught to map either age and size or age and rate to the horizontal and vertical lines. In the next phase of the experiment, the children were told that the story line represented changes in the two variables previously mapped to the horizontal and vertical lines—either age and size, or age and rate—for instance how an animal grows as it gets older, or how an animal gets faster as it gets older. In the judgment phase, children were asked to judge either the size represented by a particular line, or the rate represented by the particular story line. Note that in this context, children have not been reminded of any component variables of rate (for instance, time and distance travelled), but rather have been encouraged to conceive of rate as a first-order relation. In these experiments, both size and rate judgments corresponded to the height of the line: children judged the higher of two lines as representing greater size and greater rate, and the lower of two lines as representing a lesser size and a lesser rate. In other words, when introduced to both size and rate as first-order relations, children mapped both size and rate to height, structurally similar because they are both relations between elements.

The contrasting results of these two sets of experiments indicate that relational structures are finely differentiated during the mapping process. As structural similarity predicts, whether a relation is introduced as a relation between elements or as a higher-order relation influences the mappings of conceptual and spatial schemas. The judgment patterns described above indicate that conceptual relations are mapped to spatial relations, such as height, and higher-order conceptual relations are mapped to higher-order spatial relations, such as slope.

Interplay between the Constraints

The four previous sections on iconicity, associations, polarity, and structural similarity have attempted to establish the influence of each individual constraint on the creation and interpretation of spatial representations. Identifying multiple constraints on mapping raises the question of how multiple constraints interact, whether within a single representation, across the history of representations or across an individual's history of reasoning with representations. For instance, do iconicity, associations, polarity and structural similarity cooperate to produce a coherent mapping? What happens when the constraints lead to competing mappings? Does a particular constraint exert more influence on reasoning at a particular point in human development?

Certainly it is the case that many representations are influenced by more than one form of similarity between concepts and spatial representations. Isotypes, for instance, are a form of bar graphs in which the bars are made of multiple icons of a commodity, such as barrels of oil (see Neurath, 1936, and Tversky, this volume). Within an isotype, the icons are a uniform size, and represent a uniform quantity. A bar composed of a large number of icons (relative to another bar) conveys *more* redundantly via at least two constraints. More oil barrows, for instance, communicate "more oil" via iconicity, and the greater vertical extent of the bar communicates "more" via the association between quantity and area. The interpretation of such a graphic could also be constrained by polarity, with the weighted continuum of *big* and *small* mapped to the continuum of *more* and *less*.

The example of isotypes illustrates that it isn't always easy to know which constraints are influencing the mapping of concepts to space. In many cases, disentangling these four constraints will require clever experimentation. That task will be worthwhile, however, because doing so will help us to understand not only which constraints operate in a particular case, but also how the constraints interact. One possibility is that iconicity, associations, polarity and structural similarity are additively related. An additive relation between constraints would mean that mappings based on multiple types of similarity, such as isotypes, ought to be easier than mappings based on only one type of similarity.

An additive relation would be less likely to yield consistent patterns of mapping when multiple constraints conflict, as for example in the graphs studied by Gattis and Holyoak (1996). In those graphs, the iconic mapping between *up* in the atmosphere and *up* on a vertical line conflicted with the structural mapping of faster rate to steeper slope: if a graph preserved the iconic mapping, it violated the structural mapping, and vice versa. When adults were asked to use those graphs to make rate judgments, the structural mapping of rate to slope exerted a stronger influence on performance. These results suggest that some mappings can take priority over others. The priority of mappings may be determined by pragmatic context of the reasoning task. For example, when the reasoning task involves a higher-order relation, structural similarity may play a larger role. In contrast, when the reasoning task involves a relation within a single dimension, associations or polarity may exert greater influence. Similarly when the reasoning task involves a single element, iconicity may be the most important form of similarity.

A third plausible relation between the four constraints, which is also consistent with the results of Gattis and Holyoak is a hierarchical relation, perhaps with iconicity at the bottom and structural similarity at the top. A hierarchical view would predict that iconicity exerts an influence on mapping if it is the only similarity present, or if it is consistent with the higher-order constraints. In this view, structural similarity would be able to override any conflicting mappings created by iconicity, associations, or polarity.

It seems likely that the multiple constraints on mapping concepts to space are multiply related, much like the relation between constraints governing analogical reasoning (Holyoak & Thagard, 1997). The true relation between iconicity, associations, polarity, and structural similarity may be additive, pragmatic, *and* hierarchical. One reason to believe this is that the operation of one constraint is sometimes dependent on the operation of another constraint. For instance, in most of the graphing examples described in this chapter, the operation of structural similarity is dependent on polarity. In those examples, structural similarity calls for a mapping between rate and slope, but doesn't say how the dimension of rate should be mapped to the dimension of slope—that mapping is governed by polarity, which calls for a mapping between the weighted or marked end of each continuum, leading to a mapping of *faster* to *steeper*, and *slower* to *shallower*.

Another question worth further investigation is whether the influence of these four constraints changes across development. If some hierarchical relation does exist between constraints, it may also be the case that the hierarchy reflects a developmental progression in spatial reasoning—from iconicity to associations, and then on to polarity and structural similarity. Such a developmental progression may parallel the development of analogical reasoning in children. For instance, Gentner (1988) reported that children are able to comprehend and produce metaphors based on similarity of appearance (e.g., "Pancakes are nickels") earlier than metaphors based on relational similarity (e.g., "A tire is a shoe"). This pattern of development in analogical reasoning suggests that in spatial reasoning as well, perceptual similarity may exert an influence earlier in the life of an individual than relational similarity (see also Tverksy, this volume, for related evidence).

9.3   Summary and Conclusions

Pictures, graphs, signs, and other spatial representations play an important role in human communication and reasoning in part because we are able to interpret or infer meanings from these representations without specific instruction in how to do so. Reading pictures, in this sense, is not like reading written language, in which the connections between symbol and referent is usually arbitrary. We infer meaning from novel spatial representations by establishing correspondences, or mappings, between concepts and space. These correspondences are based on similarity between aspects of the spatial representation and aspects of the concept being represented. I have reviewed research suggesting that three types of similarity—iconicity, associations, and polarity—constrain the mapping of conceptual and spatial schemas, and proposed that recent research indicates that a fourth type of similarity, structural similarity, constrains the mapping process as well.

Iconicity constrains mapping when the spatial representation maintains some perceptual characteristics of the object or set of objects it represents. Associations constrain mapping when the spatial representation shares some properties with the object or concept being represented.

Association-based mappings differ from iconic mappings in that expressing the shared property or properties does not rely on perceptual isomorphism. Instead a perceptual property acts as a communicator or reminder of previously acquired associations between perceptual characteristics of the spatial representation and meaningful characteristics of the concept being represented. Iconic and association based constraints are similar in that both are based on experience, and are rooted in perception. In contrast, some mappings of concepts to spatial representations are based on similarity of organizational structures between the spatial representation and the concept being represented. These mappings appear not to require specific prior experience and are highly conducive for depicting non-perceptual characteristics of a concept or abstraction. One example of a constraint based on similarity of organizational structure is polarity, which constrains mappings of spatial and conceptual schemas when the spatial representation shares oppositional structure or directionality of dimension with the concept being represented.

These three constraints are insufficient, however, to account for the range and flexibility of human performance in reasoning with spatial representations. In this chapter I have argued that a fourth type of similarity, structural similarity, constrains mapping when the representation shares relational structure with the represented. Structural similarity leads to a mapping of elements to elements, relations to relations, and higher-order relations to higher-order relations between conceptual and spatial schemas. Research in two experimental paradigms supports this proposal. In studies using an artificial sign language, adults asked to interpret a novel sign chose a physical object to represent a conceptual element and a physical relation to represent a conceptual relation. This finding indicates that structural similarity constrains the mapping of simple relational structures—elements and relations between elements—in interpretions of novel spatial representations. In another set of studies, young children with no experience with graphs were asked to reason about conceptual variables using graph-like diagrams. Children's judgment patterns revealed two highly consistent mappings of concepts to spatial dimensions: first-order relations were inferred from the height of a line, and second-order relations were inferred from the slope of a line. This finding indicates that structural similarity constrains the mapping of higher-order relational structures as well. Together with previous research, these results indicate that iconicity, associations, polarity, and structural similarity influence the mapping of conceptual to spatial schemas in reasoning.

Chapter 10

Spatial Representation as Cause and Effect: Circular Causality Comes to Cognition

Brendan McGonigle and Margaret Chalmers

1   Introduction

Visual space has been both friend and foe to theories of cognitive functioning. As a metaphor for the mental representation of human adults, the properties of Euclidean space are amenable to psychological theories, providing neat models with structural principles that make intuitive sense (see, for example, the tree-like hierarchical structures of Rosch, 1973 and the network models of Collins and Quillian, 1969). Some theorists have even adopted a quite literal interpretation of spatial thinking to convincing explanatory effect. When it was first reported that adult humans use linear vectors to organize the premises of transitive inference tasks, the models were transparent, psychologically plausible as they derived from "think aloud" data, and left open the possibility, moreover, that such representations had pragmatic origins in actual space. As a result, they became a serious challenge to the prevailing approaches arising from the then dominant psycholinguistic theories of Chomsky (1966) and Miller (1963). De Soto, London and Handel (1965) and Huttenlocher (1968), for example, challenged Clark's deep-structural interpretation of choice biases and reactions times during three term series tasks (Clark, 1969) in terms of an alternative mechanism through which the agent and object of a sentence are inserted mentally one after the other along an imagined horizontal or vertical vector (depending on the relation in question), as if the meaning relations were mentally enacted with "lift and place" operations one would use in physical space. Thus, subjects, confronted with relational predicates such as "Jim is taller than Susan," "Susan is taller than Henry," etc., would often imagine a spatial vector and place the tallest item (usually at the top of a vertical one) such that the mental arrangement of logical objects would appear to enable the subject to secure inferences exclusively on the basis of relative position (e.g., "Jim must be taller than Henry," because Jim is "above" Henry).

Both spatial and non-spatial accounts of three term series research were united, however, in observing two quite distinctly different phenomena. The first is the finding of a privileged series more psychologically palatable than other forms which carry the same logical implication. Thus the *isotropic* series (Hunter, 1957, after James, 1891), in which items are presented in a connected sequence with relational direction maintained across premises (e.g., A > B; B > C) is found to be much easier than the *heterotropic* form which obtains when the temporal sequence of the predicates is incongruent with the series order (e.g. B > C; A > B), and/or the logical arguments are conveyed in a relationally inconsistent manner (e.g. A > B; C < B). These heterotropic cases are more difficult to solve as measured by both accuracy of choice during inference tests and by reaction time (Clark, 1969; Huttenlocher, 1968; Hunter, 1957). That human adults can solve these at all, at least in limited circumstances, is surely one of the clearest examples of thought in action. Yet the second form of presentation seems to derive from the subject's grasp of the *canonicality* of the series as expressed in the isotropic form: subjects solve heterotropic series (especially where there are more than 3 terms) by conversion and reordering procedures and frequently end up with an ordered isotropic series even when the predicates are indeterminate (McGonigle and Chalmers, 1986).

Despite a broad consensus on the data base, however, it has been difficult to achieve any resolution of competing and what seems at first mutually exclusive accounts. For every "imaginal" account, there is usually a competing one based on non-imaginal, language-like processes (Clark, 1969)—and not just for deductive tasks, but also for more direct assays of knowledge representation. In research on mental comparisons, Banks (1977), for example, successfully explained all the attendant phenomena of comparisons "in the minds eye" without recourse to any of the spatial processes of De Soto and Huttenlocher. These phenomena, generated using tasks in which subjects compare two items on a dimension such as size (e.g. "Which is bigger a cat or a cow?") include the well-known "Symbolic Distance Effect" or SDE (Moyer, 1973) which reflects an inverse relationship between the reaction time (RT) and the relative magnitude of the items being compared in memory. The impressive regularity of this RT function has suggested to many that subjects possess some form of analogue representation in the form of a mental line allowing item differences to be read off directly (Trabasso, 1977). However, using digit comparisons (in which a subject is typically asked to judge the larger of two numbers), for example, Banks, Fujii and Kayra-Stuart (1976) suggest that a code (established probabilistically) such as SMALL or LARGE is set for all the digits in the set under comparison. Here the representation is semantic and coded in discrete values rather than quasi-perceptual and coded along a continuous scale. A discrete code representation produces the Symbolic Distance Effect by probabilistic weightings. Adjustment to the codes thus set is made in working memory during a second stage of processing when a decision is made as to whether the codes are discriminable in relation to the specific question asked. If, for example, two codes match, one must then be converted in working memory, e.g. LARGE to LARGE+. The further apart, the more likely two items are to be tagged differently and the less likely the need for re-codification. The closer together, the more often the decision and recode process has to be repeated.

Though possibly analogue/spatial in character, therefore, the distance effect (SDE) can also be explained by these non-spatial discrete code types of explanation and, for this and other reasons, spatial models were later regarded as but one of several options for solving questions in mental comparison tasks (Potts et al, 1978). Later, in what could be seen as a convergence of approaches, the essentially *spatial* aspects of analogue representations became less figural than the *serial* processes argued to be used in their construction and in retrieval of information from them. For whether spatial or not, most approaches now focused on the serial processes allowing sustained uni-directional search in working memory from well-defined anchor points (biggest, lowest, highest, etc.) (e.g. Clark, 1970; Holyoak and Mah, 1982; Parkman, 1971). Here there was a strong analogy with the concept of "isotropy" arising from three-term series, but with the emphasis on the importance of sustained unidirectional search from the relevant end or anchor point of a series when encoding or retrieving information from long term memory. Influenced by this type of research, models for problem solution in three-term series tasks began to consider the possibly spatial aspect of the memory representation as only a part of the overall explanation of the solution processes (Sternberg, 1980)—or as one of a changing set of strategies along a path to expertise across repeated task exposure (Johnson-Laird, 1972). For some, it was simply a matter of cognitive *style* (Jones, 1970) whilst others have continued to dispute the existence of such representations (at least in reasoning tasks) altogether (Richardson, 1987). But perhaps the strongest antagonism to exclusively spatial representational accounts has come from the uncompromising view of "propositional" theorists that such concepts are epiphenomenal and can never be a basis for abstract thought. Pylyshyn (1981), for example, denounced the explanatory value of any and all analogue models on the grounds that investigators were confusing cause and effect; the true language of the mind, he argued, was based on the impenetrable silent operations of symbol manipulation for which there is, by definition, no explicit (spatial or other) expression.

Nevertheless, linear spatial representational devices may have an important enabling role in supporting isotropic or privileged search trajectories in memory and inference tasks as evidenced, at least, by protocol reports of imagined spatial arrays. As for causation, however, a chicken and egg problem expresses itself in a dilemma we represented some time ago as "mapping versus constructivism" (McGonigle and Chalmers, 1986). Are the privileged spatial vectors that subjects report the residue of a primary component in the development and evolution of relational encoding—an elementary and integral aspect of the construction of order? Or are they instead a later addition—an optional mental "map" based on the culturally expressed conventions of what Popper has described as the "third world" of books—the product of a "society of minds" rather than the product of an individual one? Forged (say) for navigation and maps of geographical space with conventionalized (polar) axes—such culturally evolved cognition takes on a format which individuals when immersed in a literate, graphic-oriented society might use as an optional but convenient "tool" to represent relational terms as objects in a linear array (McGonigle, 2000).

On this latter scenario, spatial schemas for abstract thought would emerge in adults from what once were quite separable components, now fossilized in Vygotsky's terms as an integrated scheme or data structure and subject to culturally evolved and transmitted representations of space such as geographical maps based on Cartesian co-ordinates. As for individual cognitive growth, the origins of such spatial schemas and their properties might well derive, as Clark (1970) has suggested, from functional adaptations in physical space which demand privileged meridians such as the vertical (upright) and horizontal (ground plane) to support locomotion.

However, purely spatial mechanisms, whatever their origins, will not be sufficient to explain how comparatives such as the size ones traditionally used in mental logic tasks come to be understood, get connected as a series, and mapped in "the minds' eye" to some spatial paralogical device. In short, there is a major ontological problem here centered on how the private, silent adaptations of the individual become expressed as the public conventions of row, column, ruler and array as expressed in the epi-phenomena of introspective report. And the answer, as Pylyshyn rightly insists, cannot lie within the tautology of invoking the latter to explain the former.

In this chapter, we review evidence from a developmental and comparative perspective, that, linear ordering based on comparative (e.g.) size judgements are derived from core design primitives which are neither spatial nor linguistic in origin (10.2). Evolved, we argue, as the basis of an effective *inductive* mechanism (McGonigle and Jones, 1978), we shall review evidence which suggests that series which are monotonic (linearly ascending or descending), such as the isotropic series, have simple, data reducing memory features which lead to their adoption as the most economical to operate in memory resource terms—especially as the number of elements to be managed in working memory increases (10.3). As predictable series, moreover, they are also generative and enable the subject to go well "beyond the information given" (Bruner, 1957). In an analogous way (10.4), we shall then present evidence that similar memory cost factors operate to ensure the selection of privileged vectors in actual space—such that searching locations along a principled path as determined by a vertical vector, for example, materially improves efficiency of search and reduces the self monitoring memory demands which would occur were a random search procedure adopted. Finally (10.5), we shall suggest that spatial and non-spatial search procedures may merge through a process of *externalization* when the classification and sorting of objects in actual space leads to visible forms of spatial arrangement which can then be internalized as psychologically explicit phenomena. Here too, we suggest that the merging will be motivated by a need to achieve the most powerful forms of adaptation consistent with the least possible cost to the system as a whole (McGonigle and Chalmers, 1992, 1996, 1998).

10.2   Primitive Relational Competencies and Linear Organization

Our work on relational design primitives began in 1969 when McGonigle and Jones (1975, 1977, 1978) investigated the ease with which size and brightness relations could be learned by young squirrel monkeys (*Saimiri scuireus*)—as compared with the learning of single absolute values. One group of monkeys (the relational group) was required to choose the larger/darker of two stimuli so that given two pairs, AB and BC, in which e.g. A is the smallest, C the largest, B was chosen over A, and C was chosen over B. The other group (the absolute group) were required to choose the item B in both cases. The "larger than" relation proved easier to learn than the absolute size, and so robust was the performance by the relational group over a long period of overtraining and transfer conditions, that McGonigle and Jones (1975, 1978) interpreted the asymmetric rule of relation (greater than, less than) as a primitive, not reducible to lower levels of processing, at least for squirrel monkeys. The profile for brightness was broadly similar. Our conclusions that relational encoding was a design primitive (at least in primates) was reached independently with human subjects and at around the same time by Bryant (1973).

As for linear organization, spatial or otherwise, however, relational encoding is only a pre-condition. Having established such primitives the next question was the extent to which such relational competencies support the linear organization of size related elements into a mental order, maintained as a representation without direct perceptual support. A suitable and relevant task paradigm was suggested at that time by the new work on transitivity in the 70s on children (Bryant and Trabasso, 1971). Bryant and Trabasso presented four pairs of a connected series of asymmetric relations, A > B, B > C, C > D, D > E, using pairs of colored rods arranged in a box such they protruded from the top by an equal amount (see Figure 10.1a). Verbal training using a regime of question (such as "Which is taller/shorter, red or yellow?") and answer established the correct size relationships for each pair. Once all the comparisons had been learned, test questions followed, concerning all the non-adjacent, untrained comparisons e.g. AC, BD, etc. Conventionally regarded as a test of mental ordering by measuring the extent to which subjects make transitive judgments during test, e.g. A > C, B > D, the training version of this task was adapted by McGonigle and Chalmers (1977) for use with squirrel monkeys (*Saimiri scuireus*) in the first such experiment on transitivity to be conducted with non-humans. To convey the relational differences between the test items without linguistic instructions on the one hand, or by direct perceptual means on the other, weight differences were used instead (see Figure 10.1b). Thus for each training pair of colored tins of equal size, one tin was "heavy," the other "light." Only two weight values were used throughout, so there was no correlated weight dimension

A. Bryant and Trabasso (1971)

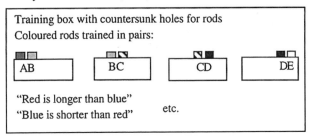

B. McGonigle and Chalmers (1977)

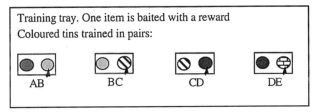

C. Chalmers and McGonigle (1984): Long tray condition

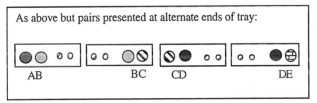

Figure 10.1
(A) The box and stimuli used during five-term series training with children by Bryant and Trabasso (1971). The tray and stimuli used in a WGTA, during five-term series training (B) with squirrel monkeys by McGonigle and Chalmers (1977) and (C) with five-year-old children by McGonigle and Chalmers (1984).

to associate with the color values to provide a possible empirical basis on which ordered decisions (for the set as a whole) could be made. Thus, as in the case of the Bryant and Trabasso task, any transitive choices would have to result from the subject's integration of pairwise information alone.

As Figure 10.1b illustrates, monkeys were trained on the four pairs using a reward/no reward basis for training A over B; B over C, etc., then, like the children in Bryant and Trabasso's study, tested on all non-adjacent pairings, where a choice to either stimulus was rewarded.

On all main points of comparison, the monkey's performance was similar to that of the children in Bryant and Trabasso's study; and in binary choice tests, all choices were impeccably transitive. As for linear representation, monkeys showed all the characteristics claimed for linear ordering at a "representational" level. For example, they showed a classical serial position effect when acquiring the five term series interpreted by Trabasso (1977) as the *sine qua non* of linear representation. When measures of reaction time were analyzed, furthermore, they showed a significant Symbolic Distance Effect (SDE)—an inverse linear relationship between RT and the degree of ordinal separation between the items compared during test. Argued by many, as we reviewed above, as evidence of an analogue device which enables subjects to read off the relative differences between test items which can be ordered on, e.g. a material scale such as size, using a form of spatial paralogical device.

However, detailed analysis of the RT data indicated that the SDE in monkeys at least is not a simple reflection of a mental line or array. For strong series asymmetry was found when the reaction times were computed from each end of the series separately (see Figure 10.2). Although every individual monkey showed an SDE, in all cases but one the distance effect obtains only from one end of the series and comparisons were uniformly fast from the other end (though monkeys varied as to whether the "fast" end was the rewarded or non-rewarded one). That this is a feature that also applies in the case of humans, moreover, was shown by our re-analyses of Trabasso's data from six and nine year old children when he tested them using a six term version of the Bryant and Trabasso task (McGonigle and Chalmers, 1998). Despite the fact that both comparatives ("longer" and "shorter") were used during training, once again, the series representation seems profoundly asymmetrical even in the older, nine year old, children—favoring comparisons from the "long" end over the "short" one, *whatever the question asked.*

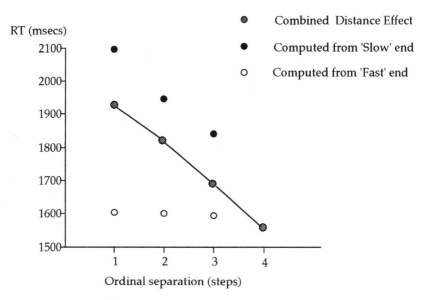

Figure 10.2
The Symbolic Distance Effect (SDE) obtained with monkeys (McGonigle & Chalmers, 1992), plotted conventionally and also separately from the 'slow' and the 'fast' end-points of the series.

Finally, when using a mental comparison paradigm with children, McGonigle and Chalmers (1984) found a similar effect, again suggesting that the SDE does not necessarily indicate that subjects consult a spatial array in memory. Using, first, the traditional method with comparative questions such as "Which is bigger, a cat or a cow?" the data revealed a significant SDE with six and nine year old children for lexical and pictorial items compared for size "in the mind's eye" as found for adults. However, when verification questions were used such as "Is a cat bigger/ smaller than a cow?" etc., then a pronounced asymmetry of series was found such that, *even at the level of choice*, six year old children were unable to verify questions which demanded series reference from the small end of the series. That is they were unable to verify that e.g. "A cat is smaller than a cow," even though their previous categorization of the items showed an accurate rank ordering. We regarded this as due to a search (procedural) asymmetry rather than a "marking" effect operating simply on a lexical level (Clark, 1969). For our results indicated that the primary bias lay in using "bigger than" over "smaller than" as a means of representing a difference relation, not in the retrieval of the meaning of the terms "bigger" versus "smaller" (for details, see McGonigle and Chalmers, 1984). Even nine year olds showed this directional asymmetry; although generally correct on all four forms of verification, their answers were significantly slower for smaller "true" and bigger "false" questions, i.e. those that forced the subject to topicalize the smaller item in the pairing (e.g. "Is a cat smaller than a cow?" and "Is a cat bigger than a cow?"). Such directional asymmetry is not entirely inimical to the idea of a spatial format, but it does considerably constrain the sense in which a mental line or array might be utilized by subjects that show such selectivity of access to the information it embodies.

Rather than interpret such phenomena as evidence of a spatially based representation device of the sort reported by De Soto and Handel, therefore, we concluded that these "suggest the early development of a mental metric or set of codes which allow for the representation of order with respect to some reference point or pole" (McGonigle and Chalmers, 1986, 152). That is, we interpreted the biased and asymmetrical representation of the memory set in both age groups, as possibly deriving from the fact that items might be coded as "big" and "not big" rather than as the polar opposites "big" and "small" and that this produces an enduring search asymmetry favoring search from the, well-defined "big" end of the continuum. This interpretation was further confirmed by two new findings. One was that six year old children were indeed faster to deny that "small" animals were "big" than to affirm that they were "small," suggesting a primary codification in terms of big and not big (see Figure 10.3).

The second was, that, when the SDE is computed for every item separately, and when the data are averaged across both "bigger" and "smaller" forms of question, the variance used to compute the distance effect is actually less than the variance arising from the relative size of the smaller item in the comparison (see Figure 10.4 for an example from nine year old children). This source of variance is known as the Min effect (Potts et al, 1978) but in adult data where it is usually observed, it is seen to be an additional effect over and above the variance due to the ordinal separation between the items being compared (producing the distance effect). Here in contrast, as in the analysis of our monkey transitivity data (McGonigle and Chalmers, 1992), we had no reason to believe that there was such a separate source of variance deriving from the separation between the comparison items on a mental line. For children and monkeys, the codification and search of items in terms of a unipolar description

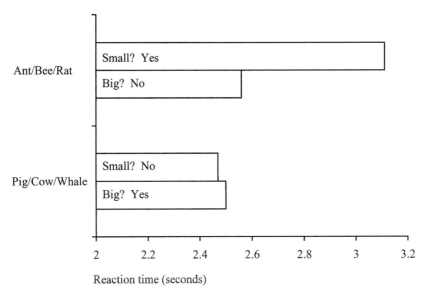

Figure 10.3
Reaction times obtained from six-year-old children in response to questions asking them to affirm or deny that depicted animals (scaled to appear the same size) were "big ones" or "small ones" (McGonigle & Chalmers, 1984).

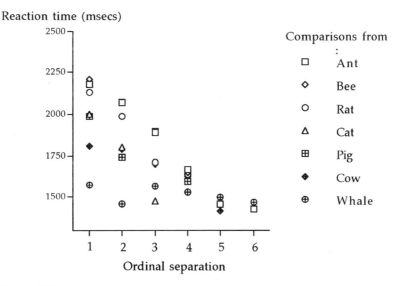

Figure 10.4
Reaction times obtained from nine-year-old children in mental-comparison experiments, plotted, as a function of ordinal separation, from every item in the set.

such as "big," and the proximity of items to a single anchor point was sufficient to explain all the phenomena we had observed.

As far as interpreting the SDE in terms of a spatial analogue device, in other words, *there was no evidence from any of the extensive analyses that we did, either on the logical tasks or on the Moyer-type mental comparison ones, that a spatial paralogical device is in operation in our subjects.* Our analyses of decision times in both domains, furthermore, cast strong doubt on the validity of claims for children's representations such as those expressed by Trabasso (1977) that the items are rank ordered from big to small and read off directly by consulting an internal spatial array. Instead a highly asymmetrical and unidirectional search process seems to operate well in advance of any more static Euclidean form of representing linearly ordered information.

This characterization of the RT data as due essentially to a serial search procedure working on-line, rather than the product of direct "read-off" from a static, off-line, representational array, was further supported by an extension of standard transitivity testing that we carried out, in which we presented three rather than the conventional two items during transitivity tests (e.g. BCD instead of BD). In our first recorded tests of this sort (McGonigle and Chalmers, 1977: Chalmers and McGonigle 1984) we found that neither monkeys nor children were able to maintain the levels of transitive choice recorded in the binary phases. Even in a later study, (in which we first recorded RTs and found the SDE with monkeys) which included more extensive experience with triadic choices by using triplets rather than pairs in training (e.g. AAB, ABB, etc.) we once again recorded an initial drop in the levels of transitivity to the triads (McGonigle and Chalmers, 1992).

Such a decrement is difficult to reconcile with an array based model, but is entirely consistent with a search based one, and emerges also from a production rule based model of transitivity by Harris and McGonigle (1994). Their modeling of monkey data was based on condition-action pairs such as (If E select E, etc.) and shows how errors, choice, and RTs are well fitted by a rule stack principle in which information is organized serially in working memory in one direction. Crucially, however, it also shows that binary and triadic choices are formally different from one another and that the latter require greater depth of search. Sixteen different rule stacks could be generated that were consistent with training and all of them predicted transitivity of choice on binary tests, showing that *binary* transitivity does not depend upon a unique ordering of the information in long-term memory. As two of the five items are end-points and lead to simple rules with no competitors, e.g. "if E, take E" or "if A, take other," however, these two are likely to be implemented first within the stack of serial decisions (E, then A, etc.)—and stacks with either of these properties offered the best fit to the data. In the case of triads, additional constraints are added—for triads that do not contain the end-item that always attract choice (E), a simple avoid—A rule does not help in the selection of which of the remaining two items are to be chosen. This creates a need for increased depth of search within the rule stack.

Depth of search apart, the number of rule stacks which optimally support transitive choice within triads are considerably reduced from those which operate effectively in binary decisions. Consistent with this, monkeys were found to converge on the use of rule stacks which now always prioritize the E rule in the stack during extended triadic testing (McGonigle and Chalmers, 1998) where it was found that monkeys spontaneously improved their levels of triadic transitive choice when exposed to triads over considerable periods, but without any selective reinforcement (McGonigle and Chalmers, 1992). This suggested that the experience of larger combinations of objects induces a data reducing strategy of simply coding only three objects derived from the 10 triads, as ranked predictors of reward. Thus a new rule stack such as: IF E then E; IF D then D; IF C then C economically catered for all the test choices without having to code all triadic combinations explicitly. These findings offered a new perspective on transitivity and suggested that depth and type of search within the decision space is a crucial aspect to the emergence of a more integrated—albeit unidirectional—form of linear representation. Whilst sharing many of the properties of directional search suggested in the literature on mental comparisons by adults (e.g. Potts et al, 1978), a key aspect of the stack model was in extending the notion of end anchoring to a sorting mechanism that allows internal rank ordering of the other items also, and doesn't simply assume that they are already somehow encoded within a linear format, spatial or otherwise.

In summary, the emergence of *serial search procedures* seems to be a crucial aspect of the emergence of linear organization in humans and non-humans alike; the evidence from our own research does not suggest that a spatial form of representation has a causal role here.

These conclusions do not sit well with those developmental accounts which place a strong emphasis on the mapping or metaphorical role that space might have in enabling the development of transitive reasoning (e.g. Halford, 1993). So strong was the assumption that space provides a natural device for representing relations, that initial claims for inference making by children were dogged by the possibility that space might even be an artifact when testing for mental integration of size relations. Specifically, doubts were raised by Riley and Trabasso (1974) that the results of Bryant and Trabasso (1971) were obtained because the children has access to a literal spatial cue to the right answer without having to think about the size relations at all. The problem arose because the authors used a five-holed box to present the pairwise premises during training. Thus the four pairs of rods used in training were of different actual lengths and countersunk in a wooden box at fixed locations along it (see Figure 10.1a). Whilst Bryant and Trabasso counterbalanced right/left positions within the pairs (by turning the box round), concern was subsequently expressed that children were nevertheless able to base their answers on the relative spatial location of the sticks (Riley and Trabasso, 1974).

Considered as a physical rather than a mental support, however, our own research, suggested that space does not operate in these experiments either to provide a map with properties congruent with choice, but rather as a device for *enabling the serial coding of the information* (see Roberts, this volume). As such, it is effective even when there is no isomorphism between the literal space and the logical order. This emerged during an attempt at replicating the study of Bryant and Trabasso (1971) but in which the training box had only two holes (Chalmers, 1977). As we experienced considerable difficulty replicating their results, we resolved the situation by using a modification of the paradigm that we had successfully used with monkeys (McGonigle and Chalmers, 1977). We also increased the age of our subjects by eighteen months to an average age of six years. Children were thus trained and tested in a Wisconsin General Testing Apparatus (WGTA) which allows the objects in a discrimination task to be selectively "baited" with a reward whilst out of view of the subject. Especially built for child testing, our WGTA was larger than that used for monkey, but identical in design: child and experimenter were seated at opposite ends of the apparatus and the experimenter baited the stimuli behind a guillotine door, separating child from adult. The rewards were colored counters which the child exchanged at the end of the experiment for a token number of sweets. For each pair, they were required to choose in a direction which was consistent across the series (e.g. B over A; C over B; D over C, and E over D). As three subjects had to be rejected shortly after starting the experiment due to extreme diffi-

Table 10.1
Results on transitivity tests with five-year-old children (Chalmers, 1977)

Short tray				Long tray			
	C	D	E		C	D	E
A	64*	47*	63*	A	73	67*	97
B		57*	83	B		83	93
C			73	C			83

* Non-significant on a binomial test ($p < 0.01$)

culty in learning the pairs, it was decided to introduce a spatial aid which might enhance learning without being itself correlated with a linear order connecting the pairs. This was a longer tray than the conventional one, in which there were two reward cavities at either end as depicted in Figure 10.1c.

The rationale was that such spatial separation might reduce proactive and retroactive interference across pairs without "giving the game away," by spatially separating linked pairs. That is pair AB, in which B is rewarded was presented at one end, whilst pair BC, in which B appears again, but is not rewarded, is presented at the other. Thereafter children were transferred to the long tray if they failed to meet criterion at any point, and no further subjects had to be rejected. Fifty percent of subjects required this aid to training. In test, the children showed significant transitive biases (on all pairs except AD). As Table 10.1 shows, however, the transitive profile was largely due to the long tray subjects, even though there was no correlation between the layout and the choice bias and the short tray was used in test.

These results suggested an enabling, but not a causal, role for spatial factors in the linear integration of the pairs. Instead, such factors seemed simply to provide extra cues which helped keep the pairs separate in long and short term memory. Similar results were later obtained by Kallio (1982) in an extensive study in which he went on to separate the serial presentation and spatial factors in a 4-way design in which he provided in four different conditions, a spatial (correlated) cue along with the serial cue provided in the separate pairs phase of training (the Bryant and Trabasso condition), only the serial cue (ordered pairs throughout), only the spatial cue or neither. Consistent with our own findings was the clear evidence that it was not necessary to have the correlated spatial cue to improve learning and transitive choice; this factor in fact made no difference in Kallio's case. What was crucial to both learning and transitive choice performance in his study was the availability of the serial cue provided by training the pairs in order from AB to DE. Although most training studies only use such serial training in the first introductory phase of the task, Kallio's results suggest that presenting the pairs in a way which is initially in the isotropic form is one key to the success of the Bryant and Trabasso paradigm when used with children and monkeys.[1]

Does this imply that separable spatial dimensions are not themselves the subject of transitive connections for young children? Recent studies have illustrated that this is far from the case. Pears and Bryant (1990), for example, have provided perhaps the most compelling evidence of transitivity mechanisms in young children in a task which required transitive choices to be made about the spatial relations "higher" and "lower." Without any training whatever, four year old children were able to predict the relative vertical positions of blocks within a tower construction on the basis of pairwise segments, composing mini-towers. When space is viewed therefore as the sole material connective on which transitive choices are founded, it shows itself to be a potent dimension along which linear constructions can be made. Viewed as a dimension of connectivity in its own right, we can therefore appreciate that it may sometimes facilitate transitive judgements about other dimensions. The question is *how* it might do so. Recently, Schnall and Gattis (1998) trained six year old children on four pairs, using a reward/no reward basis for training as used by McGonigle and Chalmers (1971), but the pairs were presented within a linear array which either preserved a congruity between temporal order of introducing the pairs in the training phase (AB, BC, CD, DE, etc.) or randomized them spatially within the linear matrix such that they were de-correlated with the training order. Schnall and Gattis found a major facilitation on transitivity tests using the former as opposed to the latter condition. Here the spatial factor was undoubtedly seen by the children as integral with the reward structure of the task, but the extent to which the temporal presentation of the training pairs might have helped to establish that structure is not clear. Certainly in that study there was a higher proportion of first phase, serial order training as compared to Chalmers and McGonigle (1984). In the latter study, although there was a great deal more training in total (the subjects were more than one year younger than those of Schnall and Gattis), it involved more extensive exposure to the second phase, random pair presentation. Under these circumstances, the spatial factor clearly did not have to be congruent with a linear construction to facilitate training and test, as both the temporal and the spatial conditions were non-linear for the major part of training.

Taking all these results together, it would seem that the "benefit" of a linear spatial layout is an additional option for subjects *who can already integrate the information by another means,* i.e. as an aid rather than a primary route to the encoding of the information. On this interpretation of the spatial aid, it might then seem anomalous that "removing" the Bryant and Trabasso box appeared to have little or no disabling effect in conditions run by Riley and Trabasso (1974) and Kallio (1982) where there was (some) isotropic input to support any such congruity. However, whilst the training box was occluded in these experiments, subjects were nevertheless shown it during pre-test. Having seen the box beforehand, therefore, it is highly likely that the relative location of the items in the spatial array was used to augment the representation of the pairwise information presented, in these particular conditions, in serial, isotropic form. As Schnall and Gattis have shown, space will be utilized by children when there is congruity between spatial and temporal inputs, but as we and others have also shown, the primary congruity must derive from the serial search procedures entrained or initiated in the task and the temporally "isotropic" form which maintains consistency of relational direction. And as Kallio has demonstrated, if this support is removed altogether, linear integration is eliminated in young children. In short, temporal mechanisms that operate to control relationally based search would appear to have primacy over spatial ones in the generation of order, creating conditions in which space might be used on-line to reduce memory demands, but does not seem to be used off-line by young children or animals to support representation in long-term memory.

If so, the mapping role for spatially based representations—at least as far as linear order is concerned—is a later, possibly strategic, development following temporally motivated search procedures which enable restricted forms of series construction. This however, creates the new problem of how and why spatial representation devices ever come to interact with temporal search based ones, and why the latter would spontaneously evolve in the isotropic form. Whilst triadic transitivity results suggest that search procedures improve dynamically in the context of more difficult problems, the conventional transitivity paradigms as a whole are too restrictive in scope to pursue these issues much further. For this and other reasons, we now turn to a task which has remained since its introduction, one of the most robust indicators of cognitive growth. The classic size ordering tasks of Piaget and Szeminska (as reported in Inhelder and Piaget, 1964) requires children to re-organize a jumbled collection of a large number of rods (up to ten) varying in size, and place them in a linear arrangement in space in ascending or descending order of size (a monotonic series)—either by instruction to "make it look like a staircase" or by copying a model. By six to seven years, the child solves the task by a principled selection procedure which involves taking, for example, the largest item then the next biggest, then the next, etc. until the test pool is exhausted and a series constructed.

The large number of items used in this task makes it, first of all, a substantial search problem. Combinatorially, the number of possible sequence which a 10 item set can generate is 3628800. Second, the emergent organization as described by Inhelder and Piaget (1964) has all the hallmarks of a privileged series of the sort that seems to be the canonical form when adults are required to mentally construct and represent a series. And, as classically administered, the task has a strong spatial component as Piaget himself recognized. Laying out the items in space both as model (with "good gestalt") and as product, makes the ensemble "look like something." As children place objects, they change the state of the array and are able to view the global consequences of their actions.

A highly explicit and demanding test of linear organization, in short, this task neatly encapsulates all of the main elements implicated in the emergence of the abstract representation of order. Unfortunately, in the classic task, factors which make the task demanding are not well separated from ones which may have ameliorative effects. Consistent with the search stance, the number of elements has been long implicated as an important element in the very slow unfolding of this competence (Inhelder and Piaget, 1964, Kingma, 1984). Yet a systematic study of the number of elements and how they increase the search requirements in seriation has not been undertaken. And if it were to be, it would need to be carried out under conditions where the visible consequences of object placement and the cumulative layout features of the series were sometimes eliminated, if the possible role of spatial and gestalt factors are to be separated from the serial control factors responsible for this skill. Finally, from a comparative standpoint as well, a fractionation of the necessary from the more accidental aspects of size seriation needs to be undertaken. It is clear that non-humans subjects are not generally competent to place objects in a neat row as required by the classic task, a fact which makes

A. Monotonic size sequencing task

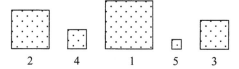

Correct touch sequence
e.g., 5, 4, 3, 2, 1

B. Colour sequencing task

Correct touch sequence
e.g., R, G, P, W, Y

Figure 10.5
(A) An example of a five-item monotonic size sequence and the touch sequence
required on a particular trial. While the sequential requirement remains the same
throughout the task, the spatial layout changes randomly from trial to trial. (B)
An example of a color sequencing task, trained under the same conditions as (A).

the question of whether animals can seriate sizes to any extent at all
critically important in evaluating how active spatial manipulation might
contribute to the evolution and development of seriation competence.

For these reasons we turned first to a version of seriation that had
no specific spatial task requirement; only a search one. Using computer
driven touch screens, we displayed a variety of icons varying in size in
random linear arrays, and required that subjects touch each one once only,
according to a sequential rule such as biggest to smallest. The randomized
arrays ensured that there was *no correlation* between the way the sizes
appeared, and (e.g.) the monotonic search path that had to be complied
with (see Figure 10.5a). In this way, we have been able to assess size
seriation, considered as an extended serial search task without manipulation requirements and spatial confounds.

10.3   Linear-Size Based Search and the Emergence of a Privileged Series

A first and obvious question was: can young children show principled
monotonic ordering of size without any privileged, invariant spatial support

for their productions? Our results (Chalmers and McGonigle, 2000) demonstrated that five year old children can be trained to seriate five and seven item size sets under conditions where the choice of stimuli did not affect the appearance of the array. Although the 7-item set proved significantly harder than the 5-item condition for the younger subjects, successful seriation was nevertheless obtained in conditions where the choice of the stimuli did not affect the appearance of the array. In children below the age of operational (spontaneous) seriation, it is difficult to say from these results alone whether such achievements reflect an "abstract" grasp of size relations, or simply the mastery of an arbitrary set of connections. Our study, however, included an entirely arbitrary serial task by way of comparison (Figure 10.5b). Here subjects were trained in exactly the same way on the touch screen to learn a fixed color sequence such as red, green yellow, blue, white, etc. Using an intra-subject design, we therefore had the basis for a subtractive metric by means of which we could measure the degree to which children were able to predict the size sequence on the basis of an understanding of the monotonic structure of an ascending or descending sequence, using a non size-based sequence as a baseline. Figure 10.6 illustrates the choice data for the seven item set, from which it can be seen that there is a measurable component of error reduction which is selective to the two size sequences. The acquisition data show a significantly higher incidence of error in assimilating successive items into the trained sequence in the case of the arbitrary sequence.

This utilization of monotonicity in size seriation does not require an invariant form of spatial layout. Instead, there are reasons to believe that the learning of a monotonic series occurs precisely because it is highly predictable and redundant, enabling subjects who pick up the simple serial structure where only a single relational code needs to be iterated to generate series well beyond the exemplars on which original training occurs. These characteristics are not shared by other possible series which derive permutatively from such ordering tasks. For example, a small increase in the numbers of elements from say 5 to just 7 items increases the number of possible sequences geometrically from 120 sequential possibilities to 5040. And in none of the other (non-monotonic) sequences can the subject profit from series predictability and achieve an economy of cognitive resource as can be achieved in the monotonic form. As an ordering task, therefore, seriation is a good example of a behavior which succeeds because the agent has achieved high levels of constraint in the face of progressive combinatorial problems.

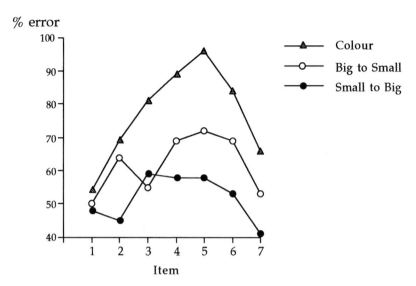

Figure 10.6
The relative error recorded on successive items within a seven-item sequence learning task by five year olds, for an arbitrary colour task (depicted by triangles) and the two monotonic size tasks (depicted by circles).

However, we cannot rule out the possibility that successful seriation by children could result from their importation of previously acquired spatially-based representational formats which they mentally map onto the size series as given in our experiments. To evaluate this possibility, we replicated some of the core conditions with monkeys under even more severe conditions of test—up to nine different elements were presented and arranged in randomly changing configurations within a 12 position matrix, as illustrated in Figure 10.7.

Based also on touch screens, six *Cebus apella* (McGonigle and Chalmers, 1998; McGonigle et al., 1999) have been trained to seriate progressively longer sequences where, in one condition (reported here), the composition of the elements was based exclusively on relative size. Within the study, which is still ongoing, three subjects (McGonigle et al., 2000) have achieved a criterion of at least 75% correct seriation across 50 trials on size series of nine items, ordered monotonically from small to big. Yet the configurations are even more deviant from the spatial arrays so favored in the conventional seriation tasks. Without a public language system, or a culture disposed towards certain forms of organization, and

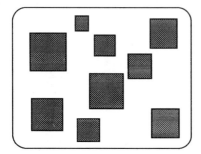

Figure 10.7
An example of a touch-screen array for size seriation as learned by *Cebus apella.*

without the means of object manipulation that enable it to display for itself the consequences of its own seriation procedures, monkeys can seriate nine sizes within configurations that are not supported by any sort of privileged spatial format. The fact that such sequence learning is generative and enables subjects to accomplish progressively longer seriation tasks without concomitant increases in learning costs (McGonigle and Chalmers, 1998), indicates, moreover, that it is the monotonic *type* of sequence (Chalmers and McGonigle, 2000), that makes serial search *economic*, and which motivates the development of linear ordering in human cognitive growth (McGonigle and Chalmers, 1996).

In none of the assays thus far have spatial factors been allowed any clear supportive role. On the contrary, the spatial configurations of the items subject to ordering rules have changed at random from trial to trial, and, on a given trial, the actions of seriating do not change the state characteristics of the arrays of icons. This of course does not deny that the implementation of the search procedures we observe has no spatial infrastructure. We have found evidence that children use the position of an icon within an array to help remember which icons have already been touched within a given trial (Chalmers and McGonigle, 2000)—rather as we found the long tray to reduce memory demands in transitivity training. What we are saying is that there is no invariant, *special spatial format* which has been found essential to the delivery of effective size seriation in both children and monkeys. Whatever the spatial contribution, however, the progressive and principled emergence of linear seriation behaviors in both simians and children indicates strongly that there are core cognitive precursors of human abstract thought that derive from individual acts of discovery and "honest toil" (Harnad, 1987). Based on temporally coded search procedures exploiting redundancy in monotonic size series, here surely is a strong, plausible, causal candidate for the *canonical* series representation in adult human subjects. In short, there is no warrant for the belief that such behaviors have a strong social or spatial determination, or indeed that they are unique to humans.

If monotonically based search procedures are as data reducing, economic and privileged as we claim, however, it should follow that *non-monotonic* ones will remain psychologically implausible in such subjects. More specifically, the degree of non-monotonicity—measured as the degree of deviance from monotonic form—should be a good predictor of series difficulty. As our touch screen techniques enable us to train any sequence from the combinatorial set under identical conditions of training and layout, we were able to test this prediction.

Using exactly the same stimuli and random layout conditions as in the monotonic search task, we trained children to follow a fixed but non-monotonic order (e.g. second biggest, smallest, middle-sized, biggest, second smallest). Here both ages of subject registered pronounced difficulty on this task even for five item sets, and the seven item sets (only attempted with seven-year-olds!) were, in the main, beyond the ability of even the "operational" aged seriators to learn. Insofar as the non-monotonic task could be solved at all by children, the data led us to the view that such disordered sequences as are learned, derive from subsets set of local monotonic sub-strings rather than as a random string of individual elements (Chalmers and McGonigle, 2000).

These results suggest a strong parallel with those which emerge following reviews of data on the selective effects of input form in logical tasks (Hunter, 1957; Glick and Wapner, 1968; McGonigle and Chalmers, 1984; 1986). Subjects who cope well with monotonically congruent (isotropic) input are generally poor in dealing with non-monotonic (heterotropic) orders. That young children's sequential encoding of relational arguments is limited to temporal strategies which preserve monotonicity, moreover, has been demonstrated by Kallio (1982) and by O'Connor and Hermelin (1972). What Piaget called the "tyranny of temporal succession" seems to make it difficult for young children to recode the logical objects in orders which differ from order of mention of the logical arguments. Significant too, the solution of heterotropic forms "in the head" is rare also in human adults where the number of predicates exceeds four (Potts et al., 1978).

The non-monotonic task, however, is not intrinsically impossible, and eventually becomes solvable during development at some point after the age of seven. Even with seven items, adult subjects will learn such sequences within a single session. However, those who do, use a number code derived from a monotonic series. The new codes are then used to tag each successor size in the series, such as 4375261. These number codes which are knowledge lean and map invariantly from one set to another show the power of the procedures which derive from the concept of iso-tropic as privileged, where each adjacent ordinal code on the number line is also the cardinally adjacent value. If constructed as a spatial layout, allowing a direct "read-off," it would mean that each spatially adjacent code *must also be cardinally and ordinally adjacent*. Within this cross-correlated structure, knowledge of the ordinal code gives a strong clue as to its cardinal value which in turn gives a strong clue as to its position (and vice-versa) and make for an exceedingly powerful, robust, data format, easy to store and search. Indeed, the well known characteristics of the privileged (canonical) isotropic series much beloved by William James (1891), where "any number of intermediaries may be expunged without altering what remains" would seem to require this type of spatial format as a representational device, providing item location as an enduring trace or scratchpad.

10.4   The Genesis of Spatial Schemas and Privileged Vectors

However, it is one thing to show the putative utility of a spatial device once it is assumed (see e.g. Hummel and Holyoak, 2000, this volume) and another to discover the route by which some aspects of spatial represen-tation leak into other parts of the cognitive system (Clark, 1997). Seeking to avoid the tautology of claiming that space is somehow prefigured into canonical arrangements along linear axes, we consider the development of literal search skills within an actual visible space. Here we evaluate the extent to which search in actual space develops gradually through the increasingly effective utilization of spatial (vector) principles and report high correlations between good spatial search performance and the use of constraining, vector based search principles.

In the spatial memory tasks we have devised (McGonigle, De Lillo and Dickinson, 1992, 1994), the paradigm is deceptively simple. The task is merely to touch in turn all dots on a touch screen, neglecting none (ex-haustive search). The task is increased progressively in difficulty, thus increasing the memory load should the subject try to keep track of icons already chosen. Failure to do so on the other hand, would make the

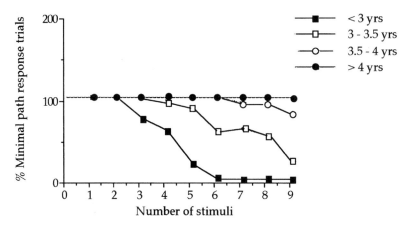

Figure 10.8
Search paths for children aged between 3 and 4 years as a function of the number of icons to be touched.

search uneconomic as reiterations would occur and delay the completion of the task in hand. As the numbers of icons increases, random, unprincipled search become more expensive in these terms. Nevertheless the question at issue was: would young children and monkeys spontaneously adopt a principled search attitude under these circumstances? And if they did, what search path(s) within the spatial layout would they choose?

No selective reinforcement is applied throughout the subject's production. The only positive feedback is at the end of a trial when the screen goes blank and the children see an icon of a man climbing a ladder towards a tree laden with apples: in the monkey experiments, a dispenser gives them a peanut. How subjects choose to search, however, is left entirely to them. Figure 10.8 shows how children respond to this task. Younger subjects (of four years and younger) soon get into difficulty when the dots increase in number beyond five. This is because they do not use a principled strategy like the older children who emerge with a consistent, (usually) vertical vector based search strategy, starting at the bottom of a column of dots and searching to the top, then moving to the adjacent column and searching down to the bottom, etc. With this search strategy, memory for keeping track of what had been searched is heavily diminished. Based on an adjacency principle combined with a search along the principal meridians, the subject merely has to follow these lines in space to keep search demands low. In contrast, younger children seem to search either at random, or use other paths though the space, such as following the contours of the matrix—then neglecting icons at its center.

These developmental results indicate that *spatial meridians* are beneficial and, if used in conjunction with search procedures of the sort we report in size seriation, would greatly benefit the subject. However, with children we find subjects who either cope with large search tasks and immediately adopt a principled search attitude or those who do not, and fail. In contrast, monkeys were tested over long periods, using tasks scaled for progressive difficulty. This efficiency is objectively measured in terms of the number of "surplus" touches which are required over the minimal number which a particular task level decreases e.g. if 6 dots, the minimum path is 6; if 9 then 9. For a subject to exit on 8 in the case of the 6 level condition, and 11 in the case of the 9 item conditions is a measure of the relative efficiency of search. As measured in these terms, it was found that their performance was a highly gradable function of task complexity; every additional icon produced a measurable difference in performance (see Figure 10.9). However, a strong indication that monkeys were able to develop effective search procedures was (a) the finding that performance was a linear rather than a geometric function of task complexity when measured during the course of learning, as Figure 10.9 also shows, and (b) that their performance improved significantly over the course of task practice but entirely without the selective feedback as given in conventional learning experiments (McGonigle and De Lillo, 1999).

10.5   A Future Interactive Scenario for Spatial Schemas and Relational Understanding: Externalization

We now have simian subjects who have developed spatial vector principles honed under conditions where there are no material differences between the icons. In the same subjects, we also have strong evidence of linear (object) relational search where there are no spatial correlates or consequences of such search. Nevertheless, it has to be recognized that under normal operating conditions, humans who seriate and classify objects will move and place them in a spatial layout where, for the seriation task as conventionally given, the objects will be seriated along a horizontal vector in a neat row. Similarly, when objects are sorted, they are frequently sorted into piles and collections where objects of the same sort are placed in regions of the test space away from others which form a

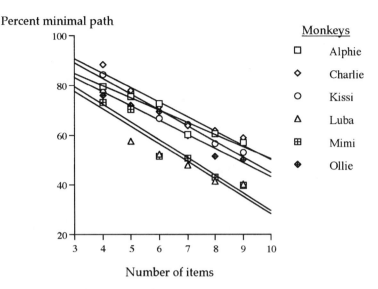

Figure 10.9
Search paths for monkeys (*Cebus apella*) as a function of the number of icons to be touched, together with their fit to a linear model.

different class or collection. So objects when manipulated and ordered in external space (e.g. within a linear spatial array) make it possible for the agent to see the global spatial consequences of a production. In the course of an ongoing task of this sort, the subject can review output and use deictic codes to achieve further cognitive economies as suggested for eye movements recently by Ballard et al (1998).

Once complete, moreover, a global image of success could create new images of achievement. And these in turn could well entrain new solutions. Economic in memory resource, furthermore, tasks may be interrupted, then resumed and completed later. The world itself has become a scratchpad, replaying an old evolutionary trick (McGonigle, 1998) and reflecting a data reducing externalizing process described by Clark (1998) as "leaky."

Whilst monkeys cannot manipulate objects and place these in a neat row in real space—the reason for switching to touch screens in the first place—we have now devised procedures which allow for a variety of action provoked changes in the spatial array as the subject is seriating, so that we can empirically evaluate the combined utility of relationally based with vector based search. To help assess the possible additional benefits of

A. Cumulative constraint with   B. Cumulative constraint
   consistent spatial array translation   without array translation

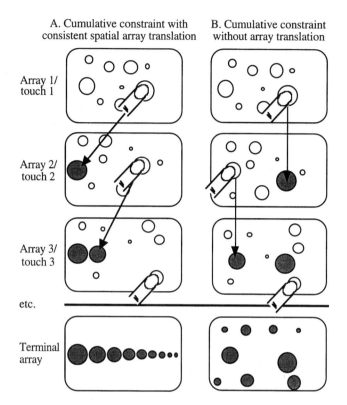

Figure 10.10
A paradigm for testing the potential benefits of externalizing principled sequencing during learning, through cumulative translation into a linearly organised spatial array (A), as compared with a control condition (B) in which touched icons are spatially fixed but in the random positions in which they were presented.

congruent externalized feedback, and when these might appear in evolution and development, we are planning new experiments which enable us to move the icons in *constrained and principled ways* following seriation and classification. These new experiments eschew the manipulative restrictions in monkeys and young children whilst preserving the essential (search) action-to-visible consequent relationship which active human primates take for granted. As Figure 10.10 shows, the program moves the icons interrogated on the screen in accordance with some spatial conventions—linear (as illustrated) in the case of linear size seriation, and in groups and collections when subjects must classify.

10.6 Summary and Conclusions

Our work has been motivated by a concern to study the evolutionary and developmental precursors to cognitive competencies as found in human adults. These have problems of being fossilized and compiled as skills; and a further problem is that later elaborations of cognitive skill may materially reduce the complexity of the procedures which formed the initial basis for problem solution. For example, the spatial representational devices used by human adult subjects, may well operate to circumvent more costly procedures which have been forged prior to spatial representational competencies. Placing logical/linguistic objects along an imagined spatial dimension, for example can provide a convenient spatial bridge between logical arguments, and allow for a variety of relative judgements to be made without requiring any retention or co-ordination of the logical arguments which informed the subject in the first place. This is the sort of mechanism, for example that Trabasso (1977) suggested in his "read off" argument in the case of the (inference-based) SDE. In real space, furthermore, the ability to lay out sets of objects as in Piaget's celebrated counting studies with rows of beads, would offer a convenient means of identifying ordinally equivalent items from set to set without those expensive, symbolic sorts of computation demanded by non-spatial methods.

As for spatial causative factors, however, there is little or no evidence that any special form of spatial format or spatially congruent feedback is a necessary condition for the primary elaboration of codes for order. With humans subjects, of course, all one can say is that the experimental tasks have eliminated conventionalized forms of spatial support. Yet spatially derived devices could well be "imported" by the subject and used "in the mind's eye." With our simian subjects, ignorant of social and cultural conventions that utilize spatial layouts, this contention is difficult to sustain. The basis for such organization in all primates, we would contend, is temporal in nature, and can be tracked through the trajectories for private individual knowledge growth in evolution and development.

However, temporally based procedures alone are unlikely to sustain some of the complex reordering and other series transformations which adult human subjects can exhibit. In short, spatial elements must bring some additional adaptive advantages: they are not optional extras but enable new competencies to develop. Here, we have speculated, that physical and cognitive space search procedures may merge when the additive benefits of both forms of organization procure discriminable systems gain for the agent. On the (relative) utility argument we have espoused here and elsewhere, such a merger is virtually guaranteed if there is sufficient payoff to be had for the combined or integrated structure over each one when used separately. Akin to earlier findings obtained under "risky" perceptual judgements by animals (McGonigle, 1967) (where it was shown that both rats and cats combined the signaling vales of cues in discrimination experiments as a direct function of their number and discriminability), we argue here that the combination of object relational and spatial codes may offer analogous enhanced returns in terms of both utility and economy.

This merger, may not simply be the result of an additive process, however. It could also be the case that later solutions based on visual arrays which are themselves the consequences of principled search procedures may enable the elimination of otherwise expensive search procedures—even relatively economic ones. Beyond additivity, where spatial (vector based) search and seriation procedures coincide, new opportunities emerge to exploit the global visuo-spatial consequences of sorting and seriating stimuli. That is, where the objects are progressively sorted according to a spatial layout rule, the production which follows acquires *state* properties —with further memory load reduction benefits when the subject is working on-line, (see Ballard et al, 1998; McGonigle, 1998). In addition, the search procedures, now instantiated as *constructed assemblies of objects with perceivable layout features*, afford the agent new means to represent solutions, both to themselves and to others. And it may well be that the changes in cognitive style which Jones (1970) proposed as characterizing those variations in solution found in adult reasoning tasks, reflect *options* available to skilled subjects, enabling them to materially reduce cognitive costs—through the use of spatial representational devices which in certain cases may *bypass* otherwise expensive processing. Indeed this "complexity reduction" (Fischer and Bidell, 1998) may be culturally transmitted by instructional means without requiring that each individual first develops all the options as a prior condition.

However, the "paleontology" of the mind as suggested by our comparative stance indicates a temporal to spatial unfolding in which initial options available to individuals (with no culturally evolved tools for shared understanding) are severely restricted and may never substantially increase without the crucial development of spatio-temporal representational factors based on externalization procedures. These critically depend, we would argue, for the *evolution* of the processes at least, on *object manipulation* as the core activity which drives the "search and see" procedures so essential to the constructivist account outlined here.

To study this dynamic interplay between cognitive and physical space further, we are conducting new experiments which eschew the manipulative constraints on monkeys and very young children, whilst preserving the essential (search) action-to-visible consequent relationship which active, mature, human primates take for granted. Cyclic and productive, circular in the causative relationships between actions and representations—where action spawns representation and representation action—the hunt is surely on for the complex of feedback loops which active, embodied, cognitive systems create for themselves as a result of their own activity.

Note

1. However, we now know from our recent experiments with *Cebus apella* that successful transitive choice can occur in the context of exclusively randomized pair presentation.

Chapter 11

A Process Model of Human Transitive Inference

John E. Hummel and Keith J. Holyoak

If you are told that job A pays more than job B and job B pays more than job C, then you can conclude that job A pays more than job C. This conclusion follows deductively because *pays-more-than*( )—or, more generally, *more-than*( )—is a transitive relation. How does the human mind reason about transitive relations such as *more-than*( ), *taller-than*( ), etc.? Transitive relations are logically well-behaved: Given that some relation, *R*( ), is transitive, and given the facts *R*(A, B) and *R*(B, C), we can conclude *R*(A, C) with certainty. As such, there are many ways in principle to reason about them. For example, it is easy to imagine a cognitive "module" devoted to transitive reasoning. Like a program written in PROLOG, the module might take statements about transitive relations as input—for example, statements of the form *pays-more-than*(A, B) and *pays-more-than*(B, C)—and generate various inferences—such as *pays-most*(A), *pays-least*(C), and *pays-more-than*(A, C)—as output. However, the behavioral evidence suggests that this is not how the human mind processes transitive relations. A logical module would not provide any inherent basis for predicting that some transitive inferences will be more difficult to make than others. But it has been known for a long time that people solve some transitive-inference problems more quickly and accurately than others (e.g., Clark, 1969; DeSoto, London & Handel, 1965; Huttenlocher, 1968; McGonigle & Chalmers, 1977, 1984).

As suggested by several other chapters in this volume, the machinery of visuospatial reasoning may provide an economical basis for reasoning about transitive relations. Our visual systems are adept at computing spatial relations—such as *above*( ), *larger-than*( )—and many of these relations are transitive: If object A is above object B and B is above C, then A will be above C. Importantly, the visual machinery that computes these relations from the information in a visual image must have this knowledge built into it implicitly. The reason is that images are quintessentially analog: If, in some image, A is above B and B is above C, then A will necessarily be above C, so the same machinery that computes A above B and B above C (from their locations in the image) also has the information necessary to compute A above C. To the machinery that computes spatial relations from visual images, the "inference" that A is above C is not an inference at all, but rather a simple observation. This is not to say that visuospatial reasoning is the only basis—or even the phylogenetically or ontogenetically "first" basis—for reasoning about transitive relations (see McGonigle & Chalmers, this volume, for a thorough review of alternative approaches; also McGonigle & Chalmers, 1977, 1984), but it does provide an efficient potential basis for solving such problems.

For this reason, numerous researchers have proposed that people reason about transitive relations by exploiting the properties of spatial arrays (e.g., Huttenlocher, 1968). The general hypothesis is that, given statements such as "A is more than B" and "B is more than C," we map A, B, and C onto locations in a spatial array (e.g., with A near the top, B in the middle and C at the bottom). Given this mapping, the machinery that computes spatial relations from visual images can easily compute that A is above (in this case more than) C, that A is at the top (in this case is most), and that C is at the bottom (least). There is empirical support for the use of a mental array to make transitive inferences in solving three-term series problems (e.g., DeSoto et al., 1965; Huttenlocher, 1968; see also McGonigle & Chalmers, 1984), and the mental array hypothesis is also supported by the inverse distance effect commonly found when people make comparative judgments in series of four to 16 items (e.g., Potts, 1972, 1974; Woocher, Glass & Holyoak, 1978). That is, the further apart two items are in an ordered series, the faster people can decide which is greater or lesser. The distance effect is readily accounted for by perceptual discriminability of items in an array (Holyoak & Patterson, 1981), or in a monotonic ordering (McGonigle & Chalmers, this volume), but has no ready explanation in terms of logical inference rules. The mental array hypothesis is also appealing for its simplicity and economy: Given that we come equipped with routines for processing transitive relations in the domain of visual perception, it seems natural to assume that these same routines might be recruited in aid of reasoning about transitive relations in non-visual domains. But in spite of the appeal of the general mental array hypothesis, a detailed account of exactly how these operations might work has remained elusive (but see Byrne & Johnson-Laird, 1989, for a process model of a related task).

The task of developing an adequate process model of transitive inference is made much more difficult by the need to incorporate mental operations that go beyond the use of a spatial array. In particular, there is clear evidence that some of the variations in the difficulty of transitive inferences are due to linguistic factors, such as negation and markedness of comparative adjectives (e.g., the marked form *worse* in premises tends to lead to slower solutions than the unmarked or neutral form *better*; see Clark, 1969; Sternberg, 1980). To accommodate such findings as well as those that support use of a spatial array, Sternberg (1980) proposed a mixed spatial-linguistic model. This model provides a good mathematical fit to data on solution times for a range of transitive inference problems, but it is not a process model. Developing a process model of transitive inference is further complicated by evidence indicating that transitive reasoning depends on limited-capacity working memory. For example, the abilities of preschool children to make transitive inferences appear to be subject to capacity limitations (Halford, 1984), and transitive inference can be greatly impaired by damage to the prefrontal cortex, the apparent neural substrate for the form of working memory required for integrating relations (Waltz et al., 1999). It thus appears that transitive inference requires both working memory resources and linguistic representations, neither of which are specifically spatial. More generally, mapping from linguistic statements of premises to spatial representations, and mapping back from spatial relations to concrete inferences about specific objects (i.e., verbally statable conclusions), requires the machinery of visuospatial processing to communicate with other parts of the cognitive apparatus. Thus, even if visuospatial processing plays a role in transitive reasoning, it cannot be the whole story (see McGonigle & Chalmers, this volume). How might non-visual representations and processes communicate with the machinery of visuospatial processing for transitive reasoning, and how might the resulting algorithms give rise to the behavioral properties of human transitive reasoning? These are the questions to which the current chapter is addressed.

11.1 Visuospatial Routines for Transitive Inference

Using visuospatial routines for transitive reasoning entails solving at least two problems. First, it is necessary to map objects onto locations in a spatial array based on their pair-wise relations. Second, it is necessary to use the resulting values (locations) to compute additional relations. The second problem—computing categorical relations based on locations in an array—is relatively straightforward, and to solve it we will borrow (and adapt) a set of routines that Hummel and Biederman (1992) developed to compute the spatial relations among object parts for the purposes of object recognition.

The first problem—mapping objects to locations based on their pair-wise relations—is more challenging. First, it is under-constrained: Knowing that A is more than B and B is more than C is not sufficient to specify any unique assignment of values to A, B and C. A system for mapping objects onto values based on their pair-wise relations must therefore be prepared to make "guesses" about the specific locations of objects in the array. A second challenge concerns the semantics of transitive relations. If transitive relations are to serve as the basis for mapping objects onto a *spatial* array, then the mental representation of non-spatial transitive relations must somehow capture what they have in common with more obviously spatial relations such as *above*( ) and *larger*( ). That is, the "language of thought" must make the mapping from non-spatial relations (such as *more-than*( ), *better-than*( ) or *smarter-than*( )) onto spatial predicates transparent, and the cognitive architecture must be configured to exploit this language. Although this latter constraint is obvious, it is less obvious how to satisfy it. Atomic symbols of the type used by traditional symbolic models of cognition do not make the relationship between different predicates explicit. In order to solve the object-to-value mapping problem, we will borrow from the literature on analogical mapping, augmenting Hummel and Holyoak's (1997) LISA model of analogical reasoning with a set of routines for mapping pair-wise relations onto locations in a spatial array ("LISA" stands for "Learning and Inference with Schemas and Analogies").

LISA's algorithm for analogical mapping forms the basis of the current model of transitive reasoning, so we will start by reviewing how that algorithm works. Next, we will describe the "Mental Array Module" (MAM), a set of routines that augment LISA by allowing it to convert pair-wise categorical relations into hypotheses about the numerical values (i.e., locations) of specific objects, and to compute additional relations based on those values. The resulting system (which we will simply refer to as "LISA" for brevity's sake) is a process model of human transitive reasoning. Given statements such as "A is more than B" and "B is more than

C," LISA can answer questions such as "Which is greatest?" and "Which is least?" And like the human, LISA solves some problems faster than others. We will conclude by presenting LISA's simulations of a large body of data on human transitive reasoning (specifically, the data from 16 of the kinds of problems that Sternberg, 1980, administered to human subjects).

The LISA Model of Analogical Thinking

LISA is an integrated model of the major stages of analogical thinking, which include access (retrieving a useful source analog from long-term memory given a novel target problem or situation as a cue), mapping (discovering the correspondences among the elements of the source and target), analogical inference (using the source to make inferences about the target), and schema induction (using the source and target together to induce a more general schema or rule). For the purposes of the current model, only LISA's mapping algorithm is important. We review that algorithm in detail below. For a more complete discussion of access, inference and schema induction in LISA, see Holyoak and Hummel (in press) and Hummel and Holyoak (1997).

Human thinking is both structure-sensitive and flexible. It is structure-sensitive in the sense that we can represent and reason about abstract relationships, appreciating for example the similarities and differences between the idea "John loves Mary" and the idea "Mary loves John" (see Fodor & Pylyshyn, 1988). It is flexible in the sense that we can tolerate imperfect matches. For example, we effortlessly understand how "John loves Mary" is similar to (and different from) "Bill loves Susan." Together, the structure-sensitivity and flexibility of human thinking constitute challenging design requirements for a model of the human cognitive architecture. Traditional symbolic models easily capture the structure-sensitivity of human mental representations, but do not naturally capture their flexibility. The proposition *loves* (John, Mary) clearly specifies who loves whom, and makes transparent the structural relations between the ideas "John loves Mary" and "Mary loves John." But it fails to specify what John and Mary have in common and how they differ.[1] It likewise fails to specify that *loves* (John, Mary) is semantically more similar to *loves* (Bill, Susan) than to *loves* (Bill, Rover). Traditional connectionist representations have the opposite strengths and weaknesses. Distributed representations of Mary, Susan and Rover can specify what these objects have in common and how they differ (i.e., capture their semantic content), but traditional connectionist models lack provisions for binding simple representations, such as feature vectors describing Bill and Rover, into symbolic relational structures, such as *loves* (Bill, Rover) (see Fodor & Pylyshyn, 1988; Holyoak & Hummel, in press; Hummel & Holyoak, 1997; Marcus, 1998).

The core of the LISA model is a basis for dynamically binding distributed (i.e., connectionist) representations of relations and objects into structured (i.e., symbolic) representations in working memory (WM), and using those representations for memory retrieval, analogical mapping, inference and schema induction. (See Holyoak & Hummel, in press, for a review of connectionist approaches to role-filler binding.) LISA uses synchrony of firing for dynamic binding in WM (Hummel & Holyoak, 1992; Shastri & Ajjanagadde, 1993). Case roles and objects are represented as patterns of activation on a collection of *semantic units* (small circles in Figure 11.1); units representing case roles and objects fire in synchrony when they are bound together and out of synchrony when they are not. Because these representations are distributed, they naturally capture the semantic content of the predicates and objects they describe; and because

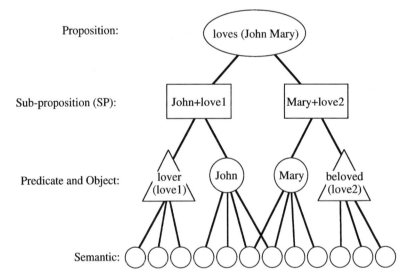

Figure 11.1
Illustration of the representation of a single proposition in LISA's LTM. The oval is a proposition (P) unit, rectangles are sub-proposition (SP) units, triangles are predicate units, large circles are object units, and small circles are semantic units. See text for details.

they bind the roles of predicates dynamically to their fillers, they also capture the symbolic structure of the proposition as a whole. The resulting representations simultaneously capture both the flexibility and structure-sensitivity of human representations of propositions.

Every proposition is encoded in LTM by a hierarchy of *structure units* (Figure 11.1). At the bottom of the hierarchy are *predicate* and *object* units. Each predicate unit locally codes one case role of one predicate. For example, *love1* represents the first ("lover") role of the predicate "love," and has bi-directional excitatory connections to all the semantic units representing that role (e.g., *emotion1, strong1, positive1*); *love2* represents the second ("beloved") role and is connected to the corresponding semantic units (e.g., *emotion2, strong2, positive2*). Semantically-related predicates share units in corresponding roles (e.g., *love1* and *like1* share many units), making the semantic similarity of different predicates explicit. Object units are just like predicate units except that they are connected to semantics describing things rather than roles. For example, the object unit *Mary* might be connected to units for *animal, human, adult,* and *female,* whereas *Rover* might be connected to *animal, dog, pet,* and *male.*

Sub-proposition units (*SPs*) bind roles to objects in LTM. For example, *love* (John, Mary) would be represented by two SPs, one binding John to lover (*love1*), and the other binding Mary to beloved (*love2*) (see Figure 11.1). The *John + love1* SP has bi-directional excitatory connections with *John* and *love1*, and the *Mary + love2* SP has connections with *Mary* and *love2*. *Proposition* (*P*) units reside at the top of the hierarchy and have bi-directional excitatory connections with the corresponding SP units. P units serve a dual role in hierarchical structures (such as "Sam knows that John loves Mary"), and behave differently according to whether they are currently serving as the "parent" of their own proposition or the "child" (i.e., argument) of another (see Hummel & Holyoak, 1997). Structure units do not encode semantic content in any direct way. Rather, they serve only to store that content in LTM, and to generate (and respond to) the corresponding synchrony patterns on the semantic units.

An analog (e.g., episode, problem or story) is represented as collections of structure units coding the propositions in that analog (see Figure 11.2). Separate analogs do not share structure units, but do share the same semantic units. The final component of LISA's architecture is a set of *mapping connections* between structure units of the same type in different analogs. Every P unit in one analog shares a mapping connection with every P unit in every other analog; likewise, SPs share connections across

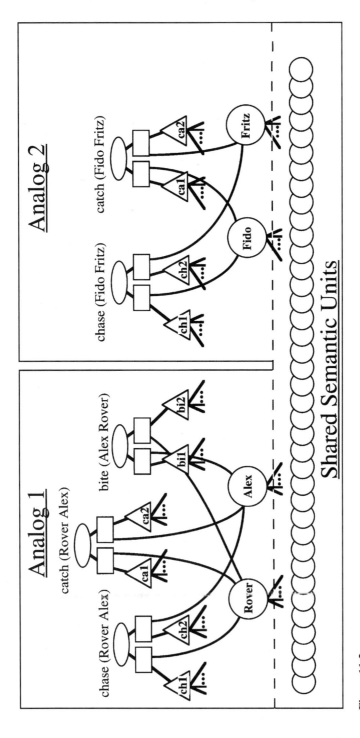

Figure 11.2
Illuatration of the representation of whole analogs in LISA's long-term memory. Analog 1 states that Rover chased Alex, Rover caught Alex, and Alex bit Rover. Analog 2 states that Fido chased Fritz and Fido caught Fritz. Each proposition is coded by a collection of structure units (as in Figure 10.1). Within an analog, a single structure unit codes a single object, predicate, or proposition regardless of how many times it is mentioned (e.g., in Analog 1, the same object unit represents Rover in all three propositions). Separate analogs do not share structure units but do share semantic units.

analogs, as do objects and predicates. For the purposes of mapping and retrieval, analogs are divided into two mutually exclusive sets: a *driver* and one or more *recipients*. Retrieval and mapping are controlled by the driver. (There is no necessary linkage between the driver/recipient distinction and the more familiar source/target distinction.) LISA performs mapping as a form of guided pattern matching. As P units in the driver become active, they generate (via their SP, predicate and object units) synchronized patterns of activation on the semantic units (one pattern for each role-argument binding): Semantic units for roles fire in synchrony with the semantic units coding their fillers, and separate role-filler bindings fire out of synchrony with one another. Because the semantic units are shared by all analogs, the patterns generated by a proposition in one analog will tend to activate one or more similar propositions in other analogs in LTM (analog retrieval) or in WM (analogical mapping).

Mapping differs from retrieval solely by the addition of the modifiable mapping connections. During mapping, the weights on the mapping connections grow larger when the units they link are active simultaneously, permitting LISA to learn the correspondences generated during retrieval. By the end of a simulation run, corresponding structure units will have large positive weights on their mapping connections, and noncorresponding units will have strongly negative weights. These connection weights also serve to constrain subsequent access and mapping: If object A maps to object B in one context, then the mapping connection thereby acquired will encourage it to map to B in future contexts. This property plays a critical role in LISA's ability to integrate multiple relations, appreciating for example, that *Jim* in *taller* (Sam, Jim) is the same object as *Jim* in *taller* (Jim, Bill).

Mapping in LISA is bootstrapped by shared semantics in objects and predicates across analogs, but an important property of LISA's mapping algorithm is that it permits objects and predicates to map even when they have no semantic overlap. For example, imagine that LISA is mapping "John loves Mary" in the driver onto "Susan loves chocolate" in the recipient, and that the representation of Mary shares no semantic features at all with the representation of chocolate. LISA will still map Mary onto chocolate by virtue of their shared binding to the *beloved* (*love2*) role of a *loves* relation. When the SP *love2* + *Mary* fires in the driver, the semantics activated by *love2* will activate *love2* in the recipient. *Love2* will activate the SP for *love2* + *chocolate* (in the recipient), which will activate *chocolate*. As a result, *Mary* (in the driver) will be active at the same time as *chocolate* (in the recipient), so LISA will strengthen the weight on the mapping connection between them. This ability to map dissimilar objects based on shared relational roles (or to map dissimilar roles based on similar arguments) plays a key role in LISA's ability to map arbitrary objects to spatial locations based on their pair-wise relations.

Mapping Objects onto a Spatial Array: The Mental Array Module (MAM)

Given a set of pair-wise relations among a collection of objects, our current goal is to use those relations to map the objects onto unique locations in a spatial array. For example, given the propositions *taller* (Bill, Joe) and *taller* (Joe, Sam), the goal is to map Bill to a location near the top of the array, Joe to a location near the middle, and Sam to a location near the bottom. To accomplish this mapping, LISA is equipped with a Mental Array Module (MAM; see Figure 11.3), a specialized module for manipulating visuospatial relations. Like any other analog in LISA, MAM contains a collection of object and predicate units, which have connections to the semantic units that are shared by all analogs. In MAM, predicate units represent the roles of the *greater-than* relation (which we will designate "greater-subject," *gS*, and "greater-referent," *gR*) and the *less-than* relation (less-subject, *lS*, and less-referent, *lR*). Object units represent locations (values) in a spatial array.[2] In contrast to an "ordinary" analog, MAM also contains an array of *location-and-relation*, $L \times R$, units (Hummel & Biederman, 1992), each of which represents a conjunction of one relational role at one location in the array. For example, the $L \times R$ unit *6-gS* represents any object whose location (value) is 6 and is greater than the location (value) of some other object. Each $L \times R$ unit has excitatory connections to the corresponding relation and location units (horizontal and vertical gray lines in Figure 11.3), and mediates the communication between them. These units make it possible to compute categorical relations (such as *greater-than* (A, B)) given specific values (such as A = 6 and B = 4) as input, and vice versa.

Representation Using MAM to compute categorical relations from specific values is straightforward, and is not the primary focus of the current effort (for details, see Hummel & Biederman, 1992). The reverse mapping—from categorical relations to specific values—is more challenging. Given only the knowledge that A is greater than B, there is no unique assignment of A and B to values in the array. In order to bootstrap the mapping from categorical relations to specific values, MAM contains two

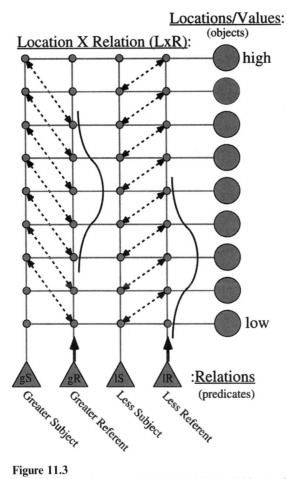

Figure 11.3
LISA's "Mental Array Module" (MAM). Object units (large circles) represent locations (values) in the mental array and predicate units (triangles) represent the roles of the relations *greater-than* and *less-than*. Location-by-Relation (L × R) units mediate the communication between location units and relation units. See text for details.

additional sets of connections, which amount to heuristic "guesses" about the likely value of an object based on the relational role(s) to which it is bound. First, the referent relations, gR and lR, activate their corresponding $L \times R$ units in a Gaussian pattern (Gaussian curves in Figure 11.3). For example, gR, the referent role of the greater-than relation, strongly excites the $L \times R$ unit corresponding to *greater-referent at location 5* (5-gR), and more weakly excites those surrounding location 5 (the strength of excitation falls off according to a Gaussian function). This pattern of excitation corresponds to the assumption: Given no knowledge about an object except that it is the referent of a greater-than relation, assume that object has a medium value. (Location 5 is the center of the array.) Similarly, lR, the referent role of the less-than relation, excites $L \times R$ units in a Gaussian pattern centered over location 3 (below the center). These connections correspond to the assumption: Given no knowledge except that an object is the referent of a less-than relation, assume that the object has slightly less than a medium value. Whereas "greater-than" is an unmarked relation, "less-than" is the marked form of the relation. We assume that markedness manifests itself in the assumption that an object has a smaller-than-average value. For example, told that Sam is taller than Fred (the unmarked form), LISA assumes that Fred (the referent) is of average height; but told that Fred is shorter than Sam, it assumes that Sam (the referent) is shorter than average (see Clark, 1969). The assumption that marked adjectives are selectively mapped onto the lower range of the array is a key representational assumption about the connection between linguistic and spatial representations of comparatives.

The second set of additional connections in MAM (dashed diagonal arrows in Figure 11.3) capture the logical dependencies among the referent and subject roles of the greater-than and less-than relations. $L \times R$ units representing the referent role of greater-than excite all $L \times R$ units representing the subject role of the greater-than relation at values two *above* themselves. For example, $L \times R$ unit 5-gR (greater-referent at location 5) excites unit 7-gS (greater-subject at location 7), and vice-versa (i.e., the connections are reciprocal): Whatever the value, V_r, of the object bound to the referent role of the greater-than relation, the value, V_s, of the object bound to the subject role must be greater than that (i.e., $V_s > V_r$). Conversely, $L \times R$ units representing the referent role of the less-than relation excite $L \times R$ units for the subject role of that relation one unit *below* themselves, and vice versa: Whatever the value, V_r, of the object bound to the referent role of a less-than relation, the value, V_s, of the object bound to the subject role must be less than that (i.e., $V_s < V_r$). Markedness manifests itself in these connections as the distance between connected L × R units representing the unmarked relation relative to the distance between L × R units representing the marked relation. The former is twice the latter, corresponding to the assumption that the arguments of an unmarked relation are likely to be less similar than the arguments of a marked relation: Told that Fred is shorter than Sam (the marked form), LISA will assign Fred and Sam to more similar heights than when told that Sam is taller than Fred. This assumption, which plays an important role in LISA's ability to simulate the findings of Sternberg (1980) (as elaborated shortly), follows as a natural consequence of the fact that the referent role of a marked relation assumes a lower value than the referent role of an unmarked relation: Because lR activates a value below the mean of the array, and because lS must activate a still lower value, the two roles are "crowded" together near the bottom of the array; as a result, the distance between lR and lS is necessarily smaller than that between gR and gS (which, by virtue of gR's placement at the center of the array, are not crowded together near the top; see Figure 11.3).

Operation   The interactions among the location, relation and L × R units cause LISA to assign objects to locations based on their categorical relations. Imagine that we tell LISA that A is greater than B and B is greater than C, as illustrated in Figures 11.4 and 11.5. ("Telling" LISA these facts means creating an analog containing the propositions *greater-than*(A, B) and *greater-than*(B, C), and designating that analog as the driver.) When the proposition *greater-than*(A, B) becomes active, *greater-subject + A* will fire out of synchrony with *greater-referent + B* (Figure 11.4a). When *greater-referent + B* fires, the predicate unit *greater-referent* (in Analog 1) will excite the semantic unit *greater-referent*, which in turn will excite gR (greater-referent) in MAM. Inside MAM, gR will excite L × R units in a Gaussian pattern centered at location 5. In turn, these units will excite L × R units for greater-subject centered at location 7 (recall that greater-referent L × R units excite greater-subject L × R units two values above themselves; see Figure 11.4). The output from L × R units to location units is gated by the activation of the corresponding relation unit. As a result, when gR fires (which it will do in synchrony with *greater-referent* and therefore object B in the problem), the L × R units for greater-referent will activate the location units surrounding location 5;

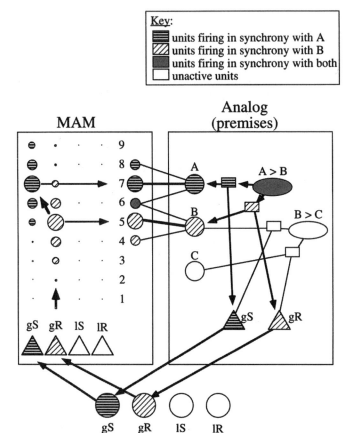

Figure 11.4
Illustration of the operation of MAM. When the proposition *greater-than*(A, B)
fires in the problem, MAM activates location 7 in synchrony with A (i.e., A maps
to location 7) and location 5 in synchrony with location B (B maps to location 5).

as a consequence, Object B in the problem will map to (i.e., develop a
positive mapping weight to) the object unit in MAM representing location
5. When greater-subject (*gS*) fires in MAM (which it will do in synchrony
with *greater-subject* and therefore object A in the problem), it will allow
the greater-subject L × R units to activate location units surrounding
location 7; Object A in the problem will therefore map to the object unit
in MAM representing location 7 (Figure 11.4).

In the course of mapping *greater-than* (A, B) to MAM, LISA thus
maps object A onto location 7 and object B onto location 5, and stores

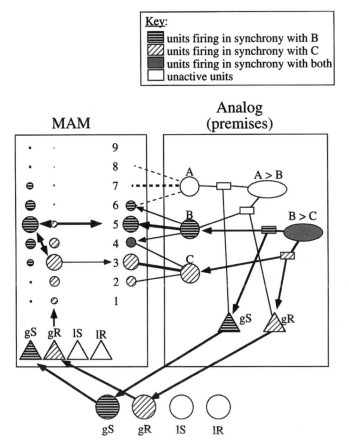

Figure 11.5
Second illustration of the operation of MAM. When *greater-than*(B, C) fires in the problem, B maps to location 5 (by virtue of the mapping connection established previously), so C maps to location 3.

these mappings as weights on the corresponding mapping connections. These connections serve as linking relations, allowing LISA to integrate the first proposition, *greater-than*(A, B), with the second, *greater-than*(B, C), based on their shared argument, B. Specifically, when the proposition *greater-than*(B, C) becomes active, *greater-subject* + B will fire out of synchrony with *greater-referent* + C (Figure 11.5). *Greater-referent* (in the analog) will tend to cause C to map to location 5, just as it caused B to map to location 5 in the context of *greater-than*(A, B). However, this time, object B already has an excitatory mapping connection to location

5, so when *greater-subject* + *B* fires, object B will activate location 5 directly, i.e., by way of the mapping connection (Figure 11.5). In turn, location 5 will activate L × R units for location 5 in the greater-subject role. Recall that in the proposition *greater-than*(B, C), B is bound to (i.e., synchronized with) the *subject* role of the greater-than relation. The greater-subject L × R units will activate greater-referent L × R units two values below themselves, i.e., centered around location 3 (recall that greater-referent L × R units activate greater-subject L × R two units above themselves, and because the connections are reciprocal, greater-subject units activate greater-referent units two values *below* themselves). The result is that, with object B activating location 5, object C will tend to map to location 3.

After both *greater-than*(A, B) and *greater-than*(B, C) have had the opportunity to fire a few times, object A will map strongly to location 7, B to location 5 and C to location 3. LISA will thus have mapped the objects to locations in a spatial array based on their pair-wise relations. As detailed shortly, these locations serve as the basis for LISA's discovery of other relations among the objects, including the fact that A is greatest, C is least, and A is greater than C. It is important to emphasize the role of the linking relation between B in the first proposition and B in the second (embodied in the mapping connection from B to location 5) in this mapping. Without the ability to learn this connection, LISA would map A to location 7 and B to location 5 in the context of *greater-than*(A, B), and map B to location 7 and C to location 5 in the context of *greater-than*(B, C). The resulting mappings would be useless for inferring any additional relations among the objects.

The example in Figures 11.4 and 11.5, based on the premises *greater-than*(A, B) and *greater-than*(B, C), was chosen for ease of illustration. Similar principles apply when the relations among A, B and C are stated differently (e.g., *less-than*(B, A) and *less-than*(C, B), or *less-than*(C, B) and *greater-than*(A, B)). However, as illustrated in the context of the specific simulations, not all premises are equally easy for LISA to process. For example, problems based on the less-than relation tend to be slightly more difficult for LISA to solve than problems based on greater-than. Recall that the marked form, less-than, tends to push the objects closer together and lower in the spatial array. This makes it more difficult for MAM/ LISA to decide which is greatest or which is least. LISA and MAM are also sensitive to other factors, such as the order in which the premises are stated.

Computing Greatest and Least

While LISA and MAM are mapping objects to locations based on their pair-wise relations, MAM also keeps track of the mounting evidence regarding which objects occupy the greatest and smallest locations/values. Each location unit, i, in MAM is associated with an integrator, I_i, which accumulates evidence from other location units, j, above and below itself. At each instant in time, t, I_i is updated according to (1):

$$\Delta I_i^t = \sum_{j<i} A_j^t - 0.8 \sum_{j>i} A_j^t, \tag{1}$$

Here A_j^t is the activation of location unit j at time t. Whenever a location lower than i (i.e., $j < i$) fires (i.e., $A_j^t > 0$), I_i is incremented, adding to the evidence that any object at location i (if there is one) has the greatest value; whenever a location higher than i (i.e., $j > i$) fires, I_i is decremented, subtracting from the evidence that any object at location i has the greatest value, and (equivalently) adding to the evidence that any object at location i has the smallest value. Negative evidence (i.e., from $j > i$) accumulates more slowly then positive evidence, as indicated by the 0.8 in (1). As a result, it takes LISA/MAM longer to decide which value is the smallest than it takes to decide which is greatest.

Equation (1) describes how each location unit accumulates evidence about whether it represents the greatest or smallest value by monitoring whether there are active locations above or below itself. As time progresses, the integrator on the highest location will accumulate a progressively larger (i.e., more positive) value, and the integrator on the lowest location will accumulate a progressively larger negative value. At each instant, t, a global integrator, Γ, monitors the values of all individual integrators, I, by computing a gated sum of their values:

$$\Gamma^t = \sum_i I_i^t A_i^t 0.2|i - 4.5| \tag{2}$$

Effectively, the value of the global integrator at any instant, t, is the value of the local integrator (I_i) associated with whichever location, i, happens to be active at instant t, weighted by the distance between i and a fixed point (location 4.5) just below the center of the spatial array. For example, if object A is mapped to location 7, and object A is active at time t, then location 7 will be active at time t. At time t, the value of the global integrator will be the value of the integrator on location 7, multiplied by the distance between location 7 and location 4.5. If LISA is seeking the object with the greatest value, and if Γ' is greater than a threshold value (+2700), then processing stops and LISA declares whichever object is currently active (i.e., the object firing in synchrony with location i—in the above example, object A) to have the greatest value. If LISA is seeking the object with the smallest value, and if Γ' is lower than a threshold value (−2700), then processing stops and LISA declares whichever object is currently active to have the smallest value. Weighting Γ' by the distance between i and the center of the array biases LISA to respond "greatest" fastest to objects mapped to very high values, and "smallest" fastest to objects mapped to very small values.

11.2   Simulations

We evaluated LISA/MAM as a model of human transitive inference by testing it on a subset of the problems Sternberg (1980) gave his subjects. We chose these data as the basis of our simulations because they represent a complete sampling of ways to state transitive inference problems (as detailed below), and are based on a large number of subjects to ensure reliability of the response-time data. In a series of four experiments, Sternberg gave subjects problems of the general form "Bill is better than Joe. Joe is better than Sam. Who is best?" and recorded how long it took them to solve them. The problems varied on four dimensions:

• The order and markedness of the stated premises. As illustrated in Table 11.1, both premises could be stated in the unmarked form (UU; e.g., "Bill is better than Joe; Joe is better than Sam"), both could be stated in the marked form (MM: "Joe is worse than Bill; Sam is worse than

Table 11.1
Order and markedness of stated premises

Condition	First	Second	Example
UU	unmarked	unmarked	"Bill is better than Joe. Joe is better than Sam."
MM	marked	marked	"Joe is worse than Bill. Sam is worse than Joe."
UM	unmarked	marked	"Bill is better than Joe. Sam is worse than Joe."
MU	marked	unmarked	"Joe is worse than Bill. Joe is better than Sam."

Joe"), the first could be unmarked and the second marked (UM: "Bill is better than Joe; Sam is worse than Joe"), or the first could be marked and the second unmarked (MU: "Joe is worse than Bill; Joe is better than Sam").

• Negation of the premises. The premises could either be stated as negations (e.g., "Joe is not as good as Bill"), or as non-negated predicates ("Bill is better than Joe").

• The question asked. Subjects were asked to specify either the top-most object (e.g., "Who is best?") or the bottom-most object ("Who is worst?").

• Presentation order. Premises were either stated in a *forward* order, so that the highest pair of objects was mentioned first (e.g., in "Bill is better than Joe; Joe is better than Sam," Bill and Joe, both of whom are higher than Sam on the dimension of goodness, are mentioned first), or the *reverse* order, so that the lowest pair of objects was mentioned first (e.g., "Joe is better than Sam; Bill is better than Joe").

In all, Sternberg recorded subjects' response times and accuracy in 32 different conditions: Markedness and order (4) × Negation (2) × Question (2) × Presentation order (2). Of these, we will consider the 16 non-negated conditions obtained by crossing Markedness and order × Question × Presentation order. (The data in the 16 negated conditions are similar to those in the 16 non-negated conditions, except that negation adds roughly a constant to subjects' response times; see Sternberg, 1980.) Some of Sternberg's conditions involved precuing, in which either the two premises or the question were presented prior to the possible answers (people's names). We only simulated data from the uncued conditions, in which all the problem information was presented at once (premise 1, premise 2, question, and alternative names, respectively, on successive vertically-arranged lines on a tachistoscopically-presented card). The data in the 16 non-negated uncued conditions are summarized below. Numbers indicate the rank order of mean response time across conditions, averaged over Sternberg's four experiments, with 1 being the shortest (fastest) and 16 the longest (slowest).

The data are complex, but several major trends are apparent. First, there is an interaction between presentation order and question asked, such that the reverse order (in which the premise containing the lower pair of items is stated first) is easier than the forward order (stating the upper pair first) when the subject must report the top-most object (e.g., "Who is

Table 11.2
Sternberg (1980) data (non-negated conditions)

Question	Presentation order			
	Forward		Backward	
Top-most	UU	3	UU	1
"Who is best?"	MM	14	MM	8
	UM	7	UM	2
	MU	10	MU	4
Bottom-most	UU	4	UU	10
"Who is worst?"	MM	12	MM	16
	UM	6	UM	13
	MU	8	MU	14

best?") and harder than the forward order when the subject must report the bottom-most object ("Who is worst?"). This pattern can be viewed as a kind of recency effect: Responses are faster when the correct answer is contained in the second premise stated (in the lower premise in the case of "Who is least?" and in the upper in "Who is greatest?"). Second, when both premises have the same markedness status (i.e., UU or MM), responses are faster in the unmarked conditions than in the marked conditions (i.e., UU is faster than MM in all four cells of Table 11.2). And third, in the mixed-markedness conditions (UM and MU), responses are faster when the upper pair is stated in the unmarked form than when the upper pair is stated in the marked form (i.e., UM is faster than MU in all four cells of Table 11.2).

Simulation Procedure

We tested LISA on the 16 conditions in Table 11.2. Premises were stated in the simple form *greater-than*(x, y) (unmarked) and *less-than*(x, y) (marked). We varied the premises (i.e., conditions UU, MM, UM, and MU) by varying which predicate (greater-than or less-than) was used to describe the upper pair of objects (A/B), and which was used to describe the lower pair (B/C). For example, condition MU stated the propositions *less-than*(B, A) (upper pair marked) and *greater-than*(B, C) (lower pair unmarked); UM stated *greater-than*(A, B) and *less-than*(C, B). We varied the presentation order by manipulating whether the upper or lower pair was presented first. In the "forward" order, the proposition describing the higher pair (H; objects A and B) was presented first, and in the reverse order, the proposition describing the lower pair (L; objects B and C) was presented first. Specifically, in the forward order, H was presented twice, then L was presented once, followed by H, then L twice, resulting in the ordering: H H L H L L.[3] We created the reverse order simply by switching the higher and lower pairs in the ordering: L L H L H H. These orderings reflect our assumption that the subject first thinks about the first premise stated (e.g., H H, in the forward order), then transitions to the second (L H), and finally concentrates on the second (L L). We asked LISA "Who is greatest?" by setting the threshold on the global integrator, Γ, to $+2700$; to ask "Who is least?" we set the threshold to -2700. A run terminated as soon as Γ crossed the threshold, and we recorded LISA's response time (i.e., the number of iterations run to solution). Although a single run entails up to three presentations of each proposition, LISA was usually able to answer the question before all six propositions had run. (If LISA was unable to answer the question after all six propositions had run, then it continued to run propositions in a random order until it could answer the question.) We ran each condition ten times. The data reported below are means over the ten runs.

Simulation Results

Figure 11.6 shows a scatter plot of LISA's mean response time in each condition (in iterations) against the mean response times of Sternberg's (1980) subjects in the same conditions. The correlation coefficient (Pearson's r) between LISA's response times and those of the human subjects is .82, or $r^2 = .67$. Sternberg reported fits of r^2 ranging from .34 to .51 across individual experiments between subjects' response times for uncued problems and his most successful mathematical model, the mixed linguistic-spatial model. Our LISA simulations thus compare favorably with the fits provided by Sternberg's models. As the parameter space for LISA is not comparable to that for Sternberg's mathematical models, and we did not perform any systematic search for a "best fit" with LISA, the relative fits are simply suggestive that LISA can account for the human pattern of data at least as well as the most successful previous model. It should also be noted that we simulated only 16 of Sternberg's 32 data points (omitting the 16 data points from the negated conditions), so LISA's correlation with the human data suffers from range restriction. This range restriction would be expected to reduce LISA's fit given that

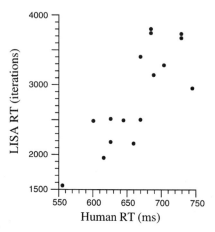

Figure 11.6
LISA's response times in 16 of Sternberg's (1980) conditions plotted against human response times in the same conditions (human response times from Sternberg, 1980).

the negated versus non-negated dimension accounts for a large proportion of the variance in Sternberg's data (see Sternberg, 1980). But the most important distinction between LISA and Sternberg's models is that LISA is a process model. That is, in contrast to Sternberg's models, LISA actually *solves* the problems and so provides an algorithmic account of how people may solve them. Sternberg's models are strictly mathematical models, the only function of which is to predict the response times themselves. Mathematical models cannot actually solve the problems, and hence provide little insight into the likely psychological algorithms underlying response times to achieve solutions.

Table 11.3 shows the rank ordering of LISA's response times by condition alongside the corresponding data from Sternberg's (1980) subjects. LISA captures most of the major trends in the human data. First, it captures the interaction between presentation order and question asked: As in the human data, the reverse order is faster than the forward order when the question is "Who is greatest?" and slower than the forward order when the question is "Who is least?" Second, when both premises have the same markedness status (i.e., UU or MM), LISA's responses are faster in the unmarked conditions than in the marked conditions (compare UU to MM in corresponding cells of Table 11.3). The one exception is in the Backward-Least condition, where LISA reversed the relative ease

Table 11.3
LISA data and Sternberg (1980) data (non-negated conditions)

	Presentation order					
	Forward			Backward		
Question		Human	LISA		Human	LISA
Top-most	UU	3	2	UU	1	1
"Who is best?"	MM	14	14	MM	8	7
	UM	7	3	UM	2	5
	MU	10	16	MU	4	4
Bottom-most	UU	4	8	UU	10	15
"Who is worst?"	MM	12	10	MM	16	9
	UM	6	6	UM	13	11
	MU	8	12	MU	14	13

of the MM and UU conditions. Third, recall that for Sternberg's subjects in the mixed-markedness conditions (UM and MU), problems were easier when the upper pair was stated in the unmarked form than when the upper pair was stated in the marked form (i.e., for humans, UM is faster than MU in all four cells of Table 11.3). LISA shows this trend in the forward condition but not in the backward condition.

11.3 Discussion

We have described a process model of human transitive reasoning that integrates the LISA model of analogical reasoning (Hummel & Holyoak, 1997) with routines for computing relations borrowed from Hummel and Biederman's (1992) model of shape perception and object recognition. The model provides the first explicit algorithmic account of mechanisms by which an internal spatial array (e.g., as used for computing spatial relations in visual perception) might be used to perform transitive inferences. By integrating a Metric Array Model, MAM, within the LISA architecture, the augmented LISA provides an account of how such a spatial module might interact with general semantic representations of word meanings and with the working-memory limits that constrain human reasoning. Rather than strictly segregating linguistic and spatial aspects of transitive inference (as in Sternberg's, 1980, mixed model), LISA shows how the meanings of comparatives such as *greater* and *lesser* can be specified in terms of the operation of the spatial module itself. One consequence of this integration of linguistic and spatial representations is that the effects of markedness (e.g., the relative difficulty of problems stated in terms of *lesser* rather than *greater*) arise from the mapping between the meanings of the comparatives and the spatial positions in MAM, rather than from strictly linguistic processes.

It is interesting to note that the internal array MAM uses to represent quantities, magnitudes, and locations is not any sort of literal "image" of objects in specific locations: To represent A at the top of the array, B in the middle and C at the bottom, MAM does not generate picture-like depictions of A, B and C on any sort of mental viewing screen. Rather, it is sufficient to bind symbolic representations of the objects (object units in the architecture of LISA) to symbolic representations of their values or magnitudes (object units in MAM corresponding to specific locations). Indeed, for the purposes of computing the relations among objects, this symbolic representation of magnitude is superior to any literal image-based representation of objects in specific locations (see Hummel & Biederman, 1992). Like the representation the Hummel and Biederman model uses to compute spatial relations, the symbolic representation of magnitude in MAM specifies all and only that which is relevant to the relation of interest—namely, the values or magnitudes that need to be compared. A literal image, by contrast, would specify (implicitly or explicitly) all manner of irrelevant information, including the size and font in which a letter is written, whether it is upper or lower case, and so on. (Note that it is impossible to draw a picture of an A without drawing some specific A.) None of these properties are relevant to the task of deciding whether the A is above or below the C. (Of course, it is an empirical question whether the representations underlying human visuospatial reasoning are as "uncluttered" by irrelevant details; the current model predicts that they will be.) This point is worth emphasizing because the contrast between analog versus discrete representations is often confused with the contrast between image-based versus symbolic representations (the assumption being that all analog representations are image-based, and all propositional, i.e., symbolic, representations must be discrete). MAM, like the visual routines from which it is derived, is an example of an analog representation that is nonetheless decidedly symbolic (see Holyoak & Hummel, in press, for a discussion of LISA as a symbolic system).

We speculate that most or all of the visual representations that make contact with higher cognition must have this property. For example, we believe the present approach could be extended to account for data concerning how people make order judgments with prestored arrays (Potts, 1972, 1974), and how they determine the relative magnitudes of concepts stored in semantic memory, such as digit magnitudes (Moyer & Landauer, 1967) and animal sizes (Moyer, 1973). In addition to routines that perform transitive inferences, routines that reason on the basis of visual relations in domains, such as graph interpretation (Gattis & Holyoak, 1996; Gattis, this volume) and sign language (Emorey, this volume), may depend on symbolic (i.e., propositional) structural descriptions that make explicit what it is necessary to know and discard the rest. (See Hummel, in press, for similar arguments about the nature of object recognition and Pylyshyn, 1973, for similar arguments about the nature of visual imagery.)

LISA also provides an account of why working memory (and in particular, the working memory associated with prefrontal cortex) is essential for transitive inference. Waltz et al. (1999) showed that patients suffering from degeneration of frontal cortex perform at chance on transitive inference problems that depend on the capacity to integrate multiple relations. For example, in order to conclude that Bill is taller than Fred given the premises "Sam is taller than Fred" and "Bill is taller than Sam," the reasoner must integrate the first premise with the second based on their common reference to Sam.[4] In contrast to frontal patients, age- and IQ-matched control patients with degeneration in anterior temporal cortex (which is presumably not as directly implicated in relational integration), perform transitive inference tasks as well as age matched controls (with near-perfect accuracy). These and other findings strongly suggest that frontal cortex must be centrally involved in the kind of working memory that is responsible for relational integration (see Waltz et al., 1999).

LISA/MAM provides a straightforward account of such findings in terms of the role of the mapping connections in the ability to integrate relations. Recall that the mapping connections play a central role in LISA's ability to integrate *greater-than*(A, B) with *greater-than*(B, C) for the purposes of mapping A, B and C to unique locations in the spatial array: It is the connection from B to location 5 (established when *greater-than*(A, B) fires) that makes it possible to keep B at location 5 and place C at location 3 when *greater-than*(B, C) fires (see Figure 11.5). Without this

Table 11.4
A simple analogy

Story 1	Story 2
Bill proposed to Mary.	Joe proposed to Sally.
Bill bought a Chevy.	Joe bought a Ford.
	Fred bought a Buick.

connection, B would map to location 7 and C to location 5 (in the context of *greater-than*(B, C)) just as A goes to 7 and B to 5 in the context of *greater-than*(A, B). The resulting representation would be useless for deciding which object is greatest and which least. And indeed, run with the mapping connections disabled, LISA, like frontal patients, performs randomly on the transitive inference task.

In this context, it is tempting to speculate that the mapping connections of LISA may be realized neurally as neurons in prefrontal cortex (see also Hummel & Holyoak, 1997). This account makes additional (and to our knowledge, novel) predictions about the role of prefrontal cortex in other reasoning tasks. One is that frontal patients should perform poorly on analogies requiring relational integration. For example, consider the simple analogy in Table 11.4. It is not difficult to realize that Bill maps to Joe rather than Fred because they both proposed marriage to their sweethearts. Based on this mapping, it is also clear that the Chevy (which Bill bought) must map to the Ford (which Joe bought) rather than the Buick (which Fred bought). But the mapping of the Chevy to the Ford is specified only because of the "proposal" statements, so discovering it requires the reasoner to integrate "Joe proposed to Sally" with "Joe bought a Buick" based on their common reference to Joe. LISA's account of transitive reasoning predicts that frontal patients should have as much difficulty discovering this simple mapping as they have reasoning about transitive relations.

It seems very likely that many other aspects of human reasoning, besides transitive inference, also depend on the integration of semantic knowledge and working-memory operations with representations derived from those that support visuospatial perception. We hope the model we have described here may provide an example of how the connections between perception and thought may be given explicit realization in a neural architecture.

Acknowledgment

This research was supported by NSF Grant 9729023.

Notes

1. Traditional symbolic models typically capture the semantic content of symbols through external devices, such as look-up tables and semantic networks. In this approach, symbols serve as "pointers" to semantic content, rather than capturing that content directly (see Hinton, 1990; Hummel & Holyoak, 1997).

2. In the current implementation, the array contains nine locations/values [units], and for simplicity location is coded in a linear fashion (e.g., the distance between the locations coded by the 8th and 9th units is the same as the distance between the locations coded by the first and second). Although this linear representation of number is not psychologically realistic, it is sufficient for our current purposes, and there are no a priori reasons to expect that adapting the algorithm to work with a nonlinear representation of number would change its properties in any substantive way.

3. "Presenting" a proposition to LISA entails activating it and allowing it's SP, object and predicate units to fire for 600 iterations (see Hummal & Holyoak, 1997).

4. By contrast, if problems are consistently stated in the order, "Bill is taller than Sam" and "Sam is taller than Fred," then it is possible to find the solution using various chaining strategies that do not require relational integration, but also do not generalize to arbitrary orderings. Patients suffering from degeneration of frontal cortex solve problems stated in this canonical ordering as well as age-matched controls (see Waltz et al., 1999).

References

Allbritton, D. W. (1995). When metaphors function as schemas: some cognitive effects of conceptual metaphors. *Metaphor and Symbolic Activity, 10* (1), 1–58.

Allbritton, D. W., McKoon, G., and Gerrig, R. J. (1995). Metaphor-based schemas and text representations: making connections through conceptual metaphors. *Journal of Experimental Psychology: Learning, Memory, and Cognition, 21* (3), 612–625.

Alverson, H. (1994). *Semantics and experience: universal metaphors of time in English, Mandarin, Hindi, and Sesotho.* Baltimore: Johns Hopkins University Press.

Anderson, J. R. (1990). *Cognitive psychology and its implications* (3rd ed.). New York: W. H. Freeman and Company.

Arnheim, R. (1977). *Dynamics of architectural form.* Berkeley: University of California Press.

Baek, Y. K., and Lane, B. H. (1988). Color, graphics, and animation in a computer-assisted learning tutorial lesson. *Journal of Computer-based Instruction, 15* (4), 131–135.

Ballard, D. H., Hayhoe, M., Pook, P. K., and Rao, R. P. N. (1997). Deictic codes for the embodiment of cognition. *Brain and Behaviour Sciences, 20* (4), 723 et seq.

Banks, W. P. (1977). Encoding and processing of symbolic information in comparative judgments. In G. H. Bower (ed). *The psychology of learning and motivation* (vol. 2). Academic Press, New York.

Banks, W. P., Clark, H. H., and Lucy, P. (1975). The locus of the semantic congruity effect in comparative judgments. *Journal of Experimental Psychology: Human Perception and Performance, 1*, 35–47.

Banks, W. P., Fujii, M., and Kayra-Stuart, F. (1976). Semantic congruity effects in comparative judgements. *Journal of Experimental Psychology: Human Perception and Performance, 2*, 435–447.

Barstow, D., Frost, E., Liben, L. S., Ride, S., and Souviney, R. (in progress). Visualizing Earth. Grant no. RED-9554504 from the National Science Foundation.

Barwise, J., and Etchemendy, J. (1995). Heterogenous logic. In B. Chandrase-keran, J. Glasgow, and N. H. Narayanan (eds.), *Diagrammatic reasoning: cognitive and computational perspectives* (pp. 211–234). Cambridge: MIT Press.

Bassok, M., and Holyoak, K. J. (1989). Interdomain transfer between isomorphic topics in algebra and physics. *Journal of Experimental Psychology: Learning, Memory, and Cognition, 15*, 153–166.

Beniger, J. R., and Robyn, D. L. (1978). Quantitative graphics in statistics. *American Statistician, 32*, 1–11.

Bennett, A. T. D. (1996). Do animals have cognitive maps? *Journal of Experimental Biology, 199*, 219–224.

Bennett, D. C. (1975). *Spatial and temporal uses of English prepositions: an essay in stratificational semantics.* London: Longman Group.

Bertin, J. (1981). *Graphics and graphic-information-processing.* New York: Walter de Gruyter.

Betrancourt, M., and Tversky, B. (in press). Simple animations for organizing diagrams. *International Journal of Human Computer Studies.*

Bierwisch, M. (1996). How much space gets into language? In P. Bloom, M. A. Peterson, L. Nadel, and M. F. Garrett (eds.), *Language and space* (pp. 31–76). Cambridge: MIT Press.

Bing, S. (1998). *Lloyd: what happened?* New York: Crown.

Blades, M., Hetherington, D., Spencer, C., and Sowden, S. (1997). Can young children recognize aerial photographs? Paper presented at the biennial meeting of the Society for Research in Child Development, Washington, D.C., April.

Blades, M., and Spencer, C. (1987a). The use of maps by 4–6-year-old children in a large-scale maze. *British Journal of Developmental Psychology, 5*, 19–24.

Blades, M., and Spencer, C. (1987b). Young children's recognition of environmental features from aerial photographs and maps. *Environmental Education and Information, 6*, 189–198.

Blades, M., and Spencer, C. (1994). The development of children's ability to use spatial representations. In H. W. Reese (ed.), *Advances in child development and behavior* (vol. 25, pp. 157–199). New York: Academic Press.

Bloom, P., Peterson, M. A., Nadel, L., and Garrett, M. F. (eds.) (1996). *Language and space.* Cambridge: MIT Press.

Bluestein, N., and Acredolo, L. (1979). Developmental changes in map-reading skills. *Child Development, 50*, 691–697.

Boroditsky, L. (2000). Metaphoric structuring: understanding time through spatial metaphors. *Cognition, 75*, 1–27.

Bowdle, B., and Gentner, D. (1995). *The career of metaphor.* Paper presented at the meeting of the Psychonomics Society, Los Angeles, November.

Bowdle, B., and Gentner, D. (1997). Informativity and asymmetry in comparisons. *Cognitive Psychology, 34* (3), 244–286.

Bowdle, B., and Gentner, D. (1999). Metaphor comprehension: from comparison to categorization. *Proceedings of the Twenty-first Annual Conference of the Cognitive Science Society*. Hillsdale, N.J.: Erlbaum.

Bowdle, B., and Gentner, D. (in preparation). The career of metaphor.

Bower, G. H. (1970). Analysis of a mnemonic device. *American Scientist, 58*, 496–510.

Boysen, S. T., and Capaldi, E. J. (1993). *The development of numerical competence: animal and human models.* Hillsdale, N.J.: Erlbaum.

Bradshaw, C. M., and Szabadi, E. (1997). *Time and behaviour: psychological and neurobehavioural analyses.* Amsterdam: Elsevier.

Braine, L. G., Schauble, L., Kugelmass, S., and Winter, A. (1993). Representation of depth by children: spatial strategies and lateral biases. *Developmental Psychology, 29*, 466–479.

Brewer, C. A. (1997). Spectral schemes: controversial color use on maps. *Cartography and Geographic Information Systems, 24*, 203–220.

Brewer, C. A., MacEachren, A. M., Pickle, L. W., and Herrmann, D. J. (1997). Mapping mortality: evaluating color schemes for choropleth maps. *Annals of the Association of American Geographers, 87*, 411–438.

Brown, L. (1979). *The story of maps.* New York: Dover.

Brown, M. F., and Moore, J. A. (1997). In the dark II: spatial choice when access to extrinsic spatial cues is eliminated. *Animal Learning and Behavior, 25*, 335–346.

Brown, M. F., and Terrinoni, M. (1996). Control of choice by the spatial configuration of goals. *Journal of Experimental Psychology: Animal Behavior Processes, 22*, 438–446.

Bruner, J. S. (1957). Going beyond the information given. In Dept. of Psychology, University of Colorado at Boulder (ed.), Contemporary approaches to cognition: a symposium held at the University of Colorado. Harvard University Press, Cambridge.

Bryant, D. J., Tversky, B., and Franklin, N. (1992). Internal and external spatial frameworks for representing described scenes. *Journal of Memory and Language, 31*, 74–98.

Bryant, P. E. (1974). Perception and understanding in young children. London: Methuen.

Bryant, P. E., and Trabasso, T. (1971). Transitive inferences and memory in young children. *Nature, 232*, 456–458.

Byrne, R. M. J., and Johnson-Laird, P. N. (1989). Spatial reasoning. *Journal of Memory and Language, 28*, 564–575.

Cacciari, C., and Tabossi, P. (1988). The comprehension of idioms. *Journal of Memory and Language, 27*, 668–683.

Calbris, G. (1990). *Semiotics of French gesture.* Bloomington: Indiana University Press.

Card, S. K., Mackinlay, J. D., and Shneiderman, B. (1999). *Readings in information visualization: using vision to think.* San Francisco: Morgan Stanley.

Carpenter, P. A., and Shah, P. (1998). A model of the perceptual and conceptual processes in graph comprehension. *Journal of Experimental Psychology: Applied, 4,* 75–100.

Carswell, C. M. (1992). Reading graphs: interaction of processing requirements and stimulus structure. In B. Burns (ed.), *Percepts, concepts, and categories* (pp. 605–645). Amsterdam: Elsevier.

Carswell, C. M., and Wickens, C. D. (1988). Comparative graphics: history and applications of perceptual integrality theory and the proximity compatibility hypothesis. Technical report, Institute of Aviation, University of Illinois at Urbana-Champaign.

Carswell, C. M., and Wickens, C. D. (1990). The perceptual interaction of graphic attributes: configurality, stimulus homogeneity, and object integration. *Perception and Psychophysics, 47,* 157–168.

Cartwright, B. A., Collett, T. S. (1983). Landmark learning in bees. *Journal of Comparative Physiology A, 151,* 521–543.

Chalmers, M. A. (1977). Transitivity and the representation of stimulus relations by young children. Unpublished Ph.D. thesis, University of Edinburgh.

Chalmers, M., and McGonigle, B. (1984). Are children any more logical than monkeys on the five term series problem? *Journal of Experimental Child Psychology, 37,* 355–377.

Chalmers, M., and McGonigle, B. (2000). *Serial versus logical structure as the genesis of ordering mechanisms: a developmental study.* Manuscript submitted for publication.

Chapuis, N., and Varlet, C. (1987). Shortcuts by dogs in natural surroundings. *Quarterly Journal of Experimental Psychology, 39B,* 49–64.

Cheng, K. (1986). A purely geometric module in the rat's spatial representation. *Cognition, 23,* 149–178.

Cheng, K. (1988). Some psychophysics of the pigeon's use of landmarks. *Journal of Comparative Physiology A, 162,* 815–826.

Cheng, K. (1989). The vector sum model of pigeon landmark use. *Journal of Experimental Psychology: Animal Behavior Processes, 15,* 366–375.

Cheng, K. (1990). More psychophysics of the pigeon's use of landmarks. *Journal of Comparative Physiology A, 166,* 857–863.

Cheng, K. (1994). The determination of direction in landmark-based spatial search in pigeons: a further test of the vector sum model. *Animal Learning and Behavior, 22,* 291–301.

Cheng, P., and Holyoak, K. J. (1985). Pragmatic reasoning schemas. *Cognitive Psychology, 17,* 391–416.

CHI 96 Conference, *Human factors in computing systems: Common Ground Chi 96 conference proceedings, Vancouver, April 13–18, 1996* (pp. 42–49). New York: Association for Computing Machinery.

Chomsky, N. (1966). *Cartesian linguistics: a chapter in the history of rationalist thought.* New York: Harper and Row.

Church, R. B., and Goldin-Meadow, S. (1986). The mismatch between gesture and speech as an index of transitional knowledge. *Cognition, 23,* 43–71.

Clark, A. (1997). *Being there: putting brain, body, and world together again.* Cambridge: MIT Press.

Clark, H. H. (1969). Linguistic processes in deductive reasoning. *Psychological Review, 76,* 387–404.

Clark, H. H. (1970). The primitive nature of children's relational concepts. In J. R. Hayes (ed.), *Cognition and the development of language.* New York: Wiley.

Clark, H. H. (1973). Space, time, semantics, and the child. In T. E. Moore (ed.), *Cognitive development and the acquisition of language* (pp. 27–63). New York: Academic Press.

Clark, H. H., Carpenter, P. A., and Just, M. A. (1973). On the meeting of semantics and perception. In W. G. Chase (ed.), *Visual information processing.* New York: Academic Press.

Clement, C. A., and Gentner, D. (1991). Systematicity as a selection constraint in analogical mapping. *Cognitive Science, 15,* 89–132.

Cleveland, W. S. (1984). Graphs in scientific publications. *American Statistician, 38,* 261–269.

Cleveland, W. S. (1985). *The elements of graphing data.* Monterey, Calif.: Wadsworth.

Cofer, C. N. (1973). Constructive processes in memory. *American Scientist, 61,* 537–543.

Cogen, C. (1977). On three aspects of time expression in American Sign Language. In L. Friedman (ed.), *On the other hand: new perspectives on American Sign Language* (pp. 197–214). New York: Academic Press.

Cohen, I. B. (1984). Florence Nightingale. *Scientific American,* March, 128–137.

Collett, T. S., Cartwright, B. A., and Smith, B. A. (1986). Landmark learning and visuo-spatial memories in gerbils. *Journal of Comparative Physiology A, 158,* 835–851.

Collins, A. M., and Quillian, M. R. (1969). Retrieval time from semantic memory. *Journal of Verbal Learning and Verbal Behaviour, 9,* 432–438.

Cooper, L. A., Schacter, D. L., Ballesteros, S., and Moore, C. (1992). Priming and recognition of transformed three-dimensional objects: effects of size and reflection. *Journal of Experimental Psychology: Learning, Memory, and Cognition, 18,* 43–57.

Cooper, W. E., and Ross, J. R. (1975). World order. In R. E. Grossman, L. J. San, and T. J. Vance (eds.), *Papers from the Parasession on Functionalism.* Chicago: Chicago Linguistic Society.

Correa, J., Nunes, T., and Bryant, P. (1998). Young children's understanding of division: the relationship between division terms in a noncomputational task. *Journal of Educational Psychology, 90*, 321–329.

Coulmas, F. (1989). *The writing systems of the world.* Oxford: Basil Blackwell.

Couvillon, P. A., and Bitterman, M. E. (1992). A conventional conditioning analysis of "transitive inference" in pigeons. *Journal of Experimental Psychology: Animal Behavior Processes, 18*, 308–310.

Cowan, R., and Daniels, H. (1989). Children's use of counting and guidelines in judging relative number. *British Journal of Educational Psychology, 59*, 200–210.

Dallal, N. L., and Meck, W. H. (1990). Heierarchical structures: chunking by food type facilitates spatial memory. *Journal of Experimental Psychology: Animal Behavior Processes, 16*, 69–84.

Danziger, E. (1999). Language, space, and sociolect: cognitive correlates of gendered speech in Mopan Maya. In C. Fuchs and S. Robest (eds.), *Language diversity and cognitive representations* (pp. 85–106). Amsterdam: Benjamins.

Danziger, E. (to appear). Cross-cultural studies in language and thought: is there a metalanguage? In C. Moore and H. Mathews (eds.), *The psychology of cultural experience.* Cambridge: Cambridge University Press.

Danziger, E., Kita, S., and Stolz, C. (2000). *Conversational gesture as spatial manipulation: language, thought and behavior in two Mayan speech communities.* Manuscript in preparation.

Danziger, E., and Pederson, E. (1998). Through the looking-glass: literacy, writing systems, and mirror-image discrimination. *Written Language and Literacy, 1*, 153–164.

Davis, H. (1992). Transitive inference in rats (*Rattus norvegicus*). *Journal of Comparative Psychology, 106*, 342–349.

DeFrancis, J. (1989). *Visible speech: the diverse oneness of writing systems.* Honolulu: University of Hawaii Press.

Dehaene, S. (1997). *The number sense: how the mind creates mathematics.* New York: Oxford University Press.

De Lillo, C., and McGonigle, B. (1998). The logic of searches in young children (*Homo sapiens*) and tufted capuchin monkeys. *International Journal of Comparative Psychology, 10*, 1–24.

DeLoache, J. S. (1987). Rapid change in the symbolic functioning of very young children. *Science, 238*, 1556–1557.

DeLoache, J. S. (1995). Early symbol understanding and use. *Psychology of Learning and Motivation, 33*, 65–114.

DeLoache, J. S., Miller, K. F., and Rosengren, K. S. (1997). The credible shrinking room: very young children's performance with symbolic and non-symbolic relations. *Psychological Science, 8*, 308–313.

De Ruiter, J. P. (1998). Gesture and speech production. Ph.D. dissertation, Nijmegen University.

Desforges, A., and Desforges, G. (1980). Number-based strategies of sharing in young children. *Educational Studies, 6,* 97–109.

De Soto, C. B. (1960). Learning a social structure. *Journal of Abnormal and Social Psychology, 60,* 417–421.

De Soto, C. B., London, M., and Handel, S. (1965). Social reasoning and spatial paralogic. *Journal of Personality and Social Psychology, 2,* 513–521.

De Vega, M., Intons-Peterson, M., Johnson-Laird, P. N., Denis, M., and Marschark, M. (1996). *Models of visuospatial cognition.* New York: Oxford University Press.

Donald, M. (1991). *Origins of the modern mind.* Cambridge: Harvard University Press.

Downs, R. M. (1981). Maps and mappings as metaphors for spatial representation. In L. S. Liben, A. H. Patterson and N. Newcombe (eds.), *Spatial representation and behavior across the life span: theory and application* (pp. 143–166). New York: Academic Press.

Downs, R. M. (1985). The representation of space: its development in children and in cartography. In R. Cohen (ed.), *The development of spatial cognition* (pp. 323–345). Hillsdale, N.J.: Erlbaum.

Downs, R. M., and Liben, L. S. (1987). Children's understanding of maps. In P. Ellen and C. Thinus-Blanc (eds.), *Cognitive processes and spatial orientation in animal and man*, vol. 1: *Neurophysiology of spatial knowledge and developmental aspects* (pp. 202–219). Dordrecht, Holland: Martinius Nijhoff.

Downs, R. M., and Liben, L. S. (1991). The development of expertise in geography: a cognitive-developmental approach to geographic education. *Annals of the Association of American Geographers, 81,* 304–327.

Downs, R. M., and Liben, L. S. (1993). Mediating the environment: communicating, appropriating, and developing graphic representations of place. In R. H. Wozniak and K. Fischer (eds.), *Development in context: acting and thinking in specific environments* (pp. 155–181). Hillsdale, N.J.: Lawrence Erlbaum Associates.

Downs, R. M., Liben, L. S., and Daggs, D. G. (1988). On education and geographers: the role of cognitive developmental theory in geographic education. *Annals of the Association of American Geographers, 78,* 680–700.

Downs, R. M., and Stea, D. (1977). *Maps in minds.* New York: Harper and Row.

Duncker, K. (1945). On problem solving. *Psychological Monographs, 58* (270).

Eliot, J. (1987). *Models of psychological space: psychometric, developmental, and experimental approaches.* New York: Springer-Verlag.

Emmorey, K. (1996). The confluence of space and language in signed languages. In P. Bloom, M. Peterson, L. Nadel, and M. Garrett (eds.), *Language and space* (pp. 171–209). Cambridge: MIT Press.

Emmorey, K., and Falgier, B. (1999). Talking about space with space: describing environments in ASL. In E. A. Winston (ed.), *Story telling and conversations:*

discourse in deaf communities (pp. 3–26). Washington, D.C.: Gallaudet University Press.

Emmorey, K., Corina, D., and Bellugi, U. (1995). Differential processing of topographic and referential functions of space. In K. Emmorey and J. Reilly (eds). *Language, gesture, and space* (pp. 43–62). Hillsdale, N.J.: Lawrence Erlbaum Associates.

Emmorey, K., Klima, E., and Hickok, G. (1998). Mental rotation within linguistic and nonlinguistic domains in users of American Sign Language. *Cognition, 68,* 221–246.

Engberg-Pedersen, Elizabeth (1993). *Space in Danish Sign Language: the semantics and morphosyntax of the use of space in a visual language.* International Studies on Sign Language Research and Communication of the Deaf, no. 19. Hamburg, Germany: Signum-Verlag.

Engle, R. A. (1998). Not channels but composite signals: speech, gesture, diagrams, and object demonstrations are integrated in multimodal explanations. In M. A. Gernsbacher and S. J. Derry (eds.), *Proceedings of the Twentieth Annual Conference of the Cognitive Science Society.* Mahwah, N.J.: Erlbaum.

Etienne, A. S. (1992). Navigation of a small mammal by dead reckoning and local cues. *Current Directions in Psychological Science, 1,* 48–52.

Etienne, A. S., Berlie, J., Georgakopoulos, J., and Maurer, R. (1998). Role of dead reckoning in navigation. In S. Healy (ed.), *Spatial representation in animals* (pp. 54–68). New York: Oxford University Press.

Etienne, A. S., Teroni, E., Hurni, C., and Portenier, V. (1990). The effect of a single light cue on homing behaviour of the golden hamster. *Animal Behaviour, 39,* 17–41.

Falkenhainer, B., Forbus, K. D., and Gentner, D. (1989). The structure-mapping engine: algorithm and examples. *Artificial Intelligence, 41,* 1–63.

Fauconnier, G. (1985). *Mental spaces: aspects of meaning construction in natural language.* Cambridge: MIT Press.

Fauconnier, G. (1990). Domains and connections. *Cognitive Linguistics, 1* (1), 151–174.

Fazzioli, E. (1986). *Chinese calligraphy.* New York: Abbeville Press.

Fersen, L. von, Wynne, C. D. L., Delius, J. D., and Staddon, J. E. R. (1991). Transitive inference formation in pigeons. *Journal of Experimental Psychology: Animal Behavior Processes, 17,* 334–341.

Fillmore, C. J. (1971). *The Santa Cruz lectures on deixis.* Bloomington: Indiana University Linguistic Club.

Fischer, K. W., and Biddell, T. R. (1998). Dynamic development of psychological structures in action and thought. In R. M. Lerner (ed.), *Handbook of child psychology*, vol. 1: *Theoretical models of human development* (5th ed., pp. 467–561). New York: Wiley.

Fiske, A. P. (1992). The four elementary forms of sociality: framework for a unified theory of social relations. *Psychological Review, 99*, 689–723.

Fodor, J. (1983). *Modularity of mind.* Cambridge: MIT Press.

Fodor, J. A., and Pylyshyn, Z. (1988). Connectionism and cognitive architecture: a critical analysis. *Cognition, 28*, 3–71.

Forbus, K. D., Ferguson, R. W., and Gentner, D. (1994). Incremental structure-mapping. *Proceedings of the Sixteenth Annual Conference of the Cognitive Science Society* (pp. 313–318). Hillsdale, N.J.: Lawrence Erlbaum Associates.

Franklin, N., and Tversky, B. (1990). Searching imagined environments. *Journal of Experimental Psychology: General, 119*, 63–76.

Franklin, N., Tversky, B., and Coon, V. (1992). Switching points of view in spatial mental models acquired from text. *Memory and Cognition, 20*, 507–518.

Fraser, J. T. (1987). *Time, the familiar stranger.* Amherst: University of Massachusetts Press.

Friedman, L. (1975). Space, time, and person reference in American Sign Language. *Language, 51* (4), 940–961.

Friedman, W. J. (1990). *About time: inventing the fourth dimension.* Cambridge: MIT Press.

Fromkin, V., and Rodman, R. (1998). *An introduction to language* (6th ed.). Fort Worth: Harcourt Brace.

Frydman, O., and Bryant, P. E. (1988). Sharing and the understanding of number equivalence by young children. *Cognitive Development, 3*, 323–339.

Frye, D., Braisby, N., Lowe, J., Maroudas, C., and Nicholls, J. (1989). Young children's understanding of counting and cardinality. *Child Development, 60*, 1158–1171.

Gallistel, C. R. (1990). *The organization of learning.* Cambridge: MIT Press.

Gattis, M. (2000a). *Perceptual and linguistic polarity constrain reasoning with spatial representations.* Manuscript in preparation.

Gattis, M. (2000b). *Mapping relational structure in an artificial sign language.* Manuscript in preparation.

Gattis, M. (2000c). *Structure mapping in spatial reasoning.* Manuscript submitted for publication.

Gattis, M., and Dupeyrat, C. (1999). Spatial strategies in reasoning. In W. Schaeken, A. Vandierendonck and G. de Vooght (eds.), *Deductive reasoning and strategies.* Hillsdale, N.J.: Erlbaum.

Gattis, M., and Holyoak, K. J. (1996). Mapping conceptual to spatial relations in visual reasoning. *Journal of Experimental Psychology: Learning, Memory, and Cognition, 22*, 231–239.

Gattis, M., and Molyneaux, J. (1999). Constraints on reasoning with spatial representations. Poster presented at the meeting of the Psychonomics Society, Los Angeles, November.

Gauvain, M. (1993a). The development of spatial thinking in everyday activity. *Developmental Review, 13*, 92–121.

Gauvain, M. (1993b). Spatial thinking and its development in sociocultural context. In R. Vasta (ed.), *Annals of child development* (vol. 9, pp. 67–102). London: Jessica Kingsley Publishers.

Gelb, I. (1963). *A study of writing* (2nd ed.). Chicago: University of Chicago Press.

Gentner, D. (1983). Structure-mapping: a theoretical framework for analogy. *Cognitive Science, 7*, 155–170.

Gentner, D. (1988). Metaphor as structure mapping: the relational shift. *Child Development, 59*, 47–59.

Gentner, D. (1989). The mechanisms of analogical learning. In S. Vosinadou and A. Ortony (eds.), *Similarity and analogical reasoning* (pp. 199–241). New York: Cambridge University Press.

Gentner, D. (1992). *Metaphor as mapping.* Paper presented at the Workshop on Metaphor, Tel Aviv.

Gentner, D., and Boronat, C. (1991). Metaphors are (sometimes) processed as domain mappings. Paper presented at the Symposium on Metaphor and Conceptual Change, Meeting of the Cognitive Science Society, Chicago.

Gentner, D., and Boronat, C. (in preparation). Novel metaphors are processed as systematic domain mappings.

Gentner, D., Bowdle, B., Wolff, P., and Boronat, C. (in press). Metaphor is like analogy. In D. Gentner, K. J. Holyoak, and B. Kokinov (eds.), *The analogical mind: perspectives from cognitive science.* Cambridge: MIT Press.

Gentner, D., Falkenhainer, B., and Skorstad, J. (1988). Viewing metaphor as analogy. In D. H. Helman (ed.), *Analogical reasoning: perspectives of artificial intelligence, cognitive science, and philosophy* (pp. 171–177). Dordrecht, Netherlands: Kluwer.

Gentner, D., and Gentner, D. (1983). Flowing waters or teeming crowds: mental models of electricity. In D. Gentner and A. L. Stevens (eds.), *Mental models.* Hillsdale, N.J.: Erlbaum.

Gentner, D., and Imai, M. (1992). Is the future always ahead? Evidence for system-mappings in understanding space-time metaphors. *Proceedings of the Fourteenth Annual Meeting of the Cognitive Science Society* (pp. 510–515).

Gentner, D., Imai, M., and Boroditsky, L. (in preparation). As time goes by: evidence for two systems in processing space-time metaphors.

Gentner, D., and Markman, A. B. (1997). Structure mapping in analogy and similarity. *American Psychologist, 52*, 45–56.

Gentner, D., and Wolff, P. (1997). Alignment in the processing of metaphor. *Journal of Memory and Language, 37*, 331–355.

Gentner, D., and Wolff, P. (2000). Metaphor and knowledge change. In E. Dietrich and A. B. Markman (eds.), *Cognitive dynamics: conceptual change in humans and machines* (pp. 295–342). Mahwah, N.J.: Lawrence Erlbaum Associates.

Gibbs, R. (1990). Psycholinguistic studies on the conceptual biases of idiomaticity. *Cognitive Linguistics, 1*, 417–451.

Gibbs, R. W. (1994). *Poetics of mind: figurative thought, language, and understanding.* Cambridge: Cambridge University Press.

Gibbs, R., and O'Brien, J. (1990). Idioms and mental imagery: the metaphorical motivation for idiomatic meaning. *Cognition, 36*, 35–68.

Gillan, D. J. (1981). Reasoning in chimpanzees II: transitive inference. *Journal of Experimental Psychology: Animal Behavior Processes, 7*, 150–164.

Glasgow, J., Narayanan, N. H., and Chandrasekaran, B. (eds.) (1995). *Diagrammatic reasoning: cognitive and computational perspectives.* Cambridge: MIT Press.

Glenberg, A. M., and Langston, W. E. (1992). Comprehension of illustrated text: pictures help to build mental models. *Journal of Memory and Language, 31*, 129–151.

Glick, J., and Wapner, S. (1968). Development of transitivity: some findings and problems of analysis. *Child Development, 39*, 621–638.

Glucksberg, S., Brown, M., and McGlone, M. S. (1993). Conceptual analogies are not automatically accessed during idiom comprehension. *Memory and Cognition, 21*, 711–719.

Gobert, J. D. (1999). Expertise in the comprehension of architectural plans. In J. Gero and B. Tversky (eds.), *Visual and spatial reasoning in design* (pp. 185–205). Sydney, Australia: Key Centre of Design Computing and Cognition.

Goodall, J. (1986). *The chimpanzees of Gombe: patterns of behavior.* Cambridge: Harvard University Press.

Goodman, Nelson. (1968). *Languages of art: an approach to a theory of symbols.* New York: Bobbs-Merrill.

Gould, S. J. (1977). *Ever since Darwin: reflections in natural history.* New York: Norton.

Greenberg, J. H. (1966). *Language universals.* The Hague: Mouton Publishers.

Halford, G. S. (1984). Can young children integrate premises in transitivity and serial order tasks? *Cognitive Psychology, 16*, 65–93.

Halford, G. S. (1992). Analogical reasoning and conceptual complexity in cognitive development. *Human Development, 35*, 193–217.

Halford, G. S. (1993). *Children's understanding: the development of mental models.* Hillsdale, N.J.: Lawrence Erlbaum Associates.

Hamilton, H. W., and Deese, J. (1971). Does linguistic marking have a psychological correlate? *Journal of Verbal Learning and Verbal Behavior, 10*, 707–714.

Harley, J. B., and Woodward, D. (eds.) (1987). *The history of cartography*, vol. 1: *Cartography in prehistoric, ancient, and Medieval Europe and the Mediterranean.* Chicago: University of Chicago Press.

Harley, J. B., and Woodward, D. (eds.) (1992). *The history of cartography*, vol. 2, book 1: *Cartography in the traditional Islamic and South Asian Societies.* Chicago: University of Chicago Press.

Harley, J. B., and Woodward, D. (eds.) (1994). *The history of cartography*, vol. 2, book 2: *Cartography in the traditional East and Southeast Asian societies.* Chicago: University of Chicago Press.

Harnad, S. (1987). *Categorical perception: the groundwork of cognition.* Cambridge: Cambridge University Press.

Harris, M. R., and McGonigle. B. O. (1994). Modelling transitive inference. *Quarterly Journal of Experimental Psychology, 47B* (3), 319–348.

Harrison, R. E. (1994). *Look at the world: the Fortune atlas for world strategy.* New York: Alfred A. Knopf.

Harrower, M., Griffin, A. L., and MacEachren, A. (in press). Temporal focusing and temporal brushing: assessing their impact in geographic visualization. *Proceedings of the Nineteenth International Cartographic Conference*, Ottawa, August 1999.

Healy, S. (ed.) (1998). *Spatial representation in animals.* New York: Oxford University Press.

Hegarty, M. (1992). Mental animation: inferring motion from static displays of mechanical systems. *Journal of Experimental Psychology: Learning, Memory, and Cognition, 18*, 1084–1102.

Hegarty, M., Narayanan, N. H., Cate, C., and Holmquist, S. (1999). Individual differences in understanding machines from diagrams, text, and hypermedia presentations. Paper presented at the meeting of the Society for Applied Research in Memory and Cognition, Boulder, Colo., June 9–11.

Hermer, L., and Spelke, E. S. (1994). A geometric process for spatial reorientation in young children. *Nature, 370*, 57–59.

Hermer, L., and Spelke, E. S. (1996). Modularity and development: the case of spatial reorientation. *Cognition, 61*, 195–232.

Hermer-Vazquez, L., Spelke, E. S., and Katsnelson, A. S. (1999). Sources of flexibility in human cognition: dual-task studies of space and language. *Cognitive Psychology, 39*, 3–36.

Hertz, R. (1973). The pre-eminence of the right hand: a study in religious polarity. In R. Needham (ed. and trans.), *Right and left* (pp. 3–31). Chicago: University of Chicago Press. Original work published in 1909.

Hicks, L. H. (1964). Effects of overtraining on acquisition and reversal of place and response learning. *Psychological Reports, 15*, 459–462.

Hinton, G. E. (1990). Mapping part-whole hierarchies into connectionist networks. *Artificial Intelligence, 46*, 47–75,

Hochberg, J. E. (1964). *Perception.* Englewood Cliffs, N.J.: Prentice-Hall.

Holyoak, K. J., and Hummel, J. E. (in press). The proper treatment of symbols in a connectionist architecture. In E. Deitrich and A. Markman (eds.), *Cognitive dynamics: conceptual change in humans and machines.* Mahwah, N.J.: Erlbaum.

Holyoak, K. J., and Mah, W. A. (1982). Cognitive reference points in judgments of symbolic magnitude. *Cognitive Psychology, 14*, 328–352.

Holyoak, K. J., and Patterson, K. K. (1981). A positional discriminability model of linear order judgments. *Journal of Experimental Psychology: Human Perception and Performance, 7*, 1283–1302.

Holyoak, K. J., and Thagard, P. (1995). *Mental leaps: analogy in creative thought.* Cambridge: MIT Press.

Holyoak, K. J., and Thagard, P. (1997). The analogical mind. *American Psychologist, 52*, 35–44.

Howard, I. P. (1982). *Human visual orientation.* New York: Wiley.

Huff, D. (1954). *How to lie with statistics.* New York: Norton.

Hughes, M. (1986). *Children and number: difficulties in learning mathematics.* Oxford: Blackwell.

Hummel, J. E., and Biederman, I. (1992). Dynamic binding in a neural network for shape recognition. *Psychological Review, 99*, 480–517.

Hummel, J. E., and Holyoak, K. J. (1992). Indirect analogical mapping. In *Proceedings of the Fourteenth Annual Conference of the Cognitive Science Society* (pp. 516–521). Hillsdale, N.J.: Erlbaum.

Hummel, J. E., and Holyoak, K. J. (1997). Distributed representations of structure: a theory of analogical access and mapping. *Psychological Review, 104*, 427–466.

Hung, D. L., and Tzeng, O. J. L. (1981). Orthographic variations and visual information processing. *Psychological Bulletin, 90*, 377–414.

Hunter, I. M. L. (1957). The solving of the three-term series problems. *British Journal of Psychology, 48*, 286–298.

Huttenlocher, J. (1968). Constructing spatial images: a strategy in reasoning. *Psychological Review, 75*, 550–560.

Inhelder, B., and Piaget, J. (1964). *The early growth of logic in the child.* London: Routledge and Kegan-Paul.

Israel, M. (1996). Polar sensitivity as lexical semantics. *Linguistics and Philosophy, 19*, 619–666.

Ittelson, W. H. (1996). Visual perception of markings. *Psychonomic Bulletin and Review, 3*, 171–187.

Jackendoff, R. (1983). *Semantics and cognition.* Cambridge: MIT Press.

James, W. (1891). *The principles of psychology* (vol. 2). London: Macmillan.

Johnson, M. (1987). *The body in the mind.* Chicago: University of Chicago Press.

Johnson-Laird, P. N. (1982). The three-term series problem. *Cognition, 1*, 57–82.

Johnson-Laird, P. N. (1996). Space to think. In P. Bloom, M. Peterson, L. Nadel, and M. Garrett (eds.), *Language and space* (pp. 437–462). Cambridge: MIT Press.

Jones, S. (1970). Visual and verbal processes in problem-solving. *Cognitive Psychology, 1*, 201–214.

Kaiser, M. K., Proffitt, D. R., Whelan, S. M., and Hecht, H. (1992). Influence of animation on dynamical judgements. *Journal of Experimental Psychology: Human Perception and Performance, 18* (3), 669–690.

Kallio, K. D. (1982). Developmental change on a five-term transitive inference task. *Journal of Experimental Child Psychology, 33*, 142–164.

Kamil, A. C., and Jones, J. E. (1997). The seed-storing corvid Clark's nutcracker learns geometric relationships among landmarks. *Nature, 390*, 276–279.

Keane, M. T., and Brayshaw, M. (1988). The incremental analogical machine: a computational model of analogy. In D. Sleeman (ed.), *Third European Working Session on Machine Learning* (pp. 53–62). San Mateo, Calif.: Kaufmann.

Kendon, K. (1980). Gesticulation and speech: two aspects of the process of utterance. In M. R. Key (ed.), *The relation between verbal and nonverbal communication* (pp. 207–227). The Hague: Mouton.

Keysar, B., and Bly, B. (1995). Intuitions of the transparency of idioms: can one keep a secret by spilling the beans? *Journal of Memory and Language, 33*, 89–109.

Kieras, D. (1992). Diagrammatic display for engineered systems: effects on human performance in interacting with malfunctioning systems. *International Journal on Man-Machine Studies, 36*, 861–895.

Kieras, D. E., and Bovair, S. (1984). The role of a mental model in learning to operate a device. *Cognitive Science, 11*, 255–273.

Kingma, J. (1984). Task sensitivity and the sequence of development in seriation, ordinal correspondence, and cardination. *Genetic Psychology Monographs, 110* (2), 181–205.

Kirsh, D. (1995). The intelligent use of space. *Artificial Intelligence, 73*, 31–68.

Kita, S. (1993). Language and thought interface: a study of spontaneous gestures and Japanese mimetics. Unpublished doctoral dissertation, University of Chicago.

Kita, S. (2000). How representational gestures help speaking. In D. McNeill (ed.), *Language and gesture* (pp. 162–184). Cambridge: Cambridge University Press.

Kita, S., van Gijn, I., and van der Hulst, H. (1998). Movement phases in signs and co-speech gestures, and their transcription by human coders. In I. Wachsmuth and M. Fröhlich (eds.), *Gesture and sign language in human-computer interaction: International Gesture Workshop, Bielefeld, Germany, September 17–19, 1997, proceedings* (pp. 23–35), Lecture Notes in Artificial Intelligence, no. 1371. Berlin: Springer-Verlag.

Klima, E., and Bellugi, U. (1979). *The signs of language.* Cambridge: Harvard University Press.

Kosslyn, S. M. (1980). *Image and mind.* Cambridge: Harvard University Press.

Kosslyn, S. M. (1985). Graphics and human information processing: a review of five books. *Journal of the American Statistical Association, 80*, 497–508.

Kosslyn, S. M. (1989). Understanding charts and graphs. *Applied Cognitive Psychology, 3*, 185–226.

Kosslyn, S. M. (1994). *Elements of graph design.* New York: Freeman.

Kosslyn, S. M., Pick, H. L., and Fariello, G. R. (1974). Cognitive maps in children and men. *Child Development, 45*, 707–716.

Krauss, R. M., Chen, Y., and Chawla, P. (1996). Nonverbal behavior and non-verbal communication: what do conversational hand gestures tell us? In M. Zanna (ed.), *Advances in experimental social psychology* (vol. 28, pp. 389–450). Tampa: Academic Press.

Lakoff, G. (1987). *Women, fire, and dangerous things.* Chicago, IL: The University of Chicago Press.

Lakoff, G., and Johnson, M. (1980). *Metaphors we live by.* Chicago: University of Chicago Press.

Lakoff, G., and Turner, M. (1989). *More than cool reason: a field guide to poetic metaphor.* Chicago: University of Chicago Press.

Langacker, R. W. (1987). *Foundations of cognitive grammar*, vol. 1: *Theoretical prerequisites.* Stanford: Stanford University Press.

Larkin, J. H., and Simon, H. A. (1987). Why a diagram is (sometimes) worth ten thousand words, *Cognitive Science, 11*, 65–99.

Laurendeau, M., and Pinard, A. (1970). *The development of the concept of space in children.* New York: International Universities Press.

Leach, E. (1976). *Culture and communication: the logic by which symbols are connected.* Cambridge: Cambridge University Press.

Lehrer, A. (1990). Polysemy, conventionality, and the structure of the lexicon. *Cognitive Linguistics, 1*, 207–246.

Levin, I., and Tolchinsky Landsmann, L. (1989). Becoming literate: referential and phonetic strategies in early reading and writing. *International Journal of Behavioural Development, 12*, 369–384.

Levine, M., Marchon, I., and Hanley, G. (1984). The placement and misplacement of you-are-here maps. *Environment and Behavior, 16*, 139–158.

Levinson, S. C. (1997). Cognitive consequences of spatial description in Guugu Yimithir. *Linguistic Anthropology, 7*, 98–131.

Levinson, S. C., and Brown, P. (1994). Immanuel Kant among the Tenejapans: anthropology as empirical philosophy. *Ethos, 22*, 3–41.

Levy, E., Zacks, J., Tversky, B., and Schiano, D. (1996). Gratuitous graphics: putting preferences in perspective. In

Li, S. C., and Lewandowsky, S. (1995). Forward and backward recall: different retrieval processes. *Journal of Experimental Psychology: Learning, Memory, and Cognition, 21* (4), 837–847.

Liben, L. S. (1981). Spatial representation and behavior: multiple perspectives. In L. S. Liben, A. H. Patterson, and N. Newcombe (eds.), *Spatial representation and behavior across the life span: theory and application* (pp. 3–36). New York: Academic Press.

Liben, L. S. (1988). Conceptual issues in the development of spatial cognition. In J. Stiles-Davis, M. Kritchevsky, and U. Bellugi (eds.), *Spatial cognition: brain bases and development* (pp. 167–194). Hillsdale, N.J.: Erlbaum Associates.

Liben, L. S. (1991). Environmental cognition through direct and representational experiences: a life-span perspective. In T. Garling and G. W. Evans (eds.), *Environment, cognition, and action* (pp. 245–276). New York: Oxford University Press.

Liben, L. S. (1997). Children's understanding of spatial representations of place: mapping the methodological landscape. In N. Foreman and R. Gillett (eds.), *A handbook of spatial research paradigms and methodologies* (pp. 41–83). East Sussex, U.K.: Psychology Press, Taylor and Francis Group.

Liben, L. S. (1999). Developing an understanding of external spatial representations. In I. E. Sigel (ed.), *Development of mental representation* (pp. 297–321). Mahwah, N.J.: Lawrence Erlbaum Associates.

Liben, L. S., Carlson, R. A., Szechter, L. E., and Mararra, M. T. (1999). Understanding geographic images. Poster presented at the Annual Convention of the American Psychological Association, Boston, August.

Liben, L. S., and Downs, R. M. (1989). Understanding maps as symbols: the development of map concepts in children. In H. W. Reese (ed.), *Advances in child development and behavior* (vol. 22, pp. 145–201). New York: Academic Press.

Liben, L. S., and Downs, R. M. (1991). The role of graphic representations in understanding the world. In R. M. Downs, L. S. Liben, and D. S. Palermo (eds.), *Visions of aesthetics, the environment, and development: the legacy of Joachim Wohlwill* (pp. 139–180). Hillsdale, N.J.: Lawrence Erlbaum Associates.

Liben, L. S., and Downs, R. M. (1993). Understanding person-space-map relations: cartographic and developmental perspectives. *Developmental Psychology, 29*, 739–752.

Liben, L. S., and Downs, R. M. (1994). Fostering geographic literacy from early childhood: the contributions of interdisciplinary research. *Journal of Applied Developmental Psychology, 15*, 549–569.

Liben, L. S., and Downs, R. M. (in press). Geography for young children: maps as tools for learning environments. In S. L. Golbeck (ed.), *Psychological perspectives on early childhood education.* Mahwah, N.J.: Lawrence Erlbaum Associates.

Liben, L. S., Downs, R. M., and Signorella, M. S. (1995). Sex differences in adolescents' success on an academic competition in geography: explanations and implications. Paper presented at the biennial meeting of the Society for Research in Child Development, Indianapolis, Ind., March.

Liben, L. S., and Yekel, C. A. (1996). Preschoolers' understanding of plan and oblique maps: the role of geometric and representational correspondence. *Child Development, 67*, 2780–2796.

Liddell, S. (1995). Real, surrogate, and token space: grammatical consequences in ASL. In K. Emmorey and J. Reilly (eds.), *Language, gesture, and space.* Hillsdale, N.J.: Lawrence Erlbaum Associates.

Linn, M. C., and Petersen, A. C. (1985). Emergence and characterization of sex differences in spatial ability: a meta-analysis. *Child Development, 56*, 1479–1498.

Loomis, J. M., Da Silva, J. A., Fujita, N., and Fukusima, S. S. (1992). Visual space perception and visually directed action. *Journal of Experimental Psychology: Human Perception and Performance, 18*, 906–922.

Loomis, J. M., Klatsky, R. L., Golledge, R. G., Cicinelli, J. G., Pellegrino, J. W., and Fry, P. A. (1993). Nonvisual navigation by blind and sighted: assessment of path integration ability. *Journal of Experimental Psychology: General, 122*, 73–91.

Lowe, R. (1999). Extracting information from an animation during complex visual processing. *European Journal of the Psychology of Education, 14*, 225–244.

Lucas, C., and Valli, C. (1990). Predicates of perceived motion in ASL. In S. D. Fischer and P. Siple (eds.), *Theoretical issues in sign language research*, vol. 1: *Linguistics* (pp. 153–166). Chicago: University of Chicago Press.

Lyons, J. (1977). *Semantics* (vol. 2). Cambridge: Cambridge University Press.

MacEachren, A. M. (1995). *How maps work.* New York: Guilford Press.

MacEachren, A. M., and DiBiase, D. W. (1991). Animated maps of aggregate data: conceptual and practical problems. *Cartography and Geographic Information Systems, 18*, 221–229.

Macken, E., Perry, J., and Haas, C. (1993). Richly grounded symbols in ASL. *Sign Language Studies, 81*, 375–394.

Mackintosh, N. J. (1965). Overtraining, transfer to proprioceptive control, and position reversal. *Quarterly Journal of Experimental Psychology, 17*, 26–36.

Mallery, G. (1893/1972). *Picture writing of the American Indians.* New York: Dover. Originally published by Government Printing Office.

Manguel, A. (1997). *A history of reading.* New York: Penguin.

Marcus, G. F. (1998). Rethinking eliminative connectionism. *Cognitive Psychology, 37*, 243–282.

Margules, J., and Gallistel, C. R. (1988). Heading in the rat: determination by environmental shape. *Animal Learning and Behavior, 16*, 404–410.

Markman, A. B. (1997). Constraints on analogical inference. *Cognitive Science, 21* (4), 373–418.

Maybery, M. T., Bain, J. D., and Halford, G. S. (1986). Information-processing demands of transitive inference. *Journal of Experimental Psychology: Learning, Memory, and Cognition, 12*, 600–613.

Mayer, R. E., and Gallini, J. K. (1990). When is an illustration worth ten thousand words? *Journal of Educational Psychology, 82*, 715–726.

McBeath, M. K., Schiano, D. J., and Tversky, B. (1997). Three-dimensional bilateral symmetry bias in judgments of figural identity and orientation. *Psychological Science, 8,* 217–223.

McCloud, S. (1994). *Understanding comics.* New York: Harper Collins.

McGlone, M. S., and Harding, J. L. (1998). Back (or forward?) to the future: the role of perspective in temporal language comprehension. *Journal of Experimental Psychology: Learning, Memory and Cognition, 24,* 1211–1223.

McGonigle, B. (1967). Stimulus additivity and dominance in visual discrimination by rats. *Journal of Comparative and Physiological Psychology, 64,* 110–112.

McGonigle, B. (1998). Pointing to see? *Brain and Behaviour Sciences, 20* (4), 754.

McGonigle, B. (2000). Getting autonomous agents to control themselves: case study 10. In O. Holland and D. McFarland (eds.), *Artificial ethology.* Oxford: Oxford University Press.

McGonigle, B., and Chalmers, M. (1977). Are monkeys logical? *Nature, 267,* 694–696.

McGonigle, B., and Chalmers, M. (1984). The selective impact of question form and input mode on the symbolic distance effect in children. *Journal of Experimental Child Psychology, 37,* 525–554.

McGonigle, B., and Chalmers, M. (1986). Representations and strategies during inference. In T. Myers, K. Brown, and B. O. McGonigle (eds.), *Reasoning and discourse processes.* London: Academic Press.

McGonigle, B., and Chalmers, M. (1992). Monkeys are rational! *Quarterly Journal of Experimental Psychology, 45B* (3), 189–228.

McGonigle, B., and Chalmers, M. (1996). The ontology of order. In L. Smith (ed.), *Critical readings on Piaget.* London: Routledge.

McGonigle, B., and Chalmers, M. (1998). Rationality as optimised cognitive self-regulation. In M. Oaksford and N. Chater (eds.), *Rational models of cognition.* Oxford: Oxford University Press.

McGonigle, B., Chalmers, M., Dickinson, A. R., and Ravenscroft, J. (2000). *Classification and nine-item size seriation by monkeys (Cebus apella).* Manuscript submitted for publication.

McGonigle, B., and De Lillo, C. (1999). Exhaustive searches in monkeys. Manuscript in preparation.

McGonigle, B., De Lillo, C., and Dickinson, A. R. (1992). Serial order induced search in children and monkeys. Paper presented at the Fifth European Conference on Developmental Psychology, Seville, Spain.

McGonigle, B., De Lillo, C., and Dickinson, A. R. (1994). Classification to order: a comparative analysis of categorical seriation in monkey and man. Paper presented Fifteenth Congress of the International Primatological Society, Bali, Indonesia.

McGonigle, B. O., and Jones, B. T. (1975). The perception of linear gestalten by rat and monkey: sensory sensitivity or perception of structure? *Perception, 4,* 419–429.

McGonigle, B. O., and Jones, B. T. (1977). Judgmental criteria and the perception of structure. *Perception, 6*, 213–217.

McGonigle, B. O., and Jones, B. T. (1978). Levels of stimulus processing by the squirrel monkey: relative and absolute judgments compared. *Perception, 7*, 635–659.

McNeill, D. (1985). So you think gestures are non-verbal. *Psychological Review, 92*, 350–371.

McNeill, D. (1992). *Hand and mind.* Chicago: University of Chicago Press.

McNeill, D. (to appear). Pointing and morality in Chicago. In S. Kita (ed.), *Pointing: where language, cognition, and culture meet.*

McNeill, D., Cassell, J., and Levy, E. (1993). Abstract deixis. *Semiotica, 95* (1/2), 5–19.

Meck, W. H., Church, R. M., and Gibbon, J. (1985). Temporal integration in duration and number discrimination. *Journal of Experimental Psychology: Animal Behavior Processes, 11*, 591–597.

Medin, D. L., Goldstone, R. L., and Gentner, D. (1993). Respects for similarity. *Psychological Review, 100* (2), 254–278.

Millar, S. (1994). *Understanding and representing space: theory and evidence from studies with blind and sighted children.* New York: Oxford University Press.

Miller, G. (1963). *Language and communication.* New York: McGraw-Hill.

Miller, G., and Johson-Laird, P. (1976). *Language and perception.* Cambridge: Cambridge University Press.

Miller, K. (1984). The child as the measurer of all things: measurement procedures and the development of quantitative concepts. In C. Sophian (ed.), *Origins of cognitive skills* (pp. 193–228). Hillsdale, N.J.: Erlbaum.

Modley, R. (1976). *Handbook of pictorial symbols.* New York: Dover.

Modley, R., and Lowenstein, D. (1952). *Pictographs and graphs: how to make and use them.* New York: Harper and Brothers.

Monmonier, M. (1993). *Mapping it out.* Chicago: University of Chicago Press.

Morris, R. G. M. (1981). Spatial localization does not require the presence of local cues. *Learning and Motivation, 12*, 239–260.

Moyer, R. S. (1973). Comparing objects in memory: evidence suggesting an internal psychophysics. *Perception and Psychophysics, 13*, 180–184.

Moyer, R. S., and Landauer, T. K. (1967). Time required for judgments of numerical inequality. *Nature, 215*, 1519–1520.

Muehrcke, P. C. (1986). *Map use* (2nd ed.). Madison, Wis.: JP Publications.

Muehrcke, P. C., and Muehrcke, J. O. (1998). *Map use* (4th ed.). Madison, Wis.: JP Publications.

Murphy, G. L. (1996). On metaphoric representation. *Cognition, 60*, 173–204.

Muybridge, E. (1957). *Animals in motion.* Edited by L. S. Brown. New York: Dover.

Nadel, L. (1990). Varieties of spatial cognition: psychobiological considerations. *Annals of the New York Academy of Sciences, 60*, 613–636.

Narayanan, N. H., Suwa, M., and Motoda, H. (1994). A study of diagrammatic reasoning from verbal and gestural data. *Proceedings of the Sixteenth Annual Conference of the Cognitive Science Society.*

National Geographic Society (1998). *Road atlas of the United States.* Washington, D.C.: National Geographic Society.

Needham, R. (ed.) (1973). *Right and left.* Chicago: University of Chicago Press.

Neisser, U. (1987). A sense of where you are: functions of the spatial module. In P. Ellen and C. Thinus-Blanc (eds.), *Cognitive processes and spatial orientation in animal and man* (vol. 2, pp. 293–310). Dordrecht, Netherlands: Martinus Nijhoff Publishing.

Nelson, B. D. (1994). Location and size geographic misperceptions: a survey of junior high through undergraduate college students. Paper presented at the Annual Meeting of the Association of American Geographers, San Francisco, March.

Neurath, O. (1936). *International Picture Language: the first rules of isotype.* London: Kegan Paul, Trench, Trubner and Co.

Newcombe, N. S. (1997). New perspectives on spatial representation: what different tasks tell us about how people remember location. In N. Foreman and R. Gillett (eds.), *A handbook of spatial research paradigms and methodologies* (pp. 85–102). East Sussex, U. K.: Psychology Press, Taylor and Francis Group.

Newcombe, N. S., and Huttenlocher, J. (in press). *Making space: taking cognitive development one domain at a time.* Cambridge: MIT Press.

Newcombe, N., and Liben, L. S. (1982). Barrier effects in the cognitive maps of children and adults. *Journal of Experimental Child Psychology, 34*, 46–58.

Newell, A., and Simon, H. (1972). *Human problem solving.* Englewood Cliffs, N.J.: Prentice-Hall.

Norman, D. A. (1993). *Things that make us smart.* Reading, Mass.: Addison-Wesley.

Nunes, T., and Bryant, P. (1996). *Children doing mathematics.* Oxford: Blackwell.

O'Connor, N., and Hermelin, B. M. (1972). The re-ordering of three term series problems by blind and sighted children. *British Journal of Psychology, 63* (3), 381–386.

O'Keefe, J., and Nadel, L. (1978). *The hippocampus as a cognitive map.* Oxford: Clarendon.

Olthof, A., Sutton, J. E., Slumskie, S. V., D'Addetta, J., and Roberts, W. A. (1999). In search of the cognitive map: can rats learn an abstract pattern of rewarded arms on the radial maze? *Journal of Experimental Psychology: Animal Behavior Processes, 25*, 352–362.

Olton, D. S., and Samuelson, R. J. (1976). Remembrance of places passed: spatial memory in rats. *Journal of Experimental Psychology: Animal Behavior Processes, 2*, 97–116.

Ortony, A. (1975). Why metaphors are necessary and not just nice. *Educational Theory, 25*, 45–53.

Osgood, C. E., Suci, G. J., and Tannenbaum, P. H. (1957). *The measurement of meaning.* Urbana, Ill.: University of Illinois Press.

Ossenkopp, K.-P., and Hargreaves, E. L. (1993). Spatial learning in an enclosed eight-arm maze in rats with sodium arsanilate-induced labyrinthectomies. *Behavioral and Neural Biology, 59*, 253–257.

Over, R., and Over, J. (1967). Detection and recognition of mirror-image obliques by young children. *Journal of Comparative and Physiological Psychology, 64*, 467–470.

Pane, J. F., Corbett, A. T., and John, B. E. (1996). Assessing dynamics in computer-based instructions. In CHI 96 Conference, *Human factors in computing systems: Common Ground Chi 96 conference proceedings, Vancouver, April 13–18, 1996* (pp. 197–204). New York: Association for Computing Machinery.

Pani, J. R., Jeffres, J. A., Shippey, G. T., and Schwartz, K. T., (1996). Imagining projective transformations: aligned orientations in spatial organization. *Cognitive Psychology, 31*, 125–167.

Parkman, J. M. (1971). Temporal aspects of digit and letter inequality judgements. *Journal of Experimental Psychology, 91*, 191–205.

Pears, R., and Bryant, P. (1990). Transitive inferences by young children about spatial position. *British Journal of Psychology, 81*, 497–510.

Pederson, E. (1995). Language as context, language as means: spatial cognition and habitual language use. *Cognitive Linguistics, 6*, 33–62.

Pederson, E., Danziger, E., Wilkins, D., Levinson, S., Kita, S., and Senft, G. (1998). Semantic typology and spatial conceptualization. *Language, 74*, 557–589.

Persky, H. R., Reese, C. M., O'Sullivan, C. Y., Lazer, S., Moore, J., and Shakrani, S. (1996). NAEP 1994 geography report card: findings from the National Assessment of Educational Progress. Washington, D.C.: U.S. Department of Education, Office of Educational Research and Improvement.

Piaget, J. (1928). *Judgment and reasoning in the child.* London: Kegan Paul.

Piaget, J. (1929). *The child's conception of the world.* New York: Harcourt, Brace.

Piaget, J. (1952). *The child's conception of number.* London: Routledge and Kegan Paul.

Piaget, J., and Inhelder, B. (1956). *The child's conception of space.* London: Routledge and Kegan Paul.

Piaget, J., and Inhelder, B. (1966). *Mental imagery in the child.* London: Routledge and Kegan Paul.

Pinker, S. (1989). *Learnability and cognition: the acquisition of argument structure.* Cambridge: MIT Press.

Pinker, S. (1990). A theory of graph comprehension. In R. Freedle (ed.), *Artificial intelligence and the future of testing* (pp. 73–126). Hillsdale, N.J.: Erlbaum.

Potts, G. R. (1972). Information processing strategies used in the encoding of linear orderings. *Journal of Verbal Learning and Verbal Behavior, 11*, 727–740.

Potts, G. R. (1974). Storing and retrieving information about ordered relationships. *Journal of Experimental Psychology, 103*, 431–439.

Potts, G. R., Banks, W. P., Kosslyn, S. M., Moyer, R. S., Riley, C., and Smith, K. H., (1978). In N. J. Castellan and F. Restle (eds.), *Cognitive theory III.* Hillsdale, N.J.: Lawrence Erlbaum Associates.

Presson, C. C. (1982). The development of map-reading skills. *Child Development, 53*, 196–199.

Pylyshyn, Z. (1973). What the mind's eye tells the mind's brain: a critique of mental imagery. *Psychological Bulletin, 80*, 1–24.

Pylyshyn, Z. W. (1981). The imagery debate. Analogue media versus tacit knowledge. *Psychological Review, 88*, 16–45.

Random House Webster's unabridged dictionary (2nd ed.) (1997). New York: Random House.

Restle, F. (1957). Discrimination of cues in mazes: a resolution of the "place-vs.-response" question. *Psychological Review, 64*, 217–228.

Richardson, J. T. E. (1987). The role of mental imagery in models of transitive inference. *British Journal of Psychology, 78*, 189–203.

Rieber, L. P., Boyce, M. J., and Assad, C. (1990). The effects of computer animation on adult learning and retrieval tasks. *Journal of Computer-Based Instruction, 17*, 46–52.

Riley, C., and Trabasso, T. (1974). Comparatives, logical structure, and encoding in a logical inference task. *Journal of Experimental Child Psychology, 17*, 187–203.

Rimé, B. (1983). The elimination of visible behaviour from social interactions: effects on verbal, nonverbal, and interpersonal variables. *European Journal of Social Psychology, 12*, 113–129.

Rimé, B., Schiaratura, L., Hupet, M., and Ghysselinckx, A. (1984). Effect of relative immobilization on the speaker's nonverbal behavior and on the dialogue imagery level. *Motivation and Emotion, 8*, 311–325.

Roberts, W. A., and Boisvert, M. J. (1998). Using the peak procedure to measure timing and counting processes in pigeons. *Journal of Experimental Psychology: Animal Behavior Processes, 24*, 416–430.

Roberts, W. A., Cheng, K., and Cohen, J. S. (1989). Timing light and tone signals in pigeons. *Journal of Experimental Psychology: Animal Behavior Processes, 15*, 23–35.

Roberts, W. A., and Phelps, M. T. (1994). Transitive inference in rats: a test of the spatial coding hypothesis. *Psychological Science, 5*, 368–374.

Robinson, A. H., Sale, R. D., Morrison, J. L., and Muehrcke, P. C. (1984). *Elements of cartography.* New York: Wiley.

Rosch, E. (1973). Natural categories. *Cognitive Psychology, 4*, 328–350.

Rosch, E. (1978). Principles of categorization. In E. Rosch and B. B. Lloyd (eds.), *Cognition and categorization* (pp. 27–48). Hillsdale, N.J.: Erlbaum.

Ryalls, B. O., Winslow, E., and Smith, L. B. (1998). A semantic congruity effect in children's acquisition of high and low. *Journal of Memory and Language, 39*, 543–557.

Sapir, E. (1944). Grading: a study in semantics. *Philosophy of Science, 11*, 93–116.

Save, E., Poucet, B., and Thinus-Blanc, C. (1998). Landmark use and the cognitive map in the rat. In S. Healy (ed.), *Spatial representation in animals* (pp. 119–132). New York: Oxford University Press.

Saxe, G. (1979). A developmental analysis of notational counting. *Child Development, 48*, 1512–1520.

Scaife, M., and Rogers, Y. (1996). External cognition: how do graphical representations work? *International Journal of Human-Computer Studies, 45*, 185–213.

Schaeken, W., Johnson-Laird, P. N., and Ydewalle, G. (in press). Mental models and temporal reasoning. *Cognition.*

Schiano, D., and Tversky, B. (1992). Structure and strategy in viewing simple graphs. *Memory and Cognition, 20*, 12–20.

Schmandt-Besserat, D. (1992). *Before writing.* Vol. 1: *From counting to cuneiform.* Austin: University of Texas Press.

Schmitt, E. (1999). Smart bombs, dumb map. *New York Times*, May 16, p. 6.

Schnall, S., and Gattis, M. (1998). Transitive inference by visual reasoning. In M. A. Gernsbacher and S. J. Derry (eds.), *Proceedings of the Twentieth Annual Conference of the Cognitive Science Society* (pp. 929–934). Hillsdale, N.J.: Lawrence Erlbaum Associates.

Shah, P., and Carpenter, P. A. (1995). Conceptual limitations in comprehending line graphs. *Journal of Experimental Psychology: General, 124*, 43–61.

Sherry, D., and Healy, S. (1998). Neural mechanisms of spatial representation. In S. Healy (ed.), *Spatial representation in animals* (pp. 133–157). New York: Oxford University Press.

Shettleworth, S. J. (1998). *Cognition, evolution, and behavior.* New York: Oxford University Press.

Shiffrar, M. M., and Shepard, R. N. (1991). Comparison of cube rotations around axes inclined relative to the environment or to the cube. *Journal of Experimental Psychology: Human Perception and Performance, 17*, 44–54.

Shin, S. J. (1991). An information-theoretic analysis of valid reasoning with Venn diagrams. In J. Barwise (ed.), *Situation theory and its applications, part 2.* New York: Cambridge University Press.

Small, J. P. (1997). *Wax tablets of the mind.* New York: Routledge.

Smith, L. B., and Sera, M. D. (1992). A developmental analysis of the polar structure of dimensions. *Cognitive Psychology, 24*, 99–142.

Smith, M. C., and McGee, L. E. (1980). Tracing the time course of picture-word processing. *Journal of Experimental Psychology: General, 109*, 373–392.

Sophian, C. (1988). Limitations on preschool children's knowledge about counting: using counting to compare two sets. *Developmental Psychology, 24*, 634–640.

Southworth, M., and Southworth, S. (1982). *Maps: a visual survey and design guide.* Boston: Little Brown and Company.

Spence, I., and Lewandowsky, S. (1991). Displaying proportions and percentages. *Applied Cognitive Psychology, 5*, 61–77.

Spencer, C., Blades, M., and Morsley, K. (1989). *The child in the physical environment.* Chichester, U.K.: Wiley.

Spencer, C., Harrison, N., and Darvizeh, Z. (1980). The development of iconic mapping ability in young children. *International Journal of Early Childhood, 12*, 57–64.

Spetch, M. L., Cheng, K., and MacDonald, S. E. (1996). Learning the configuration of a landmark array: I. touch-screen studies with pigeons and humans. *Journal of Comparative Psychology, 110*, 55–68.

Spetch, M. L., Cheng, K., MacDonald, S. E., Linkenhoker, B. A., Kelly, D. M., and Doerkson, S. R. (1997). Use of landmark configuration in pigeons and humans: II. generality across search tasks. *Journal of Comparative Psychology, 111*, 14–24.

Spinillo, A., and Bryant, P. (1991). Children's proportional judgements: the importance of "half." *Child Development, 62*, 427–440.

Staddon, J. E. R., and Higa, J. J. (1998). Time and memory: towards a pacemaker-free theory of interval timing. Manuscript submitted for publication.

Stasko, J., and Lawrence, A. (1998). Empirically assessing algorithm animations as learning aids. In J. Stasko, J. Domingue, M. H. Brown, and B. A. Price (eds.), *Software visualization* (pp. 419–438). Cambridge: MIT Press.

Stea, D., Blaut, J. M., and Stephens, J. (1996). Mapping as a cultural universal. In J. Portugali (ed.), *The construction of cognitive maps.* Netherlands: Kluver Academic Publishers.

Stenning, K., and Oberlander, J. (1995). A cognitive theory of graphical and linguistic reasoning: logic and implementation. *Cognitive Science, 19*, 97–140.

Sternberg, R. J. (1980). Representation and process in linear syllogistic reasoning. *Journal of Experimental Psychology: General, 109*, 119–159.

Sternberg, R. J. (1980). The development of syllogistic reasoning. *Journal of Experimental Child Psychology, 29*, 340–356.

Stevens, A., and Coupe, P. (1978). Distortions in judged spatial relations. *Cognitive Psychology, 10*, 422–437.

Stevens, S. S. (1946). On the theory of scales of measurement. *Science, 103*, 677–680.

Suwa, M., and Tversky, B. (1996). What architects see in their sketches: implications for design tools. In CHI 96 Conference, *Human factors in computing systems:*

conference companion (pp. 191–192). New York: Association for Computing Machinery.

Suzuki, S., Augerinos, G., and Black, A. H. (1980). Stimulus control of spatial behavior on the eight-arm maze in rats. *Learning and Motivation, 11*, 1–18.

Swinney, D., and Cutler, A. (1979). The access and processing of idiomatic expressions. *Journal of Verbal Learning and Verbal Behavior, 18*, 523–534.

Talmy, L. (1985). Lexicalization patterns: semantic structure in lexical forms. In T. Shopen (ed.), *Language, typology, and syntactic description*, vol. 3: *Grammatical categories and the lexicon* (pp. 57–149).

Talmy, L. (1987). The relation of grammar to cognition. In B. Ruczka-Ostyn (ed.), *Topics on cognitive linguistics.* Amsterdam: John Benjamins.

Talmy, L. (1996). Fictive motion in language and "ception." In P. Bloom, M. Peterson, L. Nadel, and M. Garrett (eds.), *Language and space* (pp. 211–276). Cambridge: MIT Press.

Taub, S. (in press). *Language from the body: iconicity and metaphor in American Sign Language.* Cambridge: Cambridge University Press.

Taylor, H. A., and Tversky, B. (1992). Spatial mental models derived from survey and route descriptions. *Journal of Memory and Language, 31*, 261–292.

Taylor, H. A., and Tversky, B. (1997). Indexing events in memory: evidence for index preferences. *Memory, 5*, 509–542.

TerMeulen, A. G. B. (1995). *Representing time in natural language: the dynamic interpretation of tense and aspect.* Cambridge: MIT Press.

Tolman, E. C. (1948). Cognitive maps in rats and men. *Psychological Review, 55*, 189–208.

Towler, J. O., and Nelson, L. D. (1968) The elementary school child's concept of scale. *Journal of Geography, 67*, 24–28.

Trabasso, T. (1975). Representation, memory, and reasoning: how do we make transitive inferences? In A. D. Pick (ed.), *Minnesota symposia on child psychology* (vol. 9, pp. 135–172). Minneapolis: University of Minnesota Press.

Trabasso, T. (1977). The role of memory as a system in making transitive inferences. In R. V. Kail and J. W. Hagen (eds.), *Perspectives on the development of memory and cognition.* Hillsdale, N.J.: Lawrence Erlbaum.

Traugott, E. C. (1978). On the expression of spatio-temporal relations in language. In J. H. Greenberg (ed.), *Universals of human language*, vol. 3: *Word structure* (pp. 369–400). Stanford: Stanford University Press.

Tufte, E. R. (1983). *The visual display of quantitative information.* Cheshire, Conn.: Graphics Press.

Tufte, E. R. (1990). *Envisioning information.* Cheshire, Conn.: Graphics Press.

Tufte, E. R. (1997). *Visual explanations.* Cheshire, Conn.: Graphics Press.

Tukey, J. W. (1977). *Exploratory data analysis.* Reading, Mass.: Addison-Wesley.

Turner, M. (1987). *Death is the mother of beauty: mind, metaphor, criticism.* Chicago: University of Chicago Press.

Tversky, B. (1981). Distortions in memory for maps. *Cognitive Psychology, 13,* 407–433.

Tversky, B. (1995). Cognitive origins of graphic conventions. In F. T. Marchese (ed.), *Understanding images* (pp. 29–53). New York: Springer-Verlag.

Tversky, B., Kugelmass, S., and Winter, A. (1991). Cross-cultural and developmental trends in graphic productions. *Cognitive Psychology, 23,* 515–557.

Tversky, B., and Schiano, D. (1989). Perceptual and conceptual factors in distortions in memory for maps and graphs. *Journal of Experimental Psychology: General, 118,* 387–398.

United States Department of Education (1998). *National assessment of educational progress.* Washington, D.C.: U.S. Department of Education.

Uttal, D. H. (1996). Angles and distances: children's and adults' reconstructions and scaling of spatial configurations. *Child Development, 67,* 2763–2779.

Uttal, D. H. (1999). Seeing the big picture: map use and the development of spatial cognition. Unpublished manuscript, Northwestern University.

Valli, C., and Lucas, C. (1995). *Linguistics of American Sign Language: an introduction* (2nd ed.). Washington, D.C.: Gallaudet University Press.

Vasta, R., and Liben, L. S. (1996). The water-level task: an intriguing puzzle. *Current Directions in Psychological Science, 5,* 171–177.

Wainer, H. (1980). Making newspaper graphs fit to print. In P. A. Kolers, M. E. Wrolstad, and H. Bouma (eds.), *Processing of visible language* (vol. 2, pp. 125–142). New York: Plenum.

Wainer, H. (1984). How to display data badly. *American Statistician, 38,* 137–147.

Wainer, H. (1992). Understanding graphs and tables. *Educational Researcher, 21,* 14–23.

Waltz, J. A., Knowlton, B. J., Holyoak, K. J., Boone, K. B., Mishkin, F. S., de Menezes Santos, M., Thomas, C. R., and Miller, B. L. (1999). A system for relational reasoning in human prefrontal cortex. *Psychological Science, 10,* 119–125.

Weaver, J. E., Steirn, J. N., and Zentall, T. R. (1997). Transitive inference in pigeons: control for differential value transfer. *Psychonomic Bulletin and Review, 4,* 113–117.

Wellman, H. M., Somerville, S. C., and Haake, R. J. (1979). Development of search procedures in real-life spatial environments. *Developmental Psychology, 15,* 530–542.

Werner, H. (1978a). The syncretic character of primitive organization. In S. S. Barten and M. B. Franklin (eds.), *Developmental processes: Heinz Werner's selected writings,* vol. 1: *General theory and perceptual experience* (pp. 41–64). New York: International Universities Press.

Werner, H. (1978b). Unity of the senses. In S. S. Barten and M. B. Franklin (eds.), *Developmental processes: Heinz Werner's selected writings*, vol. 1: *General theory and perceptual experience* (pp. 153–167). New York: International Universities Press.

Werner, H., and Kaplan, B. (1978). The developmental approach to cognition. In S. S. Barten and M. B. Franklin (eds.), *Developmental processes: Heinz Werner's selected writings*, vol. 1: *General theory and perceptual experience* (pp. 85–106). New York: International Universities Press.

Whiten, A., Goodall, J., McGrew, W. C., Nishida, T., Reynolds, V. Sugiyama, Y., Tutin, C. E. G., Wrangham, R. W., and Boesch, C. (1999). Culture in chimpanzees. *Nature, 399*, 682–685.

Wilcox, P. (1993). *Metaphorical mapping in American Sign Language.* Unpublished doctoral dissertation, University of New Mexico.

Willats, J. (1997). *Art and representation: new principles in the analysis of pictures.* Princeton: Princeton University Press.

Wilson, M., and Emmorey, K. (1997a). A 'phonological loop' in visuo-spatial working memory: evidence from American Sign Language. *Memory and Cognition, 25* (3), 313–320.

Wilson, M., and Emmorey, K. (1997b). Working memory for sign language: a window into the architecture of working memory. *Journal of Deaf Studies and Deaf Education, 2* (3), 123–132.

Wilson, M., and Emmorey, K. (1998a). A "word length effect" for sign language: further evidence on the role of language in structuring working memory. *Memory and Cognition, 26* (3), 584–590.

Wilson, M., and Emmorey, K. (1998b). Modality matters: spatial coding in working memory for signs. Paper presented at Theoretical Issues in Sign Language Research, Washington, D.C., November.

Winn, W. D. (1987). Charts, graphs and diagrams in educational materials. In D. M. Willows and H. A. Haughton (eds.), *The psychology of illustration.* New York: Springer-Verlag.

Winston, E. A. (1989). Timelines in ASL. Paper presented at The Deaf Way, Washington, D.C., July.

Winston, E. A. (1995). Spatial mapping in comparative discourse frames. In K. Emmorey and J. Reilly (eds.), *Language, gesture, and space* (pp. 87–114). Hillsdale, N.J.: Lawrence Erlbaum Associates.

Wolff, P., and Gentner, D. (1992). The time course of metaphor comprehension. *Proceedings of the Fourteenth Annual Conference of the Cognitive Science Society.* Hillsdale, N.J.: Erlbaum.

Wolff, P., and Gentner, D. (2000). Evidence for role-neutral initial processing of metaphors. *Journal of Experimental Psychology: Learning, Memory, and Cognition.*

Woocher, F. D., Glass, A. L., and Holyoak, K. J. (1978). Positional discriminability in linear orderings. *Memory and Cognition, 6*, 165–173.

Yates, F. A. (1969). *The art of memory.* New York: Penguin.

Yin, R. K. (1969). Looking at upside-down faces. *Journal of Experimental Psychology, 81,* 141–45.

Zacks, J., Levy, E., Tversky, B., and Schiano, D. J. (1998). Reading bar graphs: effects of depth cues and graphical context. *Journal of Experimental Psychology: Applied, 4,* 119–138.

Zacks, J., and Tversky, B. (1999). Bars and lines: a study of graphic communication. *Memory and Cognition, 27,* 1073–1079.

Zacks, J., Tversky, B., and Iyer, G. (in press). Perceiving, remembering and communication structure in events. *Journal of Experimental Psychology: General.*

Zoladek, L., and Roberts, W. A. (1978). The sensory basis of spatial memory in the rat. *Animal Learning and Behavior, 6,* 77–81.

Contributors

Peter Bryant is the Watts Professor of Psychogy at Oxford University. He does research on several aspects of children's intellectual development, including their understanding of space. He is the author of *Perception and understanding in young children* (Methuen, 1974) and co-author with Terezinha Nunes of *Children doing mathematics* (Blackwell, 1996).

Margaret Chalmers has been a Research Fellow and collaborator with Brendan McGonigle on his comparative and developmental programme for over twenty years. Now a Lecturer in the Department of Psychology at Edinburgh, she continues to collaborate with Brendan at the Laboratory for Cognitive Neuroscience, helping to develop, in particular, applications of their new touch-screen paradigms to help isolate and identify sequential control factors in children with fragile x syndrome.

Eve Danziger is Assistant Professor of Anthropology at the University of Virginia. Since 1986, Dr. Danziger has been conducting ethnographic and linguistic fieldwork with the Mopan Maya people of Southern Belize, Central America. Her interests revolve around the three-way interface of language, social identity and thought. She has published in the areas of social practice and social organization, the linguistics of Mopan, and the role of language in cognition.

Karen Emmorey is a senior staff scientist at the Salk Institute for Biological Studies in the Laboratory for Cognitive Neuroscience. Her work focuses on what sign languages can reveal about the nature of human language, cognition, and the brain. She has investigated how experience with a signed language impacts nonlinguistic visual-spatial cognition, such as face processing, memory, and imagery. She has also studied the processes involved in how deaf people produce and comprehend sign language and how these processes are represented in the brain. She is co-editor of *Language, gesture, and space* (Lawrence Erlbaum Associates, 1995) and *The signs of language revisited: An anthology to honor Ursula Bellugi and Edward Klima* (Lawrence Erlbaum Associates, 2000).

Merideth Gattis is Lecturer in Psychology at the University of Sheffield. Her research is concerned with the interaction of sensorimotor systems and cognition, including spatial reasoning, gesture, and imitation.

Dedre Gentner is Professor of Psychology at Northwestern University. Her research is on cognition and language, including analogy, similarity, metaphor, mental models and acquisition of semantics. She is a former president of the Cognitive Science Society. She is the author of numerous papers and co-editor of *Mental models* (Lawrence Erlbaum Associates, 1983) and *The analogical mind* (MIT Press, 2000).

Keith J. Holyoak is Professor of Psychology at the University of California, Los Angeles. His research focuses on human reasoning and its neural substrate. He is the co-author of *Mental leaps: Analogy in creative thought* (MIT Press, 1995) and *Induction* (MIT Press, 1986).

John E. Hummel is an Associate Professor of Psychology at the University of California, Los Angeles. His research interests include the representation and processing of relational information in perception and cognition, and the question of how neural and neural-like architectures can represent and manipulate symbolic structures.

Sotaro Kita is a Senior Researcher at Max-Planck Institute for Psycholinguistics, in the Netherlands. His main research interests are cognitive psychological, interactional, and ethnographic studies of the relationship between speech and spontaneous gestures. His research interests also include conversational analysis, semantics and pragmatics of spatial expressions, and cross-linguistic studies of spatial conceptualization.

Lynn S. Liben is Distinguished Professor of Psychology and the Director of the Child Study Center at Pennsylvania State University. One major focus of her work is on how individuals' understanding of spatial-graphic representations develops with age and experience. In addition to her basic research on developmental, individual, and sex-related differences in spatial-representational understanding, she considers implications of this research for how people use maps or aerial photographs, learn science through imagery, and appreciate the aesthetics of graphics.

Brendan McGonigle is Reader in Cognitive Neuroscience and Curator of the Laboratory for Cognitive Neuroscience, Centre for Neuroscience,

University of Edinburgh. He leads an interdisciplinary group featuring human and non-human primate, robotics and cognitive modelling research, unified within a common agenda dedicated to the understanding of complex intelligent systems. Dr. McGonigle is co-editor of *Reasoning and discourse processes* (Academic Press, 1986) and the author of over 100 journal and book articles ranging from developmental cognition to the design and testing of robots.

William A. Roberts is Professor of Psychology at the University of Western Ontario. He is author of *Principles of animal cognition* (McGraw-Hill, 1998). He studies cognitive processes in monkeys, rats, and pigeons, including how these animals process number, keep track of time, and use landmarks for spatial navigation.

Sarah Squire is a College Lecturer at St. John's College, University of Oxford. Her research investigates young children's ability to understand models of division problems, before they have been taught much about division at school. More generally, she is interested in how children's initial ideas about mathematics may relate to their informal experiences before instruction and the implications that this might have for education.

Christel Stolz is Assistant Professor for General and Comparative Linguistics at the University of Bremen in Germany. She has conducted extended fieldwork in Quintana Roo in Mexico with speakers of Yucatec Maya. Her research interests include the interface between culture, language, and cognition, particularly the question of how differences in spatial language might reflect differences in spatial conceptualization. Her typological research has focused on expressions of spatial relations and dimensional object properties.

Barbara Tversky is Professor of Psychology at Stanford University. Her research interests include spatial thinking and language, memory, and categorization, which has recently led her to study memory for the spatial and visual world (including faces, bodies, maps, graphs, and pictures); eye witness memory; memory for the events of our lives; imagery and spatial mental models of the space of the body, the space around the body, and the space of navigation; human-computer interaction; the design of interfaces, diagrams, and text; diagrammatic reasoning; event perception and cognition; inferences from categories; and the relations between language and thought.

Name Index

Subject Index